THE
SOCIAL
FRONTIER

Alan R. Sadovnik and Susan F. Semel
General Editors

Vol. 55

PETER LANG
New York • Washington, D.C./Baltimore • Bern
Frankfurt • Berlin • Brussels • Vienna • Oxford

THE
SOCIAL
FRONTIER

A Critical Reader

Edited by
Eugene F. Provenzo, Jr.

For Chet Bowers,
With many thanks
for all that you have
contributed to the field
and my understanding.

Gene Provenzo
Miami
March 2011

PETER LANG
New York • Washington, D.C./Baltimore • Bern
Frankfurt • Berlin • Brussels • Vienna • Oxford

Library of Congress Cataloging-in-Publication Data

The Social frontier: a critical reader / [edited by] Eugene F. Provenzo, Jr.
p. cm. — (History of schools and schooling; 55)
Includes bibliographical references.
1. Education—Social aspects—United States. 2. Social constructionism—
United States. I. Provenzo, Eugene F. II. Social frontier.
LC191.4.S645   302.43'2—dc22   2010048076
ISBN 978-1-4331-0918-8 (paperback)
ISBN: 978-1-4331-0919-5 (hardcover)
ISSN 1089-0678

Bibliographic information published by **Die Deutsche Nationalbibliothek**.
Die Deutsche Nationalbibliothek lists this publication in the "Deutsche
Nationalbibliografie"; detailed bibliographic data is available
on the Internet at http://dnb.d-nb.de/.

FSC

Mixed Sources

Product group from well-managed
forests, controlled sources and
recycled wood or fiber

Cert no. SCS-COC-002464
www.fsc.org
©1996 Forest Stewardship Council

The paper in this book meets the guidelines for permanence and durability
of the Committee on Production Guidelines for Book Longevity
of the Council of Library Resources.

© 2011 Peter Lang Publishing, Inc., New York
29 Broadway, 18th floor, New York, NY 10006
www.peterlang.com

BIRTHRIGHT

Birthright, woodcut by Lynd Ward, *The Social Frontier* Volume 5, Number 42, 1939, p. 133.

Table of Contents

Preface

Many of the conflicts and problems that are faced by contemporary American society resonate with the mid-1930s. There is the financial insecurity, the threat of terrorism, war and mass destruction, the opposition of conservative versus liberal and more progressive points of view, and perhaps most importantly, a seeming erosion and failure of traditional institutions such as government and schools.

It is particularly interesting therefore to consider an intellectual project such as the journal *The Social Frontier*, an unprecedented experiment in education and social writing, perhaps the most tangible source that remains for those interested in the American educational, social and philosophical movement known as Social Reconstructionism.

This work assembles the major writings from *The Social Frontier*. Published for nine years from 1934 through 1943, the journal was largely the creation of the faculty and graduates students in the Social Foundations of Education program at Teacher's College, Columbia University. The journal is not well-known today, but in its time, it was perhaps the most exciting, and certainly revolutionary experiment, in the educational writing of its era.

I wish to thank several of the people who encouraged the development of this project. My wife, Asterie Baker Provenzo, as always provided her quiet counsel and careful editing. Susan Semel and Alan Sadovnik generously invited me to include this book in their series with Peter Lang. Sonia Murrow's work on *The Social Frontier* was very useful. I appreciate having her as a colleague and friend.

Although we only discussed the project once, Chet Bowers work from the mid-1960s provided an invaluable guide for my understanding of the social and educational forces that were at work as part of the Social Reconstructionist movement. Chet's excellence as a scholar, his constant pursuit of a better world and educational system, and his sustained public advocacy set him uniquely apart in the field. It is with special appreciation and affection that I dedicate this book to him.

Eugene F. Provenzo, Jr.
University of Miami
Summer 2010

Introduction

In October of 1934 a group of faculty and graduate students at Teachers College, Columbia University launched a new educational journal, *The Social Frontier*.[1] It was the most interesting and important educational journal in the United States to emerge from the Great Depression. Largely under the intellectual leadership of George S. Counts and William Heard Kilpatrick, the journal represented a conscious act of educational criticism and social and political reconstruction.[2]

Although centered in New York City, the journal was seen as national in scope. Writing about the launch of the journal, William H. Kilpatrick hoped that it would "provide a prime medium for the development of a constructive social consciousness among educational workers."[3]

The editors and writers for *The Social Frontier* were visionaries, believing that education extended beyond the traditional institution of the schools. As Goodwin B. Watson explained in his article in the journal's first issue, "Education Is the Social Frontier," education represented a:

> complex of forces, whether intentional or unintentional, exercising a formative influence upon the rising generation. Education, as we think of it, includes the effects of family life, the movies, radio programs, newspapers, magazines, neighborhood folk-ways, vocations, recreations, the economic system, national festivals, churches, tools, machines, and the many other factors interwoven in what Dewey has called the "cradle of custom" in which each infant is laid.[4]

Essentially, the same point was made in the lead editorial in the same issue, titled "Orientation."

The Social Frontier, in many respects, was an extension of the call to arms George S. Counts had made in a series of speeches before the National Education Association in 1932, which was published in the same year under the title *Dare the Schools Build a New Social Order*.[5] In this, and other works, Counts called for the schools and teachers to be actively involved in the social reconstruction of the failed American economy and political system.

Counts and his followers believed that education, the schools and the teachers who worked in them, could play a critical role in the process of social reconstruction that had to be undertaken in order to emerge from the Depression. In the case of teachers, the writers for *The Social Frontier* saw them as a

potentially powerful social and political force and that they had an obligation
to become engaged activists.

> Their strength is strategic and functional as well as numerical. They spread over
> the country in a fine network, which embraces every hamlet and rural commu-
> nity. And the function, which they perform, brings them into close and sympa-
> thetic relations with the rank and file of the people of the nation. No
> occupational group in society is equally favorably situated. Another source of
> great strength, if the profession is regarded as a whole, is the fact that its mem-
> bership compasses all fields of knowledge and thought and is thus peculiarly
> armed to do battle in the contemporary world. Clearly, if they but utilized the re-
> sources within their grasp, teachers could become one of the major forces in
> American life.[6]

In the first of his regular columns for *The Social Frontier*, John Dewey argued
that because of the Depression, American society was "out of joint" and that
teachers could not avoid the responsibility of trying to set the culture right.
According to him: "They may regard it, like Hamlet, as a cursed spite, or as an
opportunity—but they cannot avoid the responsibility."[7]

   This type of approach—one recognizing that teachers had not only the potential but the responsibility to act as agents of social change—represented a
radical redefinition of the traditional role of the teacher in American society.
Figures such as George S. Counts, John Dewey, William Heard Kilpatrick and
the members of *The Social Frontier's* editorial board were not so concerned
 about the actual politics of the teachers involved (conservative or liberal), but
with the necessity for them to become politically and socially engaged. In doing so, they saw the teaching population in the United States as a potent political and social force, one that could, as part of an open and democratic
process, influence policy, and even determine the outcome of elections.[8]

   While seeing teachers as a potentially vital force in the process of social
reconstruction and reform, the editorial board of the journal was highly critical of the role they currently played. In a piece titled "Isolation or Leadership?"
written for the third issue of the journal, the editors explained that with most
teachers:

> Their mental horizon does not reach significantly beyond the three R's. Their
> professional equipment is limited to "special methods." Seldom is the distance
> between what a profession thinks it is doing and what it actually is doing so great
> as in the case of the teachers. Education is supposed to be concerned with "life,"
> "preparation for life," transmission of ideals, maintaining of old values, and crea-
> tion of new ones. Actually, teachers do little more than retail hackneyed facts and
> fix a few simple skills in the tool subjects. They are for the most part strangers to

literature, to music, and to the plastic arts. Politically and socially they are illiterate. Their mental picture of the world is a patchwork of newspaper stereotypes, movie sentimentality, and popular "wisdom." Socially they present a bad case of clinical isolation. Less than industrial workers, less than farmers, less than practitioners in the liberal professions, and certainly less than bankers and industrialists do teachers have a conception of their own group interests. Chiefly of middle class origin and priding themselves on a professional status which nobody takes the trouble to deny them, teachers are, objectively viewed, no higher in the economic hierarchy of contemporary society than factory workers. They have no property to depend on for an income and nothing they can sell at a profit. They must work for a school board in order to make a living. They are subject to retrenchment and, despite tenure regulations, to dismissals, often dictated by the whims of employers. Their salaries are in most communities no higher than the wages of manual laborers. But unlike most other workers, teachers do not recognize that they are workers. [9]

While potentially a powerful force, as a result of their sheer numbers, the editors of *The Social Frontier* maintained that "the mental poverty, the cultural philistinism, and the social isolation of the average teacher" made it impossible, in their opinion, for teachers to be effective.[10] They believed that with the obvious failure of the political and economic system (as a result of the Depression), teachers would have to overcome their traditional conservatism and seek social and political power for the first time in their history. It was this idea of awakening the teaching population to its potential as a social force that was the principle theme of the journal's early issues.

As pointed out by C. A. Bowers, who has chronicled the history of the journal at length, this preoccupation on the part of the editors of the journal with the potential power of teachers to "build a new social order" (Count's phrase was derived from two sources: the first being the strategic location of teachers in large numbers across every community in the country, and the second, the fact that they represented virtually every area of knowledge.)[11]

The new journal clearly saw itself as innovative and pro-active. The Depression had changed the rules by which traditional American society functioned, and new solutions were needed. As Goodwin Watson explained: "Today we conceive of society as advancing into pioneer territory, opening up new problems and trying out new solutions for old problems."[12] This would require a new type of education and a new role for the teachers who provided that education. As a result, Education literally was "The Social Frontier," and the new journal would have as its mission the exploration of "the causal interpretation of the irregular, ever-advancing line between what a society has been and what it is becoming."[13]

From its first issue, *The Social Frontier* had a "collectivist" orientation. As the main editorial in the second issue of the journal explained:

> THE SOCIAL FRONTIER has used the word collectivism in its pages. It has even taken the position, in harmony with the conclusions of the Commission on Social Studies of the American Historical Association, that "the age of individualism and laissez faire in economy and government is closing and a new age of collectivism is emerging.[14]

The editorial recognized that conservative and privileged elements in the society would provide an inevitable source of opposition and would call for the return to the "supposedly solid world of their grandparents."[15]

With a strong "collectivist" orientation, the journal was widely misperceived as communist in its orientation. This was something the editors strongly denied.[16] What they did believe was that:

> The advance of technology, bringing new forms of communication, transportation, and production, has literally destroyed the individualistic economy of the early years of the Republic. In place of the relatively independent and self-contained households and rural neighborhoods of the Jeffersonian era, the American people stand today before a vast and complicated economic mechanism embracing the entire country and reaching out increasingly to the far corners of the globe—a fait accompli having the most revolutionary consequences. And the operation of the mechanism, dependent as it is on the planful and rational character of technology, demands more and more of coordination and unified direction and control.[17]

A planned economy on a global scale was perceived as essential to stability and progress.

The editors of *The Social Frontier* declared that the interests of the wealthy needed to no longer dominate politics, but that a more just and democratic social order needed to be put in place. In doing so, the journal would "fight for a collectivism" which would "cherish, preserve, and fulfill the American ideals of freedom of speech, cultural diversity, and personal liberty, security, and dignity."[18] The editors stated, that as a publication, *The Social Frontier* abhored:

> . . . regimentation of public opinion; it swears with Jefferson "eternal hostility to every form of tyranny over the mind of man." It regards economic goods not as the chief end of life, but rather as a basis and a means for the development of the human spirit. It views the present concentration of wealth and power in the hands of a few, with its implications of class rule and domination, as an oppres-

sive obstacle to the personal growth of American boys and girls and as a perpetual threat to the liberties of the masses of the people. To those who say that collectivism means regimentation the answer is that collectivism is upon us and that the only hope for freedom for the many lies in the direction of a democratic control over the material sources of the abundant life. The only freedom, which THE SOCIAL FRONTIER would curtail, is the freedom of one man to enslave and exploit another.[19]

Opposition to *The Social Frontier* quickly materialized. Newspapers across the country reviewed the first issue of the journal, some praising its content and others condemning it as a conscious attack on American capitalism and business enterprise.[20] The journal did, in fact, propose revolutionary action—one which would bring about the creation of a more just and "collectivist" economic and social system. But the type of revolution they were defending was no different than the one advanced by the likes of Jefferson, Franklin and Addams one-hundred and fifty years earlier, a fact sometimes belied by its inclusion of authors such as Norman Thomas and Leon Trotsky.

Underlying the editorial policy of the journal, teachers were seen as a special profession with special responsibilities, one requiring special protection if they were to be able to fulfill their mission. As concluded in an editorial on Academic Freedom included in the second issue of the journal:

> An educational profession that is alive to its social responsibilities and free to function in the educational guidance of children and adults in their contemporary perplexities can do much to shift social forces from reinforcement of our price and profit economy to an alignment backing a collectivistic economy of social utility. It is these considerations, which make academic freedom an objective of paramount importance to the teachers of the nation.[21]

Statements such as these were highly provocative for the era. It is not surprising that they contributed to the perception that the journal and its editors and writers represented a communist front.

In fact, *The Social Frontier*, particularly the work of George S. Counts, rejected a Marxist approach. In editorial the article "1.105, 921," referring to the number of people working in schools and colleges across the country, the editorial board made very clear that it rejected:

> . . . the theory of doctrinaire radicals that all modern societies are fashioned after a single model, that every such society is divided rigidly into two classes, that one of these classes is devoted single-mindedly to the exploitation of the other, that the master class is undivided in its conception of its interests, that it applies this conception logically, rationally, and completely to every division of the cultural

apparatus, that the school must always and in each of its divisions be an instrument of profound and universal reaction, and that, as a consequence, all who argue that organized education can play a positive role in the reconstruction of society are either nursing delusions or engaging in deliberate professional deception.[22]

While concerned about the growth of a wealthy elite class in America, the editorial board of the journal did not consider the Marxists and their communist philosophy as providing a viable model for American culture. As C. A. Bowers has explained, their primary desire "was to abolish all vestiges of class in order to allow education to perform its function in a community of freely associating individuals."[23]

The extent to which George S. Counts, as the driving force of the journal, was opposed to communism is indicated by his opposition to Communist control of the local New York City chapter of the American Federation of Teachers. The destruction of prominent educators under Stalin had convinced Counts that collaboration with the American Communist party was not possible. In a joint letter written with the philosopher Reinhold Niebuhr, he argued that, "If liberal and labor forces cannot form a united front, if they weaken themselves in bitter factional and sectarian strife, there is no hope."[24]

What Counts and his followers represented was a collectivist or what we understand in our own era as a social/democratic philosophy. Their term for this was "social reconstructionists." As Bowers explains: "For the social reconstruction group, collectivism represented a progressive state of social development in which public morality and cooperation would make it possible for education to take its rightful place in the vanguard of social progress."[25]

In his article "Can Education Share In Social Reconstruction?"[26] John Dewey provided a clear explanation of the Social Reconstructionists position. According to Dewey, American schools were interested in educating students to accept the status quo, summed up by the phrase "rugged individualism."

> The assumption is—or was—that we are living in a free economic society in which every individual has an equal chance to exercise his initiative and his other abilities, and that the legal and political order is designed and calculated to further this equal liberty on the part of all individuals. No grosser myth ever received general currency. Economic freedom has been either non-existent or precarious for large masses of the population. Because of its absence and its tenuousness for the majority political and cultural freedom has been sapped; the legally constituted order has supported the ideal of *beati possidentes*. [blessed are those who possess.][27]

The real status quo, according to Dewey was "the increasing encroachment of the power of a privileged minority, a power exercised over the liberties of the mass without corresponding responsibility?"[28] The increasing attacks on the academic freedom of teachers that the journal had begun to chronicle were, in Dewey's opinion, an indication that reactionary forces were increasingly threatened by the possibility of the schools, and teachers, acting as vehicles of social reform.

It is clear that *The Social Frontier*, and the people who contributed to it, were seen as a threat by much of the political and economic leadership in the United States. Of particular prominence was the newspaper and publishing magnate William Randolph Hearst (1863–1951). Hearst distrusted radicals and was vehemently opposed to socialism. In his 1919 book, *The Brass Check: A Study of American Journalism*, the Socialist muck-racking writer and author of *The Jungle*, Upton Sinclair (1878–1968) explained how Hearst had given his newspapers clear instructions that they were never to talk favorably about Socialism.

> The Hearst newspapers pose as friends of the people; they print a great deal of radical clamor, but there is a standing order in all Hearst offices that American Socialism shall never be mentioned favorably. All newspapers have a rule that if any Socialist gets into trouble, it shall be exploited to the full; when Socialists don't get into trouble often enough to suit them, they make Socialists out of people who *do* get into trouble.[29]

In its fifth issue in February 1935, *The Social Frontier* undertook an examination of not only the daily press and its influence in the United States, but more specifically the efforts of William Randolph Hearst. In particular, the journal was concerned with Hearst's attacks on "teachers and students in universities and colleges who dare to examine critically the contemporary social situation and who believe that social change demands reconstruction of political and economic institutions."[30]

In a lengthy three-part article, the editors of *The Social Frontier* attempted to provide a documentary account of the Hearst papers' attacks on academic freedom in the United States. The attacks had begun the previous November, when Hearst had sent reporters out to Syracuse University, New York University and Teachers College, Columbia University. The reporters were to collect information about how these schools and their professors were supposedly acting as hotbeds for recruiting and training students to become socialists and communists.

Two of the main individuals interviewed by Hearst's reporters were members of the editorial board and contributors to *The Social Frontier*: George S. Counts at Teachers College, Columbia University and Sidney Hook at New York University. The reporters who were sent to interview Counts and Hook, as well other individuals such as John Washburne, the Chairman of the Psychology Department at Syracuse University, clearly intended to show that academics were actively engaged in converting their students into communists and socialists. In the case of Washburne and Counts, the reporters gained appointments under the pretense of being interested in becoming graduate students. Eventually they revealed that they were journalists.

In the February 1935 issue of *The Social Frontier*, Hearst's efforts to bait various scholars was described in great detail. The evidence of the data clearly demonstrated Hearst's willingness to distort the truth in order to convince people that there was a "red" threat in American colleges and universities—one in which Counts and *The Social Frontier* were playing a major role. Detailed, and often highly spurious articles, were eventually published in the Hearst newspapers that argued that a large number of major colleges and universities were coming under socialist and communist influence and that immediate measures needed to be taken to prevent this from happening.

Counts countered Hearst's attacks with a formal complaint to the McCormack-Dickstein Committee, a congressional watchdog committee, calling upon it "to investigate 'a campaign of terrorism against teachers in American colleges, universities, schools and even private schools.'" In this document, Counts accused Hearst of attacking fundamental democratic rights: "'If William Randolph Hearst succeeds in his efforts, . . . he will reduce American universities and schools to the ignominious condition of the German schools and universities under Hitler." [31]

William Heard Kilpatrick, who had been interviewed by Hearst as part of his smear campaign explained in a memo that he believed that Hearst's efforts:

> . . . would mean the destruction of the school as a preparation for intelligent democratic citizenship. On this basis pupils and students could not be encouraged to think but only made to conform to predetermined positions authoritatively promulgated. In a changing world like ours such a policy could only result in the destruction of intelligent democracy and the enthronement of some demagogic fascism." [32]

The memo sent to the McCormack-Dickstein Committee specifically asked that proceedings be undertaken to investigate "this most insidious and un-American attack upon our educational institutions."[33] This request was signed as follows:

> Charles A. Beard, former president of the American Historical Association; John Dewey, professor emeritus, Columbia University and honorary president of the National Education Association; William H. Kilpatrick, professor of education, Teachers College; George S. Counts, professor of education, Teachers College and chairman of the Progressive Education Association Committee on Economics and Sociology; Harry Emerson Fosdick, pastor of Riverside Church and member of the faculty of Union Theological Seminary; Howard L. McBain, dean of Graduate Faculties, Columbia University; William C. Bagley, professor of education, Teachers College; George W. Kirchwey, Dean Emeritus, Columbia Law School; E. C. Lindeman, New York School for Social Research; Karl N. Llewellyn, professor of jurisprudence, Columbia University; Howard Nudd, secretary Public Education Association of New York; John L. Childs, assistant professor of education, Teachers College; Robert K. Speer, professor of education, New York University; Jesse H. Newlon, director of Lincoln School, Teachers College, and former president of the National Education Association; Robert B. Raup, associate professor of education, Teachers College; Joseph K. Hart formerly of Vanderbilt University and associate editor of the SURVEY; Heber Harper, professor of education. Teachers College; Rollo G. Reynolds, principal of Horace Mann School and professor of education, Teachers College; Willard W. Beatty, President of Progressive Education Association; Clyde R. Miller, treasurer, Progressive Education Association; Frederick L. Redefer, executive secretary of Progressive Education Association.[34]

The memo's signatories were among the leading liberal academic and social leaders of the period.

What these signatories were countering represented an ongoing set of scare tactics involving the threat of a communist or socialist takeover of American schools and education that dated back to the First World War. In an article published in 1941 in *The Social Frontier* written by Harold Rugg and titled "This Has Happened Before," whose secondary Social Studies textbooks had come under widespread attack for their supposed Leftist leanings, the Teachers College professor outlined how there had occurred five separate attacks by conservative forces during the previous twenty to twenty-five years who feared communist and socialist thought taking over the educational system.[35] In this article, Rugg put forward the following intriguing hypothesis:

> Following, or in connection with, each major war or domestic crisis there ensues a dangerous period of restlessness, agitation, discontent and revolt. Labor troubles, strikes, riots, lynchings, near-financial panics, and witch-hunts of aliens, lib-

erals and racial and religious out-groups are all manifestations of this unrest. If the rise and fall of these were shown on a graph, such a graph would, I feel sure, rise quickly to its peak within two or three years, then slowly taper off through some years to a longer period of comparative quiet.[36]

The attacks on *The Social Frontier* were not only a continuation of the tradition of there being a "red" threat in the United States, but more specifically, the conscious attempt by conservative and fascist forces in the United States to take tighter control of the schools and to discredit the efforts of liberal minded progressive educators. In this regard, a fundamental battle was at work, one which involved who was to control the schools and what role teachers were to play in the social and political order.

The attacks on *The Social Frontier* were actually part of a larger political fight that was playing itself out in the Roosevelt administration. As Bowers has explained, the Social Reconstructionists views closely paralleled those of the early efforts of the New Deal "to create an organic economy and a co-ordinated society."[37] By 1935, however, the tactics of the New Deal shifted toward restoring an economically competitive society. Bowers quotes Arthur Schlesinger to the effect that the early New Dealers were "social evangelists, with a broad historic sweep and a touch of the visionary, seeing America at a great turning point in history."[38] Social Reconstructionists such as Counts, Rugg and Kilpatrick were similarly minded. But unlike Roosevelt, they did not back off from their original vision. Instead they expanded the idea that there was a social and class struggle at work in American society—one that was profoundly linked to the work of teachers.

In February 1936 the John Dewey Society was formed. Much of the energy of *The Social Frontier's* editorial board was dedicated to the new organization. The journal, which had increasingly emphasized the class struggle in education, began to lose a significant portion of its readership.[39] Running short of funds and energy, the editors of *The Social Frontier* turned to the Progressive Education Association to see about merging their journal with the official organ of the association, *Progressive Education.*

While there was some support for the merger, a survey sent to 750 members did not show strong support for the combination of the two publications. To a large degree, the Progressive Education Association represented the child-centered followers of John Dewey, who sent their children to Progressive—typically private—schools. Counts described them in *Dare the Schools Build a New Social Order?* as:

> . . . persons who are fairly well-off, who have abandoned the faith of their fathers, who assume an agnostic attitude towards all important questions, who

pride themselves on their open-mindedness and tolerance, who favor in a mild sort of way fairly liberal programs of social reconstruction, who are full of good will and humane sentiment, who have vague aspirations for world peace and human brotherhood, who can be counted upon to respond moderately to any appeal made in the name of charity, who are genuinely distressed at the sight of *unwonted* forms of cruelty, misery, and suffering, and who perhaps serve to soften somewhat the bitter clashes of those real forces that govern the world; but who, in spite of all their good qualities, have no deep and abiding loyalties, possess no convictions for which they would sacrifice over-much, would find it hard to live without their customary material comforts, are rather insensitive to the accepted forms of social injustice, are content to play the role of interested spectator in the drama of human history, refuse to see reality in its harsher and more disagreeable forms, rarely move outside the pleasant circles of class to which they belong, and in the day of severe trial will follow the lead of the most powerful and respectable forms of society and at the same time find good reason for doing so.[40]

Counts went on to explain that these individuals, as a result of their relatively high levels of income, had the luxury of focusing on the needs and interests of their children, whom they wished to protect as much as possible from the harsh realities of life, and to have them succeed to the "standards of their class and be a credit to their parents."[41]

While Counts saw these people as well meaning, he felt that they were a distraction from the true mission and cause of Progressive Education. As he argued:

If Progressive Education is to be genuinely progressive, it must emancipate itself from the influence of class, face squarely and courageously every social issue, come to grips with life in all its stark reality, establish an organic relationship with the community, develop a realistic and comprehensive theory of welfare, fashion a compelling and challenging vision of human destiny, and become less frightened than it is today at the bogies of *imposition* and indoctrination. [42]

Counts concluded that Progressive Education could not place its trust in a "child-centered school."[43]

It should be no surprise that the Progressive Education Association did not readily embrace the political activism of *The Social Frontier*. *The Social Frontier* editors and writers were also men and women of action. As such, they were unusual compared to most academics. They not only believed in what they studied, but felt that their ideas required them to take action. This is also why they were perceived as a significant threat by conservative forces such as Hearst. Essentially, the American intelligentsia was seen as needing to be kept under social control. According to Harold Rugg, writing in a 1935 article for the journal titled "The American Scholar Faces a Social Crisis," American scholars had, in fact, not really been a threat to the political and social status quo, since they reflected the values of the privileged social and economic class. As he explained:

> The chief reason for the hiatus between the content of American scholarship and the vital problems of the people lies in the fact that the rank and file of American scholars are molded into defenders of the status quo by the dominant social milieu in which they have been brought up, and by the special concepts of their own intellectual climate. Like the stock-brokers and the professionals in general, most of them are members of the upper middle class. They are sons of native stock and are possessors of a small property and of prestige in the community—both of which they earnestly desire to keep. But, true to the American tradition, they are thoroughgoing individualists and practice the concept of freedom to compete and—many of freedom to exploit. Also they are still convinced that, even in the new industrialism, the ladder of opportunity really stretches upward before anyone who conforms, works hard, saves, and invests. Their economic-social creed is a synthesis of the concepts of the First Industrial Revolution. Outstanding among these are: scarcity, laissez faire, building for immediate profits, accelerating growth, production for sale, and a hierarchy of social classes in which the entrepreneur and the politician occupy the loftiest positions and the creative person is either ignored or held in contempt. [44]

Rugg called for a new breed of scholars, ones who would engage thought with action. Citing the philosopher Ralph Waldo Emerson's argument that, "Without action thought can never ripen into truth," Rugg called on his fellow academics and, by implication teachers, to be part of a politically oriented progressive movement and function as agents of social change. In this regard, he was completely in line with the philosophy of Counts, and thus, a potential threat to the status quo and the existing political and educational systems in the United States.

In an editorial included in the issue immediately following Rugg's article, titled "Seeds of Revolt," the journal's editorial board declared that: "...education properly conducted in the modern world, is an enemy and not a benign supporter of inherited ways of doing things. Education in its profoundest meaning is revolution."[45] The editors declared that the task at hand was not to hold on to traditions and outdated practices "by uttering a string of ancient platitudes," but instead by asserting a type of education that "naturally leads to the remaking of human institutions."[46] According to the editorial board, "teachers must sow the seed and society must learn not to fear the whirlwind."[47]

Considering the position of the editorial leadership of *The Social Frontier* concerning the potential role of teachers at all levels of the educational system to challenge the status quo and existing power structure in the United States, it should not be surprising that the discussion of teacher loyalty oaths became a major theme in the journal.

In his article, "Loyalty Oaths-A Threat to Intelligent Teaching," William Heard Kilpatrick cited Thomas Jefferson to the effect that it is the obligation of citizens in a democracy, such as the United States, to challenge the opinions of the government and to provide alternative interpretations of what may be best for us as a nation. In this context, teachers as public servants and citizens:

> . . . must be strong characters, with strong human sympathies, with strong convictions—always held, however, subject to change upon better knowledge or deeper insight. Such teachers cannot be mere yes-men, timid of thought or action where either truth or the public welfare is involved. And all that the rest of us, as citizens and lawmakers, do or say in this connection ought to help select such characters to man our schools and teach our children.[48]

Kilpatrick condemned Loyalty Oaths for teachers as being undemocratic in their intention in "that they mean to discourage criticism of our institutions, mean to keep teachers from considering controversial issues, mean to keep the schools from intelligent preparation for change."[49]

Much of the journal's content reflects the emergence and increasing power of the labor movement in the United States. Teachers were seen by the editorial board as being aligned with labor. It was their duty to challenge those in power who reinforced their privilege to the detriment of the larger democratic system. As Kilpatrick explained: "The interests of labor are now the interests of society. The teacher should consider that if he does not consciously identify himself with labor he unwittingly sanctions the continuation of the reign of the small group, which now holds power over the life of the nation."[50]

*   *   *

In the spring of 1937, George Counts resigned as the editor of *The Social Frontier* in order to lead the anti-Communist opposition to the takeover of the New York local of the American Federation of Teachers. In February of the same year, the journal's board had been greatly expanded to include figures such as John Dewey, Edward O. Sissons, Sidney Hook, Edgar W. Knight and John L. Childs. Yet the expanded board made relatively little difference. In June 1937, Norman Woefel and Mordecai Grossman, the two graduate students who had founded the journal with Counts and Kilpatrick, resigned. The editorship was taken on by George W. Hartmann, an associate professor at Teachers College. [51]

Financial problems plagued the journal throughout 1937 and, as mentioned earlier, various proposals were undertaken to have the journal be taken over by the Progressive Education Association. By June 1939, the Progressive Education Association had agreed to publish the journal, becoming one of the two main publications of the Association. Renamed *Frontiers of Democracy*, as a part of a deliberate attempt to deemphasize the radical orientation given to the journal by its founders, the first issue of the publication to appear under the new name and sponsorship took place in October 1939.

After its takeover and renaming by the Progressive Education Association, the journal lost much of its radical and critical edge. Bowers attributes this to the fact that the social reconstructionists had retreated from their initial position once they realized that it had relatively little support from the broader educational community. In addition, the deterioration of conditions in Europe and the justified fear of war, directed the public's attention elsewhere. [52]

Initially, the social reconstructionists leading *The Social Frontier* tried to avoid having the United States enter into the war. It was not until 1940 that the journal's editors urged its readers to consider the possibility that the United States might have to defend itself. In October 1941, twelve of the journal's fourteen board members signed a statement arguing for "full responsible participation on the part of the United States in the democratic struggle against the Axis to the extent, if necessary, of actual participation in the war." [53] For the editorial leadership of the journal, the war had become the struggle between democracy and totalitarianism.

In 1943 Kilpatrick resigned from the editorial board of *The Frontiers of Democracy*. Other members of the board withdrew from the journal in order to take part in the war effort. In a secret meeting of the Executive Committee for the Progressive Education Association held late in 1943, it was decided that the journal would no longer be published. In December 1943, the journal published a statement from the Progressive Education Association that they could not afford an anticipated deficit of $2,200 if they continued to publish the journal. [54] Despite the effort of figures such as Rugg, the journal ceased publication by the end of 1943.

Although intimately connected to the founding of the field of the Social and Cultural Foundations of Education, the pioneering efforts of *The Social Frontier* have largely been forgotten. The journal represented the most critical systematic and radical critique of American education to emerge not just in the first half of the twentieth century, but in the nearly seventy-five years since.

In many respects, the efforts of *The Social Frontier* editors and writers went far beyond the radical educational theorists of the 1960s, 1970s and 1980s, or any figures in more recent years.

The intellectual movement that the journal represented probably failed because of the Second World War and the economic recovery that went with it. The virulent opposition that emerged against the journal and its ideas did not go away. The attacks against the journal and its editorial policy, as well the key leaders of the Social Foundations of Education group at Teachers College, was part of a larger anti-left and conservative movement in education that would continue during the post-war era with the witch-hunts led by Senator Joseph McCarthy of Wisconsin as part of the House Un-American Activities Committee.

This movement against the Social Foundations of Education as a field has continued, albeit less provocatively and overtly into the present. As an active scholar in the field for nearly forty years, the editor of this work does not believe it is an accident that positions in the field have systematically devolved to the disciplines and been increasingly eliminated from colleges and universities. Disciplinary knowledge in the Academy is safe, essentially conservative and often elitist. It rarely encourages social action or engagement of the type needed by those in professional areas such as Education.

While disciplinary knowledge is essential to those in a field such as the Social Foundations, it is also sufficiently conservative to act as a drag on meaningful action and reform. American society, while born in revolution, is essentially much more conservative than it admits. I wonder if the supposedly radical critics of Education—Henry Giroux, Joel Spring, Peter McLaren, Joe Kincheloe, Michael Apples and to be fair perhaps myself, are not a bit like the intellectuals in Aldous Huxley's *Brave New World*. Banished to their comfortable reservations in the South Seas, or the Falkland Islands, they are provided comfortable and interesting lives on their "academic reservations," but they have very few of their ideas circulate or be used in the culture. Were the figures who edited and wrote for *The Social Frontier* a little closer to the real world and the types of ideas that drive educational reform in meaningful ways?

In the pages that follow are a selection of some of the most important articles found in the nine years that *The Social Frontier* was published. Many of the ideas that are discussed remain highly relevant today. This alone justifies the republication of these works. They, however, also suggest how much certain fundamental ideas remain as part of the contemporary educational discourse and extend back in history nearly one-hundred years, how contemporary issues in education reflect much more powerful divides in our culture than we tend to admit, and are related to issues of power and control and who rules in the United States, and finally, what it actually means to be an American.

Notes

[1] For background on *The Social Frontier* see: *The Social Frontier Journal: A Historical Sketch*; C. A. Bowers, *History of Education Quarterly*, Volume 4, No. 3. (Sep., 1964), pp. 167–180; C. A. Bowers, *The Progressive Educator and the Depression: The Radical Years* (New York: Random House, 1969); George J. Harrison, "An Historical Analysis of the Social Frontier: A Journal of Educational Criticism and Reconstruction" (Dissertation, Rutgers, The State University of New Jersey, 1968); Maureen O'Neill, "The Social Frontier and Frontiers of Democracy (1934–1943): Visions for Curricular Reconstruct (Dissertation, Rutgers, The State University of New Jersey 1986).

[2] Norman Woefel and Mordecai Grossman came up with the original idea for the journal, which they felt would provide an outlet for authors who were not able to find outlets for publishing articles on the schools as agents of social reform. Late in 1933 the sought the help of William Heard Kilpatrick, who talked with members of the Teachers College, Columbia University faculty about the project. These included George S. Counts, John L. Childs, Jesse Newlon and Harold Rugg. See: C. A. Bowers, *The Social Frontier Journal*, p. 168. Recent studies on Social Reconstructionism as movement include: Karen L. Riley, editor, *Social Reconstruction: People, Politics Perspectives* (Greenwich, CT: Information Age Publishing, 2006); and Michael E, James, editor, *Social Reconstruction Through Education: The Philosophy, History, and Curricula of a Radical Idea* (Norwood, N.J.: Ablex Publishing Company, 1995). Included in the James work is James R. Giarelli's essay, "The Social Frontier 1934–1943: Retrospect and Prospect."

[3] William H. Kilpatrick, "Launching the Social Frontier," *The Social Frontier*, Volume 1, Number 1, 1934, p. 2.

[4] Goodwin B. Watson, "Education Is the Social Frontier," *The Social Frontier* Volume 1 Number 1, 1934, p. 22.

[5] George S. Counts, *Dare the Schools Build a New Social Order?* (New York: John Day, 1932). See also Counts's *The Social Foundations of Education* (New York: Scribner's, 1934) and William Heard Kilpatrick, *Education and the Social Crisis* (New York: Scribner's, 1934).

[6] Editorial, "1,105,921," *The Social Frontier*, Volume 1, Number 4, pp. 5–6.

[7] John Dewey, "The Teacher and His World," *The Social Frontier*, Volume 1, Number 4, 1935, p. 7.

[8] *Ibid.*

[9] Editorial, "Isolation or Leadership?" *The Social Frontier* Volume 1, Number 6, 1935, p. 7–8.

[10] *Ibid.*

[11] Bowers, *The Progressive Educator and the Depression*, p. 113.

[12] *Ibid.*

[13] Goodwin B. Watson, "Education Is the Social Frontier," *Social Frontier* Volume 1, Number 1, 1934, p. 22.

[14] Editorial Board, "Collectivism and Collectivism,"*Social Frontier*, Volume 1, Number 2, 1934, p. 3-4

[15] *Ibid.*

[16] *Ibid.*

[17] *Ibid.*

[18] *Ibid.*

[19] *Ibid.*

[20] See: "Editorial Comments On The Social Frontier," *The Social Frontier*, Volume 1, Number 2, 1934, p. 22-22. This compilation of quotes is included in this anthology on pages 39-43.

[21] "Academic Freedom," *The Social Frontier*, Volume 1, Number 2, 1934, p. 4-6.

[22] "1,105,921," *The Social Frontier*, Volume 1, Number 4, 1935, p. 5-6.

[23] Bowers, *The Progressive Educator and the Depression*, p. 112.

[24] Quoted by Bowers, *op. cit.*, p. 166.

[25] *Ibid*, p. 108.

[26] John Dewey, "Can Education Share In Social Reconstruction?" *The Social Frontier*, Volume 1, Number 1, 1934, p. 11-12.

[27] *Ibid.*

[28] *Ibid.*

[29] Upton Sinclair, *The Brass Check: A Study of American Journalism* (New York: Pasadena, CA: by the author, 1919). See Chapter LII. Source available online at: www.teleread.org/brasscheckfull.htm.

[30] W. R. Hearst Baits College "Reds," *The Social Frontier*, Volume 1, Number 4, 1935, p. 3-4.

[31] "The Hearst Attack on Academic Freedom," *The Social Frontier*, Volume 1, Number 5, 1935, p. 25-34.

[32] *Ibid.*

[33] *Ibid.*

[34] *Ibid.*

[35] For background on the attack on Rugg's Social Studies textbooks see: Ronald W. Evans, *This Happened in America: Harold Rugg and the Censure of Social Studies* (Charlotte, N.C.: Information Age Publishing, 2007). Also see Evans's book *The Social Studies Wars: What We Should Teach Our Children* (New York: Teachers College Press, 2004). In particular see Chapters 3 and 4.

[36] Harold Rugg, "This Has Happened Before," *The Frontiers of Democracy*, Volume 7, Number 58, 1941, p. 105-108.

[37] Bowers, "The Social Frontier Journal," p. 171.

[38] *Ibid*, quoted by Bowers.

[39] *Ibid*, p. 172.

[40] *Dare the Schools Build a New Social Order?*, pp. 7-8.

[41] *Ibid*, p. 8-9.

[42] *Ibid*, pp. 9-10.

[43] *Ibid*, p. 10.

[44] Harold Rugg, "The American Scholar Faces a Social Crisis," *The Social Frontier*, Volume 1, Number 6, 1935, pp. 10-13.

[45] "Seeds of Revolt," *The Social Frontier*, Volume 1, Number 7, 1935, p. 8-8

[46] *Ibid.*

[47] *Ibid.*

[48] William Heard Kilpatrick, "Loyalty Oaths—A Threat to Intelligent Teaching," *The Social Frontier*, Volume 1, Number 9, 1935, p. 10-15.

[49] *Ibid.*

[50] *Ibid.*

[51] Bowers, *the Progressive Educator, and the Depression*, p. 166.

[52] *Ibid*, pp. 175-176.

[53] "This War and America," *The Frontiers of Democracy*, Volume 8, No. 63, pp. 10-11.

[54] "The Directors of the Progressive Education Association Vote 12 to 3 to Discontinue Publication," *Frontiers of Democracy*, Volume 10, Number 81, 1943, p. 70.

ORIENTATION*

The Editorial Board

The following editorial, almost certainly written by George C. Counts, but signed by the Editorial Board, sets the tone for the new journal. The piece is remarkably prophetic. It argues that American and world culture has gone through a profound transformation from an agrarian to a "highly complex urban and industrial order." A new era is underway.

A strong "collectivist" orientation underlies Counts's philosophy and the journal's orientation. As he explains: "THE SOCIAL FRONTIER assumes that the age of individualism in economy is closing and that an age marked by close integration of social life and by collective planning and control is opening."

Counts declares that the new journal "makes no pretense to absolute objectivity and detachment, knowing such a goal to be impossible of achievement in that realm of practical affairs to which education belongs and in which positive decisions must be made. It represents a point of view, it has a frame of reference, it stands on a particular interpretation of American history."

In addition, Counts argues that education needs to be interpreted "as an aspect of a culture in the process of evolution." Thus, while recognizing that schools are the central institutional agency of education and schooling in American culture, they are by no means the only means by which people learn things. In this context, other sources of learning and socialization, from the family to religion, as well as various forms of media such as film and radio, all need to be understood as instruments in the education and socialization of Americans.

* * *

American Society, along with world society, is passing through an age of profound transition. This fact has been proclaimed with ever greater emphasis and frequency by the march of ideas and events since the Civil War and particularly since the opening of the present century. It is proclaimed in the advance of science, technology, and invention, in the growing mastery of natural forces, in the changing forms of economy and government, in the increasing instability of the whole social structure, in the swelling armaments and the intensification of international rivalries, and in the wars, revolutions, and social calamities which seem to have become the order of the day throughout the world. Also it is proclaimed in the obsolescence of inherited conceptions of human relationships, in the decline of faith in traditional moral and religious

* **Source:** *The Social Frontier*, Volume 1, Number 1, 1934, pp. 3–5.

doctrines, in the popularity of cults of cynicism and disillusionment, and in the appearance of revolutionary political theories, philosophies, and programs.

While the transition presents many facets, in its basic terms in the United States it is a movement from a simple agrarian and trading economy to a highly complex urban and industrial order with agriculture transformed into single-crop specialties. Since the days of Andrew Jackson the nation has evolved out of a loose aggregation of relatively self-contained rural households and neighborhoods into a vast society marked by minute differentiation of structure and function, close integration of parts, and common dependence on a far-flung productive and distributive mechanism whose operation requires an ever increasing measure of cooperation, general planning, and unified direction. In a word, for the American people the age of individualism in economy is closing and an age of collectivism is opening. Here is the central and dominating reality in the present epoch.

This fact means that the nation has entered a period freighted with unmeasured opportunities and responsibilities—a period when, in the words of Emerson, "the old and the new stand side by side, and admit of being compared; when the energies of all men are searched by fear and by hope; when the historic glories of the old can be compensated by the rich possibilities of the new era." In the years and decades immediately ahead the American people will be called upon to undertake arduous, hazardous, and crucial tasks of social reconstruction: they will be compelled to make some of the grand choices of history, to determine in which direction they are to move, to make decisions which will deeply affect the life of their country for generations and indeed for centuries—decisions concerning the incidence of economic and political power, the distribution of wealth and income, the relations of classes, races, and nationalities, and the ends for which men and women are to live. Moreover, owing to the revolutionary conquest of mechanical energy during the past one hundred years, the American people stand today on the threshold of unprecedented and unimagined potentialities of material and spiritual development. Also they stand in the imminent presence of economic collapse, political reaction cultural regimentation, and war. They must choose among the diverse roads now opening before them. In particular they must choose whether the great tradition of democracy is to pass away with the individualistic economy to which it has been linked historically or is to undergo the transformation necessary for survival in an age of close economic interdependence.

In the making of these choices persons and institutions engaged in the performance of educational functions will inevitably play an important role. To the extent that they operate in the real world they will make their influence felt. Indeed, even if they should pursue a policy of evasion, in actual fact they would be throwing their influence on the side of outmoded anarchy and disorder. Whatever course they pursue they will either retard or hasten the adjustment to the new realities, they will either make easy or difficult the transfer of the democratic ideal from individual to social foundations. They will be called upon, not only to bring the heritage of knowledge, thought, and attitude abreast of general social advance, but also to make broad choices concerning alliances to be consummated, values to be preserved, interests to be defended, social goals to be striven for.

Already a few voices have been raised within the ranks of educational workers in acceptance of the challenge of social reconstruction. But as yet these voices are too timid to be effective, too tentative to be convincing, and too individual to speak a language of clear-cut purpose. They belong to persons who singly and in isolation have captured this or the other meaning of unfolding events. Before these persons, and perhaps countless others who have thus far remained inarticulate, can hope to become a positive creative force in American society and education, they must come into closer communication, clarify their thought and purposes, draw like-minded individuals into their ranks, and merge isolated and discordant voices into a mighty instrument of group consensus, harmonious expression, and collective action. To contribute to the achievement of this object is being launched.

The journal makes no pretense to absolute objectivity and detachment, knowing such a goal to be impossible of achievement in that realm of practical affairs to which education belongs and in which positive decisions must be made. It represents a point of view, it has a frame of reference, it stands on a particular interpretation of American history. It accepts the analysis of the current epoch presented above and outlined in greater detail in *Conclusions and Recommendations, Report on the Social Studies* of the Commission of the American Historical Association.

THE SOCIAL FRONTIER assumes that the age of individualism in economy is closing and that an age marked by close integration of social life and by collective planning and control is opening. For weal or woe it accepts as irrevocable this deliverance of the historical process. It intends to go forward to meet the new age and to proceed as rationally as possible to the realization of all possibilities for the enrichment and refinement of human life. It will nurse no fantasies of returning to the simple household and neighborhood economy of the time of Thomas Jefferson; it will seek no escape from the responsibilities of today, either by longing for a past now gone beyond recovery or by imagining a future bearing the features of Utopia. It proposes to take seriously the affirmation of the Declaration of Independence that "all men are created equal" and are entitled to "life, liberty, and the pursuit of happiness." Also it proposes, in the light of this great humanist principle applied to the collective realities of industrial civilization, to pass every important educational event, institution, theory, and program under critical review. Finally, it will devote its pages positively to the development of the thought of all who are interested in making education discharge its full responsibility in the present age of social transition. Its editorial staff and board of directors hope that it will help fight the great educational battles—practical and theoretical—which are already looming above the horizon. And they trust that it will engage in the battles of the twentieth and not of the eighteenth century.

THE SOCIAL FRONTIER acknowledges allegiance to no narrow conception of education. While recognizing the school as society's central educational agency, it refuses to *limit* itself to a consideration of the work of this institution. On the contrary, it includes within its field of interest all of those formative influences and agencies which serve to induct the individual—whether old or young—into the life and culture of the group. It regards education as an aspect of a culture in process of evolution. It therefore has no desire to promote a restricted and technical professionalism. Rather does it address itself to the task of considering the broad role of education in advancing the welfare and interests of the great masses of the people who do the work of society—those who labor on farms and ships and in the mines, shops, and factories of the world.

THE IVES LAW *

The Editorial Board

The Ives law, which was passed in New York during the summer of 1934, required every professor, instructor and teacher employed in any school, college or university in the state to swear to uphold their allegiance to both the state and federal constitutions. The law was seen by the editors of *The Social Frontier* as a deliberate attempt to strong-arm or "muscle" teachers in the area of free speech—a right guaranteed to them under the First Amendment.

*   *   *

On August 10, 1934, Governor Lehman of New York signed the Ives bill. In view of the fact that the bill affects directly the work and status of the teacher and is not unlike legislative measures pending or enactments in force in a number of American states, *The Social Frontier* is convinced that the profession should lose no time in developing a policy with respect to legislation of this character. The future may see much more of it.

According to the provisions of the law, every professor, instructor, or teacher employed in any school, college, or university in the state must subscribe to the following oath or affirmation: "I do solemnly swear (or affirm) that I will support the Constitution of the United States of America and the Constitution of the State of New York, and that I will faithfully discharge, according to the best of my ability, the duties of the position to which I am now assigned."

The reaction of teachers to such a governmental measure is naturally one of resentment. It bears the guise of discriminatory legislation and impugns the loyalty to the deepest interests of the American people of the members of a great profession. Also, it was fathered by reactionary elements in the state and was professedly designed to muscle teachers and institutions attempting to introduce their pupils to what President Hoover's Research Committee on Social Trends called "the stark and bitter realities of the social situation." Moreover, it unquestionably violates the spirit of the Constitution itself and of the revolutionary epoch that gave the nation birth. Consequently, many teachers rightly opposed the bill and petitioned the governor not to sign it.

---

* **Source:** *The Social Frontier*, Volume 1, Number 1, 1934, pp. 7–9.

There is grave danger that the new law will have the effects desired by its sponsors, not however, because of any restrictions inherent in the oath itself but rather because of the traditional timidity and ignorance of teachers. Yet forward-looking members of the profession can find in this oath a direct mandate for broad participation in the alteration of the now existing pattern of American society. If its authors assumed that the requirement of the oath would necessarily curb the thought and action of teachers in the realm of economics and politics, they were unfamiliar either with the fundamental law of the land or with the facts of American life.

That basic provisions of the federal constitution have been violated repeatedly in every one of the forty-eight states during recent years is known to all informed persons. It is to be greatly regretted that in the face of such violations teachers have for the most part remained silent and inert. If they are to be loyal to their oath of office, they can be silent and inert no longer. They are now required to play an active role in the life of state and nation and to assume responsibility for the full realization of the historic ideals of the American people. Let it be hoped that the teachers will take this oath more seriously than have many of the occupants of public office in the United States.

The nature of the obligations which teachers are now required to assume may be revealed by an examination of some of the more common and flagrant violations of the Constitution. The questions of justice and free speech, which are fundamental to the operation and preservation of democratic institutions, will serve to illuminate the problem. "To no one will we sell, to no one will we refuse or delay right or justice." Thus did the Great Charter proclaim the ideal more than seven centuries ago—an ideal that has been reaffirmed in one form or another in the federal constitution and in the constitution or the statutes of every one of the American states. In the preamble to the former the founding fathers set down the establishment of justice as one of the six great objects of the union of states which it was to call into being. The Fourteenth Amendment, adopted in a period of civil strife, explicitly guarantees that no state shall "deny to any person within its jurisdiction the equal protection of the laws." Freedom and equality of justice have been called "the twin fundamental conceptions of American jurisprudence."

At this point the Constitution is violated daily in New York and in every other state of the union. To a degree justice is bought and sold, refused and delayed. And in the measure that justice is thus administered it is not justice. The conclusion is thoroughly documented by the observations of eminent jurists and the findings of scholars that the poor, racial and cultural minorities, and social and political non-conformists receive something less than justice at the hands of American courts. The Ives Law requires that New York teachers become familiar with the facts and then proceed to do what they can to halt this perpetual violation of the Constitution. But any such course will carry them far beyond the study of laws and courts and legislatures and into an examination of the complicated operations of the economic system and the modes of producing and distributing wealth and income.

Perhaps the second most common violation of the Constitution occurs in the sphere of free speech. The First Amendment to the Constitution states "Congress shall make no law . . . abridging the freedom of speech, or of the press; or the right of the people peaceably to assemble, and to petition the government for a redress of grievances." During recent years these rights of the people have been trampled upon repeatedly by agents of government and self-constituted guardians of the public welfare. If this is permitted to continue, even the semblance of democracy can scarcely be expected to survive. The Ives Law summons teachers to the battle for freedom of speech and assemblage.

Finally, it should be observed that, if teachers are to support the Constitution intelligently, they must become familiar with the thought of the period that produced it. They must read the debates on the Constitution and that other great document of the period—the Declaration of Independence. They must examine the writings of the English and French philosophers of the eighteenth century; and of such men as John Adams, Alexander Hamilton, Thomas Jefferson, John Taylor, and Tom Paine. Then, having observed that the architects of the Constitution provided for its amendment, they should proceed to a consideration of the changes in its provisions, which the rise of industrial civilization is making desirable or necessary. And in doing all of this, they should endeavor to carry their pupils with them. Along such lines should teachers of state and nation conduct the fight with those reactionary elements in the community, which under the guise of patriotism would seek to protect their special privileges and vested interests.

CAN EDUCATION SHARE IN SOCIAL RECONSTRUCTION? *

John Dewey

During the first half of the Twentieth century, John Dewey (1859–1953) was the preeminent philosopher in the United States. He not only served on the editorial board of *The Social Frontier*, but eventually wrote a regular column for the journal. In this article, his first contribution to *The Social Frontier*, he argues that the schools in the United States had contributed to the crisis of the Depression and the economic system's failure by their role in helping to maintain the existing status quo. Quoting Roger Baldwin, Dewey outlines how groups such as the Daughters of the American Revolution, the American Legion, Christian Fundamentalists, the Ku Klux Klan, and the War Department had employed compulsory political rites such as flag saluting, required patriotic readings, teaching of the Constitution by prescribed routine; making the teaching of evolution a crime, loyalty oaths for teachers, the promotion of conservative and ideologically driven history textbooks, restrictions or bans on teachers unions affiliated with the labor movement, and compulsory military training in both high schools and colleges, common activities throughout the country. He concludes the article with a call for action by those concerned with creating a set of more "just and humane conditions," ones which would overcome the reign of "educational fascists" and which would lay the basis "intellectual and moral, for a new social order."

*   *   *

THE STATUS QUO—EXPRESSIVE OR REPRESSIVE?

That upon the whole the schools have been educating for something called the status quo can hardly be doubted by observing persons. The fallacy in this attempt should be equally evident. There is no status quo—except in the literal sense in which Andy explained the phrase to Amos: a name for the "mess we are in." It is not difficult, however, to define that which is called the "status quo"; the difficulty is that the movement of actual events has little connection with the name by which it is called.

For the alleged status quo is summed up in the phrase "rugged individualism." The assumption is—or was—that we are living in a free economic society in which every individual has an equal chance to exercise his initiative and his other abilities, and that the legal and political order is designed and calculated to further this equal liberty on the part of all individuals. No grosser myth over received general currency. Economic freedom has been either non-existent or

---

* **Source:** *Social Frontier*, Volume 1, Number 1, 1934, pp. 11–12.

precarious for large masses of the population. Because of its absence and its tenuousness for the majority political and cultural freedom has been sapped; the legally constituted order has supported the ideal of beati possidentes.

There is no need here to review the historic change from a simple agrarian order, in which the idea of equal opportunity contained a large measure of truth, to a complex industrial order with highly concentrated economic and political control. The point is that the earlier idea and theory persisted after it had lost all relevance to actual facts, and was then used to justify and strengthen the very situation that had undermined it in practice. What then is the real status quo? Is it the condition of free individuality postulated by the ruling theoretical philosophy, or is it the increasing encroachment of the power of a privileged minority, a power exercised over the liberties of the mass without corresponding responsibility?

It would not be difficult to make out a case for a positive and sweeping answer in favor of the latter alternative. Let me quote, as far as schools are concerned, from Roger Baldwin. "On the whole, it may be said without question that the public schools have been handed over to the keeping of the militant defenders of the status quo—the Daughters of the American Revolution, the American Legion, the Fundamentalists, the Ku Klux Klan, and the War Department. Look at the twelve-year record! Compulsory patriotic rites and flag saluting by law in most states; compulsory reading of the Protestant Bible in eighteen states, contrary to the provision for the separation of church and state; compulsory teaching of the Constitution by prescribed routine; making a crime of the teaching of evolution in three states; special oaths of loyalty not required of other public servants in ten states; loyalty oaths required of students as a condition of graduation in many cities; history textbooks revised under pressure to conform to prejudice; restriction or ban on teacher's unions affiliated with the labor movement; laws protecting tenure beaten or emasculated; compulsory military training in both high schools and colleges, with inevitable pressure on students and teachers by the military mind." To these forms of outward and overt pressure may be added—as indeed Mr. Baldwin does add—more powerful, because more subtle and formulated, pressure that acts constantly upon teachers and students.

FORCES AND TENDENCIES NOW IN CONFLICT

It might seem then that, judged by the present situation, limitation upon the efforts of teachers to promote a new social order—in which the ideal of freedom and equality of individuals will be a fact and not a fiction—tremendously outweighs the element of possibility of their doing so. Such is not the case, however, great, as are the immediate odds against effort to realize the possibility. The reason is that the actual status quo is in a state of flux; there is no status quo, if by that term is meant something stable and constant. The last forty years have seen in every industrialized society all over the world a steady movement in the direction of social control of economic forces. Pressure for this control of capital—or if you please for its "regimentation"—is exercised both through political agencies and voluntary organizations. Laissez faire has been dying of strangulation. Mr. Hoover, who gave currency to the phrase "rugged individualism" while President, acted repeatedly and often on a fairly large scale for governmental intervention and regulation of economic forces. The list of interferences with genuine educational freedom that has been cited is itself a sign of an effort, and often a conscious one, to stem a tide that is running in the opposite direction—that is, toward a collectivism that is hostile to the idea of unrestricted action on the part of those individuals who are possessed of economic and political power because of control of capital.

I hope the bearing of these remarks upon the theme of the limitations and the possibilities of educational effort for establishing a new social order is fairly evident. Teachers and administrators often say they must "conform to conditions" rather than do what they would personally prefer to do. The proposition might be sound if conditions were fixed or even reasonably stable. But they are not. They are highly unstable; social conditions are running in different, often opposed directions. Because of this fact the educator in respect to the relation of educational work to present and future society is constantly compelled to make a choice. With what phase and direction of social forces will he throw in his energies? The chief evil is that the choice is so often made unconsciously by accommodation to the exigencies of immediate pressure and of estimate of probability of success in carrying out egoistic ambitions.

THE OBLIGATION UPON EDUCATORS

I do not think, accordingly, that the schools can in any literal sense be the builders of a new social order. But the schools will surely, as a matter of fact and not of ideal, share in the building of the social order of the future according as they ally themselves with this or that movement of existing social forces. This fact is inevitable. The schools of America have furthered the present social drift and chaos by their emphasis upon an economic form of success, which is intrinsically pecuniary and egoistic. They will of necessity, and again not as a matter of theory, take an active part in determining the social order—or disorder—of the future, according as teachers and administrators align themselves with the older so-called "individualistic" ideals—which in fact are fatal to individuality for the many—or with the newer forces making for social control of economic forces. The plea that teachers must passively accommodate themselves to existing conditions is but one way—and a cowardly way—of making a choice in favor of the old and the chaotic.

If the teacher's choice is to throw himself in with the forces and conditions that are making for change in the direction of social control of capitalism—economic and political—there will hardly be a moment of the day when he will not have the opportunity to make his choice good in action. If the choice is conscious and intelligent, he will find that it affects the details of school administration and discipline, of methods of teaching, of selection and emphasis in subject matter. The educator is, even now, I repeat, making this choice, but too often is making it blindly and unintelligently. If he or she is genuinely committed to alliance with present forces that tend to develop a social order which will, through collective control and ownership, make possible a genuine and needed "rugged individualism" (in the sense of individuality) for all members of the community the teacher will, moreover, not be content with generalities about the desired future order. The task is to translate the desired ideal over into the conduct of the detail of the school in administration, instruction, and subject matter. Here, its seems to me, is the great present need and responsibility of those who think the schools should consciously be partners in the construction of a changed society. The challenge to teachers must be issued and in clear tones. But the challenge is merely a beginning. What does it mean in the particulars of work in the school and on the playground? An answer to this question and not more general commitment to social theory and slogans is the pressing demand.

In spite of the lethargy and timidity of all too many teachers, I believe there are enough teachers who will respond to the great task of making schools active and militant participants in creation of a new social order, provided they are shown not merely the general end in view but also the means of its accomplishment. Dr. Kandel, at the close of a somewhat scornful article as to the part of the schools in this task of social reconstruction, says of society in general: "It would welcome help from any direction to correct the existing abuses and make it true to itself; beyond that it would not permit the schools to go. If the teaching body, whose duty it is to define and interpret society's culture and ideal to the oncoming generation, undertook much it would still be faced with a formidable task; it may lay the basis for a new social order, but society and not the teaching body will determine its particulars."

There are, in this statement, many words and phrases that I am tempted to underscore: correction of abuses; the duty of the teacher; the basis for a new social order; leaving particulars to society. But I content myself with asking what more can any educator, however "radical," want? Abuses cannot be corrected by merely negative means; they can be eliminated only by substitution of just and humane conditions. Laying the basis, intellectual and moral, for a new social order is a sufficiently novel and inspiring ideal to arouse a new spirit in the teaching profession and to give direction to radically changed effort. Those who hold such an ideal are false to what they profess in words when they line up with reactionaries by ridicule of those who would make the profession a reality. That task may well be left to educational fascists.

COLLECTIVISM AND COLLECTIVISM *

The Editorial Board

In the second issues of the new journal, the editorial board addresses the question of what is collectivism? Social change, which is a major theme that is evident throughout the journal's nine years of publication, is discussed. The editors assume that a new era is coming into being, one in which: "The advance of technology, bringing new forms of communication, transportation, and production, has literally destroyed the individualistic economy of the early years of the Republic."

Collectivism, as interpreted by the editors of *The Social Frontier*, is seen as bringing about an end to the "self-contained household and rural neighborhoods of the Jeffersonian era." It encompasses ideologies including communism, socialism, syndicalism and fascism, to name just a few. The term is one that Counts and others wrestled with—not wanting to be associated with communism, but at the same time not wanting to deemphasize the fact that a group process was increasingly at work in society.

The editors of the journal make clear that they are "not engaged in any battle for collectivism as such." Collectivism is simply the new reality, a reality that "has literally been decided by the forces of history." It is an unavoidable force that has emerged on the global scene.

The editors believe that collectivism could be good or bad. What they oppose is "the present concentration of wealth and power in the hands of a few, with its implications of class rule and domination, as an oppressive obstacle to the personal growth of American boys and girls and as a perpetual threat to the liberties of the masses of the people." In doing so, it should not be a surprise that the ideas explicated in the journal came to be seen by its opponents as representing a significant potential threat to the dominant capitalist system in the United States.

The editors of the journal felt they were participating in a major cultural upheaval, one involving "a vast and complicated economic mechanism embracing the entire country and reaching out increasingly to the far corners of the globe—a fait accompli having the most revolutionary consequences." Remarkably prophetic, the editors' descriptons suggest many of the characteristics of the world's current global economic system.

*   *   *

THE SOCIAL FRONTIER has used the word collectivism in its pages. It has even taken the position, in harmony with the conclusions of the Commission on Social Studies of the American Historical Association, that "the age of individualism and laissez faire in economy and government is closing and a new

---

* **Source:** *The Social Frontier*, Volume 1, Number 2, 1934, pp. 3-4 age of collectivism is emerging." This has disturbed those conservative elements in society who cherish their special privileges above all else and those timid souls, both inside and outside the educational profession, who see a bogey in every political bush and long for supposedly solid world of their grandparents. The result has been some calling of names, confusion of issues, and unnecessary dissipation of energy. The thing needed is a definition of terms so that all who are interested may know where the battle lies and on which side they are fighting.

The first point to be driven home is that THE SOCIAL FRONTIER is not engaged in any battle for collectivism as such. That issue has been decided by the forces of history. As Professor Walton Hamilton says in the last paragraph of a brilliant article in the Encyclopedia of the Social Sciences, the "commitment to collectivism is beyond recall." The advance of technology, bringing new forms of communication, transportation, and production, has literally destroyed the individualistic economy of the early years of the Republic. In place of the relatively independent and self-contained households and rural neighborhoods of the Jeffersonian era, the American people stand today before a vast and complicated economic mechanism embracing the entire country and reaching out increasingly to the far corners of the globe—a fait accompli having the most revolutionary consequences. And the operation of the mechanism, dependent as it is on the planful and rational character of technology, demands more and more of coordination and unified direction and control. The alternative, as recent experience has shown, is chaos for all and deepening misery for the masses of the people. Moreover, already through the spread of the corporation, the formation of the trade associations, the organization of labor, and the growth of governmental functions during the past two generations, the collectivist character of the new age has been recognized.

But the term collectivism means both less and more than those who have been frightened by it would seem to assume. It is much less definite in its implications and far more diverse in its potentialities than they appear to imagine. As a matter of fact, to say that the American people are entering an era of collective economy is to say little in detail regarding either the structure of the society to be fashioned or the pattern of the life to be lived in the future. Such a generalization merely gives the orientation and the general direction in which the nation is moving. As Professor Hamilton says in his article, while "the commitment to collectivism is beyond recall," its "form remains to be determined." Collectivism is an extremely broad category. There is collectivism and collectivism. The term may be applied to such different systems of social thought and organization as communism, socialism, syndicalism, and fascism, as well as to social doctrines, conceptions, and practices which have been outmoded by the rise of industrial civilization or which remain to be conceived and developed. Wherever the community asserts itself, whether through class or popular rule, at least the beginnings of collectivism may be observed.

At this point in the argument THE SOCIAL FRONTIER takes a positive stand. Accepting the rise of a collectivist order as irrevocable, it refuses to adopt a fatalistic attitude toward the question of the form which collectivism is to take in the United States. It believes that within the broad limits set by technology many choices are possible and that education, the school, the teacher will play a role, commensurate with the power of the institutions and persons involved, in the making of those choices.

The most crucial and fundamental of the choices which the American people will be called upon to make, which they are being called upon to make, has to do with controlling purposes and interests. Is the emerging collectivist economy to be managed primarily in the interests—material and cultural—of that small fraction of the population, which by one means or another has gained title to most of the wealth of the country? Or is it to be managed openly and honestly in the interests of the great masses of the people who do the work of the nation and live by the services, which they render society? THE SOCIAL FRONTIER is persuaded that here lies a genuine and irreconcilable conflict of interests, that here the American people must make in the years ahead one of the truly grand choices of history.

With respect to this fundamental issue THE SOCIAL FRONTIER will not, cannot, remain neutral. The editors are convinced that no educational journal can actually remain neutral on a question of this kind, whatever its professions. THE SOCIAL FRONTIER will throw all the strength it possesses on the side of those forces, which are striving to fashion a form of collectivism that will make paramount the interests of the overwhelming majority of the population. It will fight in its pages, both in season and out of season, for a social order in which no child will be starved and dwarfed, coddled and pampered, by reason of the accidents of birth and circumstance. It will battle for the fulfillment in the advancing age of the ideal of equality of opportunity, which has always constituted fire core of the American democratic tradition. In taking this position it is confident that it will have the support of at least ninety per cent of the teachers of the country.

THE SOCIAL FRONTIER also will fight for a collectivism, which will cherish, preserve, and fulfill the American ideals of freedom of speech, cultural diversity, and personal liberty, security, and dignity. It abhors regimentation of public opinion; it swears with Jefferson "eternal hostility to every form of tyranny over the mind of man." It regards economic goods not as the chief end of life, but rather as a basis and a means for the development of the human spirit. It views the present concentration of wealth and power in the hands of a few, with its implications of class rule and domination, as an oppressive obstacle to the personal growth of American boys and girls and as a perpetual threat to the liberties of the masses of the people. To those who say that collectivism means regimentation the answer is that collectivism is upon us and that the only hope for freedom for the many lies in the direction of a democratic control over the material sources of the abundant life. The only freedom which THE SOCIAL FRONTIER would curtail is the freedom of one man to enslave and exploit another. In the achievement of this goal if it is to be achieved without protracted and nation-wide strife, education must play an important role in the clarification of issues and the alignment of forces.

ACADEMIC FREEDOM *

The Editorial Board

I n this article, the journal's editorial board assumes that forces were in play in American culture which would deliberately try to limit the role of teachers in shaping broader social policy. The increasingly common practice of imposing loyalty oaths on American teachers was seen by them as a means of deliberately controlling the ability of teachers to voice their own opinions about pressing social issues, and "to accelerate and enhance those forces and tendencies in society, which will make for a free education—free to aid in the creation of a social order equal to the demands and opportunities of contemporary life." Of all of the tasks facing American teachers, maintaining academic freedom was seen by the journal's editorial board as the single most important task facing them as professionals. The theme of academic freedom was one that would reoccur again and again in the journal, Several key articles on this subject were contributed by John Dewey.

*   *   *

First in importance among the tasks, which face American teachers, is the achievement of genuine academic freedom. Moreover, the logic of unfolding events both within and outside the school will increase the significance of this task and intensify the issues clustering about it.

Already signs of an impending struggle for such status of the educational profession as would enable it to discharge its responsibilities in this crucial period of our national history is becoming visible. Likewise visible is the tightening of the lines for the battle, which seems to be impending.

On the one hand, certain sections of our community are busy devising instruments that would secure our inherited social order against the influence of teachers with a vision of the future. On the other hand, the teachers of the nation are coming to realize that their sphere of action is the full context of social life and their goal a new way of social living. Note the following plank in the platform of the NEA:

ACADEMIC FREEDOM OR THE AMERICAN CHILD'S RIGHT TO UNFETTERED TEACHING—Teachers should have the privilege of presenting all points of view, including their own, on controversial issues without danger of reprisal by the school administration or by pressure groups in the community. Teachers should also be guaranteed the constitutional rights of freedom of speech, press, and assembly and the right to support actively organized movements, which they consider to be in their own, and the public inter-

---

* **Source:** *The Social Frontier*, Volume 1, Number 2, 1934, pp. 4-6.

est. The teacher's conduct outside the school should be subject only to such controls as those to which other responsible citizens are subjected. The sudden singling out of teachers to take an oath of allegiance is a means of intimidation, which can be used to destroy the right of academic freedom.

Equally significant are the multiplication within recent years of cases of summary discharges, compulsory resignations, non-renewal of contracts at all levels of the profession because of holding or presenting in or out of class "novel," "bizarre," un-American," and "subversive" views, as well as the tendency to subject candidates for teaching positions to the political inquisitions. In a recent letter Dr. George J. Ryan, President of the Board of Education of New York City admonished the Board of Examiners to shut the door of the school system to those who do not accept our present institutional framework as the final phase in the process of God's self-realization. Vigorously Dr. Ryan commands: "Let us close the door now against any who may seek a teaching position for the purpose of teaching American children un-American or subversive doctrines. . . . We do not want them in the public schools and I call upon the Board of Examiners to keep them out."

The success of teachers in the oncoming struggle for academic freedom depends much upon their realization of the social importance and necessity of this objective, a clear picture of what genuine academic freedom is, and the adoption of a strategy adequate to its attainment.

The social importance of academic freedom arises from the crisis that is facing contemporary civilization—a crisis which imposes upon teachers grave responsibilities and affords them unprecedented opportunities. It is becoming ever more manifest that the conflict between a technological civilization essentially collectivistic and an institutional culture based on irresponsible individualism, between obvious economic inequalities and pretensions of political and ethical equality, cannot be resolved without a radical change in the basic structure of society. The social order is disjointed; its equilibrium is sorely disturbed. The life of every sensitive individual presents a drama of conflict of ideas and ideals. As long as this condition obtains—and it must obtain as long as economic inequalities give the lie to the fundamental ideals of equality upon which American society is ostensibly based—movements and overt actions tending toward social stability and individual integration and adjustment must inevitably continue.

That much is certain. What is not certain—and it is in this realm of uncertainty that education can prominently figure—are the lines along which stabilization will eventuate and the manner in which such stabilization will be effected. With respect to the social pattern that will come to take the place of the chaos of our present social structure the alternative possibilities are first, an economic and social hierarchy of classes held together by an authoritarian state with a propaganda calculated to turn free men into slaves, and second, a complete economic democracy which alone can give meaning to political and ethical democracy. Nor is the road to stabilization clearly marked out. Here too alternative possibilities suggest themselves. The sequence of events leading to social equilibrium may be consummated in protracted civil strife or in such change of the correlation of forces of society as will make catastrophe unnecessary. Which will it be? That nobody can predict. But it does seem that the educators of the nation can weight the historic process so as to improve the prospects for the desirable alternatives in each case. An educational profession that is alive to its social responsibilities and free to function in the educational guidance of children and adults in their contemporary perplexities can do much to shift social forces from reinforcement of our price and profit economy to an alignment backing a collectivistic economy of social utility. It is these considerations which make academic freedom an objective of paramount importance to the teachers of the nation.

Academic freedom in a socially significant sense is not limited to university and college levels. It does not exhaust itself in the liberty to reflect on issues and propositions in a non-partisan spirit. It means more than the individual's liberty to teach according to the dictates of his conscience in an institutional set-up dominated by a spirit which he has no hand in creating. The liberty to teach under given conditions without effective power for changing these conditions confines the scope of education within hopelessly narrow limits. What guidance in the social dilemmas of the present can education afford, if for example, teachers are handpicked by external authority for the points of view they hold? And yet this is precisely what Dr. Ryan is attempting in the elementary and secondary levels of New York City schools and what President Sproul of the University of California is attempting on the higher levels. For sheer sophistry, defined by Aristophanes as the art of making the wrong cause seem right, very few public statements can compare with the following excerpt from President Sproul's 1934 report:

> "Essentially the freedom of a university is the freedom of competent persons in the classroom. In order to protect this freedom, the university assumes the right to prevent exploitation of its prestige by unqualified persons or by those who would use it as a platform for propaganda. It therefore takes great care in the appointment of its teachers."

Academic freedom can be of moment only if conceived as that state of affairs which makes it possible for the educators of the country to stimulate the efforts of individual men and of social classes to the quest for a democratically stable form of living. The issue of academic freedom hinges on the right of the educational profession to take sides in the conflict between the inherited social order and that rendered possible by modern socio-economic realities. Freedom within the academy may be important enough but freedom of the academy—in all its branches, the kindergarten, elementary and secondary school, and the university—to give direction to social change is far more important. For the academy to function effectively: in the large sphere of social action teachers must have the right to shape educational institutions by devising curricula and determining methods, by selecting textbooks, by having a voice in administrative control, and by participating in the selection of new teachers and in the elimination of the unfit. In short, academic freedom can only be genuine if it means a high degree of self-determination for the educational profession.

A clear conception as to what constitutes socially significant academic freedom is essential to its attainment. But the how is quite as important as the. A shift of emphasis in the struggle for professional freedom is clearly indicated. All too often the emphasis in the past struggles has been on the violation of the "rights of man" or of the "civil rights" of individual teachers, on the spirit of philistinism, ignorance, and prudery that would retard the progress of the biological and social sciences. Continuation of the battle along these lines cannot be expected to result in that broad liberation of the educational profession, which is necessary for its fuller functioning in the present social situation. The "rights of man," "civil rights," and "science" are concepts altogether too vague to serve as points of departure for the creation of conditions which will facilitate enlarged educational functions. The task of the educator of today is not to re-fight the battles of the 18th century. It is that of bringing professional activities to bear in giving direction to the social tendencies of today. In the struggle for academic freedom the emphasis should be on the main issue—securing such conditions for the educational profession as would make it possible for education to participate in laying the foundations for a new social order.

It is by no means an easy task, which confronts the teacher. And yet the effort is worthwhile. For it is only by such effort that the educational profession can secure its place in the shaping of the destinies of the nation and thus help to create a social environment where the work of the educator can result in the "good life" in its individual and social aspects. By his intelligent and determined effort he can accelerate and enhance those forces and tendencies in society, which will make for a free education—free to aid in the creation of a social order equal to the demands and opportunities of contemporary life.

EDITORIAL COMMENTS ON THE SOCIAL FRONTIER *

The Editorial Board

Newspapers from across the country responded to the publication of *The Social Frontier*. The response was decidedly mixed; praise for the effort coming from *The New York Times* and *The Portland Oregonian*, and accusations of traces of "Russian Sovietism" from *The Indianapolis News* and *The Springfield Evening Union*. The latter accused the journal of being "devoted to the abolition of the profit system in American business and industry." Quotes from newspaper responses to the initial issue of the journal were printed in its second issue and are included below. They provide an interesting insight into the political conservatism of the period, and the belief that Columbia University was a center for Leftist thought and revolution.

* * *

The New York Times, September 18, 1934

The appearance of an educational monthly which will not only discuss social problems but also "definitely take sides" is noteworthy because of its personnel. The free air of the frontier will blow through its pages. The editor and the members of the board are nearly all men who were born on what was but lately our physical frontier or at a distance from the great urban centres: Kansas, Nebraska, Indiana, Georgia, Vermont. They come for the most part from old American stock. They know the traditions of America. They had first-hand knowledge of its individualistic virtues. They are realists who have as much at heart the welfare of this nation as any company of passionate idealists. That men of such high professional knowledge and strong patriotic purpose should undertake this venture will at any rate lead to fresh appraisement of educational values in the face of the changing order and make against the lethargy into which fixed systems are so apt to lead.

. . . It is a good thing for society to have such educational leaders out on the frontier, ever in search for the better.

The Indianapolis News, September 22, 1934

Dr. George S. Counts, professor of education at Teachers College, Columbia University—whence came some members of the brain

---

* **Source:** *The Social Frontier*, Volume 1, Number 2, 1934, p. 22.

trust—is to edit a new magazine called "THE SOCIAL FRONTIER."
Prof. John Dewey is to be connected with the editorial management. .
. . The announcement which is a trifle vague, shows a trace of Russian
sovietism and it definitely opposes the right of the individual to better
his condition if he can. It would be interesting to know whether the
editor of the new publication and his associates have been taking advantage of the profit system since they were old enough to shift for
themselves. They have sold their intellectual products to the highest
market and their lives have been ordered on a basis of attempting to
have something set aside for their old age after they had met the cost
of living. . . . The end of individualism and the substitution of collectivism and "classlessness," means finally the reducing of all persons to
the same level of mediocrity.

The Dayton Herald, September 26, 1934

In this connection it is interesting to note that a new monthly magazine. THE SOCIAL FRONTIER, one of whose objects will be the
abolition of the profit system, is to be established by a number of university professors and others, with Dr. George S. Counts, professor of
education at Teachers' College, Columbia University, as editor, and
Dr. John Dewey, professor of philosophy at Columbia, as a contributing editor. . . . Columbia is the university, which furnished Dr. Ray-
mond Moley and Dr. Rexford Guy Tugwell to the national
administration. So far as one may judge their expressions of opinion,
they do not concur in the opinion of Dr. Counts and Dr. Dewey that
"collectivism and classness" [sic] ought to be substituted for the profit
system. Nor is there any reason to believe that in the privacy of their
own souls they do in fact concur with these other Columbia educators. Yet the establishment of this new magazine, and the source from
which it receives the gift of life, makes it clear that the idea has a certain degree of earnest advocates.

The Worcester Evening Gazette, September 18, 1934

The profit system has taken some pretty hard blows in the last few
years. Any system that can stand a loss of a hundred billion dollars,
and still survive, is some system. And there must be profits somewhere. Because a new magazine is going to be started, with some-
body's profits, to combat the system. . . . The new monthly, which will
be called the SOCIAL FRONTIER, aims to make this the kind of
country in which such a periodical could not be published. In Russia,

which is the only collectivist state we have, literature, art, and education are controlled by the government in the interest of propaganda. No professor in Moscow can start a magazine in opposition to the established order.

If THE SOCIAL FRONTIER could limit its activities to showing us how to correct such defects in the profit system, everybody might hope that the magazine would make profits enough to continue in the field until its mission was accomplished.

The Bridgeport Telegram, September 18, 1934

Columbia University has long been a hotbed of Communism.

Now there is to be a new "educational monthly" which presumably the students at Teachers' College will be encouraged to buy, which will further the principles of "the cause." The new publication is to be known as "THE SOCIAL FRONTIER."

Russia today is the prime example of the society for which Dr. Counts and his fellow workers, Dr. William H. Kilpatrick and Professor Dewey are striving. It has abolished the profit system and its "social motivation is a collective classlessness," to paraphrase the academic phraseology of Dr. Counts.

If these phrases have any precise meaning in English, they mean the Communist system, and we are not using "Communist" in any loose sense. We mean the specific ethics, policy, and program of the Communist party as exemplified in Russia. This is the glorious goal to which "The New Frontier" [sic] is dedicated.

The Springfield Evening Union, September 26, 1934

Columbia University, to which Walter Scott [sic] and his "Technocracy" brought much publicity of a dubious nature, is in for more of the same nature, apparently. Dr. George S. Counts, professor of education in Teachers College, will edit a new magazine, "THE SOCIAL FRONTIER," devoted to the abolition of the profit system in American business and industry. Associated with him in this capacity will be Professor John Dewey . . . Who is financing this new publishing venture is not stated. Leaders of the Federal Administration have disclaimed a purpose to war on the profit system, and none of the men who have been picked for Dr. Counts' editorial staff is definitely enrolled as a New Dealer, apparently. The inevitable effect will be to increase public distrust of colleges as a breeding place of opposition to our present form of government.

Harry Elmer Barnes in the New York World-Telegram, October 26, 1934

Many who heartily sympathized with the tenor and content of the Report [of the Commission on Social Studies of the American Historical Association] feared lest its effect might be highly temporary—a flash in the pan soon to be forgotten in the hurly-burly of tabulating grades and quizzing reluctant sophomores. Such persons will be delighted to know that their fears have proved ill founded.

Most of the men who signed the famous report of last spring, together with other sympathetic and distinguished educators, have launched the most promising and realistic educational journal of our generation. It is entitled "THE SOCIAL FRONTIER."
The contents of the first number are indeed gratifying.

The Portland Oregonian, October 18, 1934

Twenty-six distinguished academicians of New York City have banded themselves together and launched a magazine, "THE SOCIAL FRONTIER—a journal of educational criticism and reconstruction," which fills a need and deserves a distinguished career.

Apparently the enterprise results partly from disappointment with the National Education Association, which at its last session took the stand that education, should modify itself to fit changing social conditions, rather than take the bull by the horns and seek to change conditions. With this modest stand of the N. E. A., the New York group (which plans to expand into a national group) has no sympathy. It believes the professors have the brains and the right to a voice in affairs.

Announcement is made that THE SOCIAL FRONTIER subscribes to the historical association's analysis and prophecy—that it believes individualism done with and collectivism approaching. That seems to us to be jumping unnecessarily far ahead, but at least it will be interesting to watch the unfolding of the academic argument, and if the articles by John Dewey, Charles A. Beard, Henry P. Fairchild, Sidney Hook, and Goodwin Watson, contained in the first issue, are a fair indication of what is to come, at least the new collectivism is to have brilliant and clear advocacy. That will be an advance; for the public has been much confused.

CHAMPIONS OF FREEDOM [*]

The Editorial Board

In this article, the journal's editorial board calls on teachers to consider what is meant by "freedom" in the United States, its purpose and whom it serves. The authors make clear that that the rhetoric of freedom is often invoked by business interests to serve their own class-based social, political and economic needs—not the needs of the culture. There is the perhaps naïve assumption on the part of *The Social Frontier's* editorial board that teachers have not only the interest but the actual potential power to shape the political discourse of the period.

*   *   *

It is an important function of the educational profession to clarify the meaning of those ideas that ostensibly constitute the basis of our national traditions and institutions. To this proposition few would take exception. Even self-proclaimed patriots would readily assent to it. Somewhat more daring, but in fact incapable of frightening any but the fossilized, is the view that it is a legitimate function of education to re-interpret national ideals in the light of the changing context of group life.

Yet axiomatic as these propositions appear, the active application of them might well have profound social consequences. It might achieve a shift in popular thought and opinion with respect to the sacred cows of private property and individual profit and lead to the new conception of shared utilization of cultural and economic resources. Unfortunately, most teachers are too busy handing out cut-and-dried subject matter in classrooms and chewing the pedagogic cud in conferences and convention halls to discuss the present day implications of basic national and human ideals. The consequence of their preoccupation with trade wares is that such conceptions as "freedom," "liberty," and "opportunity" have become the private property of those who at present wield power. These concepts are used as instruments for denying to the large masses freedom to work, to consume, to live significantly, and for perpetuating existing inherited inequalities in opportunity.

In recent months the American people have been treated to an avalanche of declamations on the beauties of freedom and to a deluge of warnings about the dangers to freedom lurking behind efforts at social experimentation. In this tearful chorus industrialists, financiers, statesmen, politicians, professional patriots, and owners of large metropolitan dailies have all participated. Some

---

[*] **Source:** *The Social Frontier*, Volume 1, Number 3, 1934, pp. 8–9

distinguished physicists and college administrators have seen fit to add their voices to the rest. Silent and unheard, however, were those whose professional function it is to transmit and interpret the ideas, ideals, and attitudes of the American people—the teachers of the nation.

It is important that the teacher lift his eyes from the textbook to view the various interpretations of the idea of freedom and to examine the uses to which it is to be put. He might inquire: Whose freedom are these eager votaries interested in safeguarding? Freedom for what and from what? What social system do those who sail under the flag of "freedom" wish to preserve or bring into being? There is a strong likelihood that the teacher would discover the current interpretations to be either incorrect or outworn and the applications socially undesirable.

He would probably discover that few if any of the latest devotees of freedom are devoured by a consuming passion for the freedom of the masses of the people to live rich, meaningful, and creative lives. When Chairman Weir of the National Steel Corporation speaks of freedom he means both the freedom of a small group of industrialists to hire and fire and the denial of the right of labor to organize strong and independent labor unions. James Warburg of the Bank of Manhattan means by freedom the freedom of bankers to manipulate the fluid national capital and freedom from governmental control. Representative Beck of Pennsylvania means by freedom the freedom of businessmen to profit and accumulate wealth, unchecked by taxation. Lieutenant Governor Bacon of Massachusetts is concerned over the freedom of property from social control. Vice-President Sulzberger of the NEW YORK TIMES means by freedom the freedom of newspaper owners to sell space to whomever they please unhampered by governmental supervision over the veracity of the advertisement and the quality of the article advertised. Similar interpretations of freedom are given by Theodore Roosevelt, Herbert Hoover, Alfred E. Smith, James Wadsworth, and the surprisingly enough, by such eminent scientists as Robert A. Millikan and Arthur Compton. The fallacy that the freedom to profit is essential to cultural creativeness which underlies the argument of the latter is so lucidly brought out in Dr. Watson's article in the present issue of THE SOCIAL FRONTIER as to make further comment on this point unnecessary.

In fine, the chief concern of the authors of the various recent jeremiads is the freedom of merchants, manufacturers, and the bankers to buy anything—including human labor—and to sell everything; the freedom to bring about or maintain a state of affairs in society which will enable the individuals in the owning classes to conduct selling and buying transactions with a view to maximum profits, regardless of social consequences—in short, the freedom of those who now wield power in society to retain and to increase their power. Of course, they speak of freedom within the law. But by law they mean the present law under which both rich and poor have an equal right to starve, to acquire culture, to gain control over the agencies which form public opinion, and to organize lobbies and liberty leagues.

It is scarcely probable that teachers will unanimously accept such interpretations of the idea of freedom. The dissenters who take seriously their professional duties to society should find it difficult to refrain from correcting the untrue and socially harmful notions about freedom, which enjoy currency.

Such dissenters—and they may be many—could contribute to the reshaping of the American mind by directing public attention to the following fairly obvious propositions:

1. Freedom does not exhaust itself in the socially guaranteed right to buy and sell at a profit. It means rather a state of affairs, which facilitates the optimum expression of all the impulses and capacities of man. Where freedom to buy or sell seriously conflicts with the broader conceptions of freedom, the need for the elimination of the narrower meaning is clearly indicated.

2. The only defensible conception of the "good life" is one which affords the greatest freedom to the greatest number. When the exercise of freedom by a small group within a certain area carries as a consequence impoverishment of life for the bulk of the population, the freedom of that group should be curtailed.

3. While it is historically true that in its rise to power the class of industrialists, financiers, and merchants has contributed much to the liberation of human activities from the bonds of authority and outworn routine, that class is no longer the carrier of the idea of freedom. In fact, it is now holding the rest of society in bondage. It is those groupings in society whose interest is to substitute the motives of creativeness and social utility, as the basis of life, for the now dominant profit motive that, for this day, can give genuine content to freedom. The champions and carriers of freedom are industrial workers, farmers, teachers, technicians, and all persons engaged in the performance of useful service.

4. The rise of modern technology renders individual freedom within the realm of the control of economic resources unworkable. Within this realm there can be only shared freedom—the collective ownership and democ-

ratic control of the wealth of the nation. Shared freedom in the economic area is the only possible method of guaranteeing both individual and shared freedom in the cultural area.

Clear and vigorous dissemination of these propositions by the teachers of the nation should contribute considerably to the preparation of the public mind for an active participation in the reconstruction of American economic, political, and social institutions.

OUR REVOLUTIONARY TRADITION *

MERLE CURTI

Merle Curti began his career at Smith College where, in 1929, he published his first book, *The American Peace Crusade, 1815–1860.* In 1931 he took a position at Teachers College. One of the founders of peace and conflict studies, Curti left Teachers College in 1942 to take an endowed chair in history at the University of Wisconsin. In1944 he won the Pulitzer Prize for his book *The Growth of American Thought.*

In the following article, Curti defends the "right of revolution" as one of the founding principles of American democracy. While recognizing that the evolution of modern American history had led to increasing restrictions being placed on those interested in taking revolutionary action in American culture, Curti concludes his article by arguing that the "radicals" in the United States rather than the Daughters of the American Revolution and "kindred societies," are the true upholders of the American revolutionary tradition.

* * *

If the fathers of our country could, by some miracle, revisit the United States today they would, no doubt, be surprised to find that in a considerable number of states the advocacy of the right of revolution is legally regarded as a very serious crime. Historically, our criminal and syndicalist laws have, in fact, not a foundation stone on which to rest. On the contrary, the right of revolution by violence has been a doctrine subscribed to by the great majority of our leading statesmen.

THE ENGLISH BACKGROUND OF OUR REVOLUTIONARY TRADITION

The doctrine of the right of resistance to authority and of revolution itself was part and parcel of the colonial inheritance from England. Colonists, particularly New England parsons, were well aware of the arguments used by Milton, Sydney, and Locke to justify the seventeenth century civil wars and revolution in the mother country. On the hundredth anniversary of the execution of Charles I, Jonathan Mayhew of Massachusetts clearly expressed the generally accepted view that under certain circumstances governments and kings could be overthrown by popular action. This doctrine, which is implicit in the natural rights philosophy, was frequently heard in the days before the Declaration

---

* **Source:** *The Social Frontier,* Volume 1, Number 3, 1934, pp. 10–13.

of Independence, and throughout the Revolution it was popularized by publicists and pamphleteers. Indeed, it would have been difficult to justify the acts of committees of public safety, the harsh treatment of the Tories, the quasi-dictatorship of Washington, and the Revolution itself without the revolutionary philosophy to which all the leaders of the revolt against England subscribed. That revolutionary philosophy was, of course, clearly expressed in the Declaration of Independence.

LEFT AND RIGHT AGREE ON THE LEGITIMACY OF REVOLUTION

Even the more conservative leaders of the Revolution, who were determined to prevent the radicals from carrying too far their program of confiscation of estates, universal suffrage, and humanitarian reforms, did not cease to pay lip service to the right of revolution in the uncertain and disintegrating years that followed the recognition of our independence. Writing in THE FEDERALIST, Alexander Hamilton, a leader in the conservative reaction against what the "wise and the well born" regarded as revolutionary excess, declared that the people, if betrayed by their representatives, might exert their original right of self-defense and overthrow their usurpers. They would have an "infinitely better prospect of success," he added, if their action were that of a people united in a single body politic; their revolutionary action would stand less chance of success if they remained separate sovereign states. In the very year when Daniel Shays frightened property owners of the whole land by a formidable revolt, John Adams, who was the exponent of conservative rule, wrote in his diary: "It is an observation of one of the profoundest inquirers into human affairs that a revolution of government is the strongest proof that can be given by a people of their virtue and good sense." Years later, in a somewhat more restrained fashion, the second president of the land expressed the belief that "revolutions ought never to be undertaken rashly, nor without deliberate consideration and sober reflection." Yet not even then did he deny the right of revolution itself. Our sixth president, the son of John Adams, also paid a glowing tribute to revolution when he wrote in his diary that "the Revolutionary age and the Constituent age were the times for great men; the administrative age is an age of small men and small things."

Madison, another leader of the conservative reaction against the attacks on property interests during the post-Revolutionary period, did not for a moment deny the right of revolution. On the contrary, in offering a series of amendments to the Constitution he placed as first in the series one in which it was declared that "the people have an indubitable, inalienable, and indefeasible right to reform or change their Government, whenever it may be found adverse or inadequate to the purposes of its institution."

If the more conservative fathers of our country continued to recognize the right of revolution after independence was a farce, the more radical men, of whom Jefferson was the leader, were naturally even more explicit. In 1787, just after Shays' Rebellion, Jefferson wrote to Madison from Paris that "a little rebellion now and then is a good thing, and as necessary in the political world as storms in the physical." Unsuccessful rebellions, he continued, "generally establish the encroachments on the rights of the people which have produced them. An observation of this truth should render honest republican governors so mild in their punishment of rebellions, as not to discourage them too much. It is a medicine necessary for the sound health of government." And to John Adams he wrote that the spirit of resistance to government was so valuable that he wished it always to be kept alive. "It will often be exercised when wrong but better so than not to be exercised at all." In writing to John Jay of the honorable way in which Shays had conducted his rebellion Jefferson declared: "God forbid that we should ever be twenty years without such a rebellion . . . what country can preserve its liberties if their rulers are not warned from time to time that their people preserve the spirit of resistance?"

Even the generation of statesmen that had not participated in the American Revolution continued to adhere to the doctrine of the right of a violent overthrow of government by the people. They did not repudiate the statement in the Declaration of Independence which asserted "That whenever any Form of Government becomes destructive of these ends, it is the Right of the People to alter or abolish it, and to institute a new Government, laying its foundations on such principles and organizing its powers in such form, as to them shall seem most likely to effect their safety and happiness." It is somewhat striking that the right of revolution should have been so generally subscribed to in view of the fact that the thirties and forties saw one after another underprivileged group resort to violence to effect a redress of grievances—the anti-rent wars in New York, the Dorr war, and the slave insurrections led by Vesey Denmark and Nat Turner were not the only examples of such flare-ups. Yet in spite of all this Daniel Webster, defender of national unity, champion of property interests, upholder of law, order, and conservatism generally, did not hesitate to admit that "the people may, if they choose, overthrow the government." In the famous debate with Hayne he declared: "We all know that civil institutions are established for the public benefit, and that when they cease to answer the ends of their existence they may be changed." Thoreau did not exaggerate things much when he wrote in his Essay on Civil Disobedience that "all men recognize the right of revolution."

To those who have thought of Abraham Lincoln as a kind of American Bismarck utilizing blood and iron to prevent the Southerners from determining their own destiny as they saw fit, it is interesting to find in his writings explicit statements on the right of revolution. While a member of Congress in 1848 Lincoln declared: "any people anywhere being inclined and having the power have the right to rise up and shake off the existing government and form a new one that suits them better. This is a most valuable, a most sacred right; a right, which we hope and believe, is to liberate the world. Nor is this right confined to cases in which the whole people of an existing government may choose to exercise it. Any portion of such people that can may revolutionize and make their own of so much of the territory as they inhabit."

Moreover, Lincoln added that "it is a quality of revolutions not to go by old lines or old laws; but to break up both, and make new ones." In his first inaugural, Lincoln said that the country with its institutions belonged to the people, and that whenever "they shall grow weary of the existing government, they can exercise their constitutional right of amendment, or their revolutionary right to dismember or overthrow it."

Of the outstanding public men during the years proceeding and during the Civil War only Charles Sumner seemed, on pacifist grounds, to question the right of revolution. And even he did not deny such a right, for, in an address before the American Peace Society in 1849 Sumner said that "sympathy with our fathers, and with the struggles for freedom now agitating Europe, must make us hesitate to question its existence." Reluctantly he admitted that if the right of revolution were upheld then the three millions of slaves were justified in "resisting to death the power that holds them." But the right of revolution was, Sumner continued, to be based on expediency and success and to be invoked with "reluctance and distrust." However much he abhorred the inherent barbarism of revolution, he felt compelled to admit that even lovers of peace must recognize that in the state of the world at that time an exigency for its use might arise.

Public men after the Civil War continued, in more or less qualified terms, to admit the right of revolution. President Grant's sympathy with captains of industry and the status quo generally did not keep him from writing in his Memoirs that "the right of revolution is an inherent one. When people are oppressed by their government, it is a natural right they enjoy to relieve themselves of the oppression, if they are strong enough, either by withdrawal from it, or by overthrowing it and substituting a government more acceptable." But Grant seems to be the last president who stated so unequivocally this traditional American theory.

NATIONAL LEADERS EXECUTE AN ABOUT TURN

Writing in his diary in 1888 ex-President Hayes expressed the belief that revolutions and "bolts" are alike. 'They are sacred when the facts justify them. When not so justified they are blunders of the sort that is worse than crime!" When ex-President Harrison took the wealthy to task for their indifference to social abuses he too, in qualified terms, expressed a conviction that under certain circumstances revolution was inevitable:

"When the house is so rotten that it is beyond repair, there is a call for him the crusader to dear the ground. But if the foundations and walls are strong and plumb, and it is only a question of a new roof or of improved internal arrangements, the man of destructive tendencies should be clubbed off the premises. . . . The tenants will stand together against the destructionists and the fire-bugs; but have a care, for if repairs are not promptly and wisely made; if the dwellers in the first floor cut off the heat and water from the dwellers in the attic, things may become so intolerable that the tenant of the attic will open the doors to the firebugs."

McKinley, Roosevelt, and Taft do not seem to have expressed themselves on the right of revolution. Wilson, indeed, was apparently the last of the presidents to speak of revolution in anything like the way his earlier predecessors had regarded it. "America was the first to set the example, the first to admit that right and justice and even the basis of revolution was a matter upon which mankind was entitled to form a judgment," declared the weary champion of the League of Nations in an address at San Francisco in 1919. Earlier, in calling attention to the fact that it was by revolution that the United States had come into existence, he had asserted that the right of revolution was too precious to be limited. Yet Wilson does not seem to have thought of the fathers of 1776 as real revolutionists for, as a constitutionalist, he once wrote that they did not stand for revolution at all, but for the maintenance of accepted practices. And in one of the last messages he gave to the American people, in 1923, "The Road Away from Revolution," he took a position somewhat similar to that of President Harrison: revolution would come unless the world were regenerated, unless the abuses of capitalism were speedily remedied.

In spite of Wilson's somewhat half-hearted recognition of the right of revolution, the temper of the times had changed. It was exceptional, not representative, when an ex-Senator, R. F. Pettigrew, wrote in 1922 that the right of revolution, "so clearly proclaimed in the Declaration of Independence, and so emphatically stated by Lincoln, remains today the avenue left to the American people as a means of escape from the intolerable plutocratic tyranny that the Constitution has drawn up." Herbert Hoover expressed the dominant attitude of public men in declaring that we had demonstrated that "our system is responsive enough to meet any new and intricate development in our economic life," without—how clear the implication!—revolution.

Indeed, by 1931 thirty-four states made the advocacy of a violent overturn of the government a penal offense. New York and New Jersey led the way in 1902, Wisconsin followed in 1903, Washington in 1909, and a large number of states in 1917, 1918, 1919, and 1920. Three years ago the Civil Liberties Union reported that most of the states without such criminal anti-syndicalist legislation were those south of the Mason-Dixon line where old reconstruction laws, aimed at penalizing incitement to insurrection and rebellion, were frequently invoked against strikers and communists. In Pennsylvania and in California the anti-syndicalist laws were frequently invoked, as they have been, from time to time, in seventeen other states. This record, taken with the changing attitude of public men toward the right of revolution, virtually indicates an about face in our public thought and action.

FEAR OF REVOLUTION CONQUERS
THE REVOLUTIONARY TRADITION

If one looks for an explanation for this change in point of view several factors come to mind. It is probably no accident that it was in the eighties and nineties that public men began to qualify the doctrine of the right of revolution. For after long eras of steady if turbulent "progress," those were the decades of hard times. In those days it was commonly feared that the American working class might fall prey to the radical agitators who were trying to inculcate the doctrines of anarchism and socialism. Labor troubles were frequent and accompanied by widespread violence and bloodshed. The memories of the great strikes of 1877, the far-reaching implications of the Homestead and Pullman affairs, the rise of a militant labor group in the western mining regions—all these instilled fear into the minds of propertied men and upholders of the status quo. The assassinations of Garfield and McKinley added coals to the fire; that of McKinley was made the pretext of the first anti-syndicalist legislation.

The Russian Revolution was another fact that doubtless has had much to do with the changing attitude toward the right of revolution! Events in the land of the czars made it clear that revolution could be successfully used by an exploited, underprivileged class to overthrow the capitalist system itself. The flood of criminal anti-syndicalist laws in the years following the rise of the Bolsheviks was the defiant answer of the ruling class in America to radical agitators who preached a new kind of revolution in the land of liberty. Traditionally, the right of revolution had been associated in men's minds with the overthrow of feudal, aristocratic, and monarchical institutions. The American Revolution, in addition to bringing about national independence, was an important step in the rise of the middle class: the Revolution saw the abolition of such feudal and aristocratic survivals as union of church and state, entails, primogeniture, and the like. A revolution that was associated in men's minds with the triumph of the middle class was one thing; a revolution which threatened to overthrow the middle class and substitute the rule of the proletariat, was another. It was not until such a revolution became a possibility that our public men began to qualify their adherence to the traditional right of revolution, and to enact laws making its advocacy a high crime.

Still another factor explains the changing attitude noticeable in the statements of the presidents after the time of Grant. As long as there was an abundance of cheap or free lands in the West, the discontented could leave the seaboard factory towns and make a new start more to their liking. Even if the cost of acquiring an equipment to go to the frontier was more than the newest immigrants and the poorest workers could afford, at least the possibility of "going west" was ever present. The frontier, in short, was, as students of Frederick Jackson Turner are well aware, a kind of safety valve. It was relatively safe to talk freely about the right of revolution when the vast, cheap lands of the West kept alive the idea of equality of opportunity, of easy escape from cramped and intolerable conditions. But in 1890 the census bureau called attention to the fact that the frontier had come to an end. The disappearance of the great substitute for revolutionary action for the redress of grievances was accompanied, naturally enough, by a qualification on the part of the ruling class of the right of revolution itself.

Other factors, no doubt, contributed to the changed attitude. The revolutionary insurrection of the Filipinos after the Spanish-American war was clear proof of the danger of the doctrine of the right of revolution, once a formidable group acted upon it. The reform movement of the first decade of the twentieth century, in which the initiative, referendum, and recall the direct election of senators, and other governmental devices seemed to put government into the hands of the people, likewise must have made the right of revolution seem less necessary and excusable.

THE FATHERS VERSUS THE DAUGHTERS

In spite of the contemporary denial in our public thought of the right of revolution, American liberals and radicals may at least call attention to the fact that throughout most of our history our leading public men have unequivocally subscribed to that right. Mr. Justice Wilson's hope that the right of revolution would be taught as a principle of the federal constitution will probably remain a hope. Yet here and there an educator may, in spite of the conservative forces controlling the schools, point out that the radicals, rather than the D.A.R. and kindred societies, are today the true upholders of the American revolutionary.

NON-PARTISAN EDUCATION FOR POLITICAL INTELLIGENCE *

HARRY D. GIDEONSE

T̶he problem of indoctrination and education is one that is discussed throughout the pages of *The Social Frontier*. It was a subject that was addressed at length by figures such as William H. Kilpatrick and George S. Counts. In the following article by the economist, and future President of Brooklyn College and the New School for Social Research, Harry D. Gideonse assumes that to some extent indoctrination is an inevitable function of education. What he questions, however, is whether or not this should be a conscious process.

*   *   *

THE ISSUE: CONSCIOUS INDOCTRINATION VERSUS EDUCATION

Indoctrination is probably an essential and inevitable function of education in the broadest sense of the term. Social cohesion and the very notion of a "society" may depend upon some such process of "making" citizens. The real question is not whether we should have freedom or indoctrination in the schools, but rather whether we should make a conscious and deliberate attempt at imposition there. There will be plenty of unconscious indoctrination resulting from the fact that the school operates in a given social setting. Society has other agencies—such as the family, the church, the press, and the political party—to attend to the process of conscious indoctrination. Is there not peril to the school and to society in a program that seeks to make the school an instrument of conscious inculcation of purposes and of values? Can an educator who subscribes to the purpose of deliberately propagandizing his students according to his own particular insight and values really object to the sort of propaganda that currently swamps curricula from the side of various vested interests of a social, commercial, or "patriotic" sort?

The issue of indoctrination versus education has arisen because of a commendable concern for the social distress, which surrounds us, and as a reaction to the aimless drift, which is characteristic of much of our teaching. It is assumed that our "social order" has "broken down" and the need for a new school program is proclaimed which will train the young to think in terms of the new society that will arise from the ashes of the old. Usually the issue is simplified in the slogan that "laissez-faire" has failed us and that a new "collective" society is dawning. In the language of the Report of the Commission on

* **Source:** *The Social Frontier*, Volume 1, Number 4, 1935, pp. 15–18.

Social Studies of the American Historical Association, "The age of individualism and laissez-faire in economy and government is closing and a new age of collectivism is emerging."

NEEDED: EDUCATION FOR INTELLIGENT APPROACH TO THE EXISTING SOCIAL SYSTEM

Now these are in part technical economic questions, which go far beyond the special competence of professors of education. It would be easy, however, to cite a score of examples—that would be within the understanding of the layman—to prove that much of our generalizing about the breakdown of laissez-faire or capitalism is just depression.

People, for instance, speak of our banking troubles as evidence of the "breakdown" of capitalism. Canada and Western Europe are just as "capitalistic" as we are, however, and they have not experienced banking difficulties comparable in any way with ours. Sometimes our corrupt local politics is cited as evidence of an inevitable tendency under our institutions. Again it is observed that similar trends do not exist abroad (England or Scandinavia, for instance), or in some of our own cities. Or people blame everything on the newspapers, which are supposed to mislead the public and to be as bad as they are, because they are "in it for profit." Cool and illuminating afterthought reveals, of course, that we also have some excellent newspapers and that they are not the least profitable.

In every one of these cases it is clear that some of the difficulty lies in the use people make of their institutions rather than in the institutions themselves. We have antiquated banking institutions for the simple and satisfactory reason that we do not care enough about the problem to go out and get ourselves better ones. We have corrupt local politics and a yellow press for the same reason. If we wanted a change, it wouldn't be necessary to change the nature of the "social order." Both the desirable and the undesirable conditions can be found in the United States or in other countries with the same social institutions. What is missing in America is a vital and significant sense of the importance of political intelligence and action. Dreaming away about the future Utopia is as fruitless as a defeatist withdrawal into the supreme glories of the past. After all, we are to live in the "here and now," and not in the Utopia to be or in the glory that was. This means that the school should give a vigorous introduction into the operation of our present institutions, which would enable the student to understand the conditions and forces at work. There is an important difference—as John Dewey has recently pointed out— between education with respect to a changing society and indoctrination into settled convictions about that society.

It might be added that this is not mere conservatism. It will require plenty of training and moral courage in the teaching profession to carry this task out with some standard of excellence. Much of the criticism of the new "indoctrinators" will come from those who are aroused by any effort to stimulate thought about present conditions and who fear that the new trend will expose the indoctrination for a reactionary social order that is so common in our schools. To keep these various pressure groups in leash is a task sufficient for the day. It will take every bit of our professional resources to see this through in a time of growing social strife and tension. It may well be that the effort to carry out this "conservative" program will aid in solving the problem of the "new social order" at the same time.

THE DANGERS AND COSTS OF PROPAGANDA

Such a program, however, requires a broader training than our teachers, or teachers' teachers, now receive. It will reject vague general criticism of the status quo leading to a futilitarian sophistication. It will insist on the best available technical assistance in studying technical problems. It will not go to sociologists or political scientists for its guidance on economic questions, and vice versa. The first issue of THE SOCIAL FRONTIER, for instance, has an article on an economic subject by a New York University sociologist. Aside from the gentleman's personal merits, has it ever occurred to the editor to ask New York University economists what they think of the qualifications of their colleague in connection with this subject? Or did the editor inquire amongst his own colleagues at Columbia University who are qualified to deal with these problems? Or is the new education "celebrating" the amateur irrespective of technical qualifications? Again, the Charter for the Social Sciences[1] by Charles A. Beard presents a "distillation of American history" which states that the American nation "seems to have set for itself the goal of "national planning" and the expansion of "insurance systems to cover protection against sickness, old age, unemployment, disaster, and hazards to civilized life." Now it is one thing to consider these things desirable objectives for future policy. It is still another to observe that this is our present program, but it is a flat untruth (misstatement of historical fact) to say that they can be discovered as the goals which the American nation has set for itself according to its own history. This is a view of history that is almost as far from Ranke's "wie es eigentlich gewesen ist" as Henry Ford's famous dictum that "history is bunk." The peril of it all might well be that "history" (or "social studies") under such a definition is likely to become a controversial subject comparable to religion and un-suitable for instruction in the schools for the same reason. Whatever propa-gandists may call such new "education," it smells like propaganda—and a viciously untruthful sort—under any other name. We might leave these things to the American equivalents of Moscow and of Dr. Goebbels. A free school should have no truck with it.

Study of our contemporary social difficulties should increase our doubts as to the wisdom of indoctrination as a remedy. Some of the most serious dif-ficulties confronting the American people today are the result of past indoc-trination. So much of our monetary tradition was "fixed" in the election of 1896 that many current attitudes towards wholly different monetary problems are determined by it. We were "taught" that "sound" money won in Bryan's defeat. Had we been taught the merits of the underlying social issue, it might have been possible to carry a more flexible attitude over into our contempo-rary problem. Our instruction in monetary matters has been so largely imposi-tion that even those who "free" themselves to the "gold fetish" fall right back into Father Coughlin's arms (and incidentally those of the Committee for the Nation with its depreciated equities) with new if lower gold rigidities. Few out-side the circle of academic economists seem to be able to recognize the obvi-ous fact that 90% of our media of exchange are created by banks and that their expansion or contraction has little to do with the old commodity money, whether it be silver or gold. Similarly "training" in the Constitution has been so rigid that it actually overlooked the Constitution's chief historical merit, to wit its flexibility in the face of emergency and new facts. These rigidities in our training are the result of indoctrination. After breaking our way painfully through the hard shell of one cake of custom, shall we promptly bake our-selves into another? Isn't that the very danger we should avoid in view of the obvious speed of transition that characterizes our current social situation?

THE VITAL PROMISE OF UNRECONSTRUCTED LIBERALISM

This is the viewpoint of an unreconstructed liberal. "Unreconstructed" needs no further explanation. "Liberal" does in a time in which both Donald Richberg and John W. Davis lay claim to the title. Just how the term "Liberal" in America has come to signify its exact opposite, is an interesting query for the historian of ideas. Suffice it for me to say that I use "Liberal" in its John Stuart Mill sense, that is to say, its "laissez faire" sense. In other words most of our contemporary "liberals" have no valid claim to the label. They are on the one hand defenders of the privileges of the corporate status quo, and on the other, various groups of contemporary neo-mercantilists classified according to the intensity of their creed as radicals, progressives, socialists, or communists. Most of them wish to return to the sort of bound and regulated society that preceded Adam Smith, and they are making The Wealth of Nations up to date again. Thirty years of NRA and AAA will make John Stuart Mill seem a revolutionary author.

Now laissez faire never was a mere do-nothing policy, even if that is one of the illusions of our historically illiterate contemporaries. Properly understood, it was a vigorous—and at times revolutionary—attack upon entrenched social, commercial and industrial privilege. "Freedom" never can mean absolute freedom. It always means freedom within a given social framework of institutional practices and standards. As the institutional framework changes, difficulties may arise. Some are inclined to blame these on the freedom. They naively prescribe detailed regulations and interferences by the collectivity as a remedy. Essentially this is an anti liberal position. Others seek such shifts in the institutional setting as will allow a free, that is, competitive situation to emerge again as the ultimate agency of control—that is the genuine liberal position. In the political field this may well mean a vigorous program of monetary, fiscal, and corporate reform, for instance. It would set the public authority against such outgrowths of competition as would end in the destruction of competition. It certainly is not a "status quo" philosophy. In the end, however, it relies upon freedom for the producer and consumer, and it regards it as the function of the state to establish and maintain such conditions that it may avoid the necessity of regulating the "heart of the contract" —that is to say, the necessity of regulating prices themselves.[2]

Such a program preserves the economic freedom that is the essential basis of the equality of opportunity and the democratic way of life, which are supposed to be the basic social ideals of America. On such a platform we could seek to make the schools as free of conscious inculcation of purposes and of values as it is socially possible to make them. With some such ideal we could confidently confront those who—as Oliver Wendell Holmes said—would "think of waterproofing the American mind against the questions that heaven rains down upon it." Education could then be, in Goodwin Watson's splendid words, "humanity on its knees, confessing the inadequacy of what has been." Its moral strength would lie in the study and interpretation of contemporary American society in the light of the best technical knowledge available. Considering the quality and the training of our teaching personnel such would seem to be a sufficient task for the next decade or so.

The moral and intellectual bankruptcy of some of our professional educators is almost as pathetic as that of some of the new era leaders in other fields.

On the one hand, an attractive group of able young men are bartering the moral freedom of the school for a mess of ill-digested collectivist pottage. On the other, professional administrators still hold solemn assemblies and talk to one another about the regrouping of the number of years in one educational unit when compared with another. Solemn disputes are carried on concerning the arithmetic of the twelve years under the college level. Meanwhile public confidence in education dwindles and the fascist wolf is at the door. It sounds like a dispute about the cabin decorations while the ship has a hole in her bottom.

FAITH IN INDOCTRINATION BELONGS
IN THE SCRAP HEAP OF HISTORY

Even if we allow for all of our modern social hedging about such absolutes, is it old-fashioned to point to the old precept about the truth that "will make you free"? And is it malicious to inquire why Professor Henry Johnson's Report for the American Historical Association's Commission on the Social Studies doesn't get more attention from those who are so enthusiastic about that body's final recommendations? It contains a direct answer to some of the current questions, an able historical essay on the history of the teaching of history. Education seems for a long time to have been a process of "adjustment to a changing world." Most of our leading "progressive" notions are found to be of venerable age and if "some eighteenth century ideas are still useful, there might be a certain economy in taking them out of the eighteenth century instead of taking them out of our own creative energies." On the other hand, "there might be a certain economy in knowing that the nineteenth century abandoned some eighteenth century ideas which we are now discovering."

Conscious indoctrination seems to have been one of these.

References

1 Part I: Report of the Commission of the Social Studies of the American Historical Association.

2 Cf. Henry C. Simons, A Positive Program for Laissez-Faire, Public Policy Pamphlet No. 15, University of Chicago Press.

THE HEARST ATTACK ON ACADEMIC FREEDOM *

THE EDITORIAL BOARD

The following article outlines the attempts of the Hearst newspaper chain to demonstrate how the leaders of the Social Reconstruction Movement were supposedly trying to politically indoctrinate students at schools such as Syracuse University, Teachers College, Columbia University and New York University. While William Randolph Hearst's right to oppose Communism is maintained, the editors of *The Social Frontier* strongly asserts that: "He has no right to try to choke off free discussion of Communism or anything else, to dominate economic inquiry in the universities or to interfere with the sanctity of the classroom. He has no right to paint impartial study as a "plague of radicalism." His actions were seen as a direct attack on the free speech in the United States. The article includes a series of newspaper editorial responses to Hearst's attack, as well as a reporting of those opposed to and supporting Hearst's position.

*   *   *

In the pages that follow the editors of THE SOCIAL FRONTIER have endeavored to give a documentary account of the Hearst attack upon academic freedom. While much available material from the press of the country has been left out because of limitations of space, the materials here assembled are thought to give a fair representation of what has happened to date. The account will be divided into three parts: first, the attack by the Hearst press; second, the counter-attack by the teachers involved; and third, the repercussions and alignments of some of the social groups and forces in the country. A concluding word will be said about Mr. Hearst and the ethics of the press.

The Attack at Syracuse University

The attack began in Syracuse last November. The following excerpt is taken from a two column front page editorial with the seven column news-head "Drive All Radical Professors and Students from University" in the Syracuse JOURNAL, November 22, 1934.

"The great champion of genuine Americanism, Mr. W. R. Hearst, recently wired the editor of this paper as follows:

'PLEASE SUPPORT THE ACTIONS OF THE UNIVERSITIES IN THROWING OUT THOSE COMMUNISTS, AND SAY, FURTHER-

---

* **Source:** *The Social Frontier*, Volume 1, Number 5, 1935, pp. 25–34.

MORE, THAT THEY OUGHT TO BE THROWN OUT OF THE COUNTRY.

"ANY ONE WHO PLOTS TO OVERTHROW THE GOVERNMENT SHOULD FORFEIT HIS CITIZENSHIP. PLEASE USE STALIN'S DEFINITION OF COMMUNISM. NO ONE WHO SUBSCRIBES TO THAT DEFINITION HAS ANY RIGHT TO BE CONSIDERED A LOYAL AMERICAN CITIZEN."

Further excerpts from this editorial read as follows:

"Obviously Syracuse University offered a field for investigation. Plainly it was the proper procedure to investigate the reports of radical doctrines and activities at that institution.

"PROFESSOR WASHBURNE INTERVIEWED

"It was, therefore, decided to look into the beliefs and activities of Prof. John N. Washburne, head of the educational psychology department at Syracuse University. It was found that Professor Washburne talked freely enough when in company of those whom he knew well, but was shy of making direct statements to people who were trying to draw him out. So, the Journal resorted to an expedient. Richard Smith, a member of the Rochester Journal staff, and Gordon Druehl, a member of the Syracuse Journal staff, both bright and reliable young men, were assigned as investigators and to interview Professor Washbume. The reports of these investigations are published herewith and make interesting reading. They are published as they were turned in by the investigators, and readers may draw their own conclusions.

"These young men represented to Professor Washburne that they were Communists hoping to go to Russia next summer for study and they wanted to take up a special course in Syracuse University along Communist lines. They expressed themselves to the effect that they thought the United States Government should be overthrown by force, that they were extreme radicals and wanted a special course in the University to fit them along this line. Of course, Mr. Smith and Mr. Druehl manufactured their story and were acting a part.

"Professor Washburne was willing and even eager to help them along. "What occurred between these young men and the professor is revealed in the reports of the investigators published herewith.

"At the outset, having decided upon a line of action to get the professor off his guard, Mr. Smith on Nov. 10, wrote Professor Washburne from Rochester as follows:

'Dear Professor Washburne:

I have been thinking about going to Columbia, but a friend of mine in Syracuse says Syracuse is nearer and cheaper and I can get good courses in sociology at Syracuse.

"Down at Columbia they give you the real stuff about Capitalism and Socialism, but my friend says I can get the same thing at Syracuse, that you are a Liberal and not afraid to give the Liberal side that the University here does not give.

'Please tell me when I could come to Syracuse and see you about attending college there. Also, do they have any Liberal clubs there where students can get the truth about things, and can students get into the Communist clubs? Also, is Syracuse less expensive than Columbia to go to? Thanking you,

'Respectfully yours,

(Signed) DICK SMITH.'"

The editorial with its introductory flashes placing suspicion of growing communism at Syracuse university under the very eyes of the Chancellor, continues at this point to give Professor Washburne's letter in reply, goes on to report the visits of the emissaries of the editor, and gives the test of Editor Bunill's letter to the professor. This letter called for direct answers to questions demanding a rather complete public declaration of personal conviction about socialism, communism, and Americanism. The text of Professor Washburne's reply to the editor's letter is then given as follows:

"Sir:
"I am in receipt of yours of Nov. 19. Since I am not and never have been directly or indirectly connected with any Communistic organization or activities, I object to the implication of your questions.
"Please be advised that since my university work is restricted to the field of psychology, I find no occasion to discuss my political views, either in the classroom or for publication, nor am I willing to do so.

"Yours truly,

(Signed) JOHN N. WASHBURNE.

"If you see fit (as I trust you will not) to publish your questions you will please also publish in full this letter, a copy of which is being sent to the publicity department of the University.

"JOHN N. WASHBURNE."

The editorial ends by giving a few biographical facts about Professor Washburne among which are included reference to his collaboration with Miss Ruth Kennell in writing a comedy with a Russian background, to the fact that his wife was a native of Russia, and to the fact that his mother ran as a candidate for the Assembly on the Upton Sinclair ticket in California in the recent election.

Along with this front page editorial appeared a large photograph of Professor Washburne and a leading news story purporting to give the gist of the reported conversations between the admittedly faking reporters and Professor Washburne. The implications about Professor Washburne's convictions, which this published conversation was supposed to bring out are clear from the following excerpts: (Capitalization as in the original.)

"SMITH: I intend to go to Russia next summer and I thought I might study some subjects here which would be of aid.

"WASHBURNE: NOW, let me look. Here is one (using course catalog) Political Science 101. I think you would find this very interesting as well as helpful. (Turns several pages) Here is another. Political Science 111. THESE WOULD BE GOOD AND ONE, CONDUCTED BY PROFESSOR BEYLE, WHO IS VERY. VERY LIBERAL INDEED, WOULD BE OF ESPECIAL VALUE.

"SMITH: Oh, there are other liberals here?

"WASHBURNE: OH, YES. SYRACUSE HAS FOR YEARS BEEN ONE OF THE MOST LIBERAL COLLEGES IN THE COUNTRY. OF COURSE, NOT ALL OF THE FACULTY IS LIBERAL. Suppose you go up and see Doctor Crawford, the dean of the School of Education. He is very conservative, so be careful what you say.

"SMITH: Well, if I tell him some of my views, he would most likely turn me down.

"WASHBURNE: Don't do that. Wait until you're in. Once you are in they can't do anything. Give Crawford the impression you are a conservative. You look something like one.

"SMITH: Thanks. If you think so, ask the New York police.

"WASHBURNE: If you want to, you could tell Crawford you are interested in the Russian experiment.

"SMITH: Personally, I am, and principally because I believe the experiment will be repeated here when the government is overthrown.

"WASHBURNE: (Leaning forward and in whisper) SO DO I.

"WASHBURNE: I'll call Crawford. You see him and then come back. We've got to get you in here.

"WASHBURNE: Well, then, all that remains is to register. Now wait. I'll call the dean of admissions.

"Washburne telephoned, gave prospective student's name, address and home [sic] to admissions office. He was told three character reference letters would have to accompany application, one, from a pastor, being especially important.

"WASHBURNE: You've got to, rather, should have a letter from your pastor.

"SMITH: Sorry, I don't know any pastors, and if I did, there is a grave doubt they would recommend me for anything besides deportation.

"WASHBURNE: (Laughs) We can get around it if you can get two other letters. I'll write you one if it will be any help.

"V: What, as my pastor?

"WASHBURNE: Ha! Well, not exactly, but I believe it would do as the third reference letter.

"SMITH: I'll see you tomorrow then.

"WASHBURNE: That will be fine. It was nice of you to come in and see me. By the way, how did you hear of me?

"SMITH: Friend of mine (giving name) in Rochester who graduated from here about three years ago.

"WASHBURNE: Oh yes. I think I may have met him down at the Socialist club.

"SMITH: I doubt it. He's a Republican.

"WASHBURNE: Well, how did he happen to mention me?

"SMITH: Oh, he's a neighbor. We frequently have political arguments, and he told me he thought I should know you.

"WASHBURNE: OH, HA, HA! I DIDN'T REALIZE MY RADICALISM WAS SO WELL KNOWN. See you tomorrow then.

"SMITH: DID YOU SIGN THE TEACHER'S OATH OF ALLEGIANCE TO THE STATE AND UNITED STATES CONSTITUTION?

"WASHBURNE: YES, BUT WHAT DID IT MEAN?

"SMITH: THAT'S TRUE, WHAT DID IT MEAN?

"WASHBURNE: AS THE UNITED STATES CONSTITUTION IS WRITTEN, I APPROVE OF IT, BUT IT DOESN'T MEAN ANYTHING.

SO FAR AS THE STATE CONSTITUTION IS CONCERNED, I HAVEN'T THE SLIGHTEST IDEA WHAT IT'S ABOUT. AND I DON'T THINK ANYBODY ELSE HAS.

"SMITH: SO YOU BELIEVE IN THE UNITED STATES CONSTITUTION?

"WASHBURNE: YES, WITH MY OWN INTERPRETATION.

"SMITH : YOU TOOK THE OATH?

"WASHBURNE: YES. AFTER ALL WHAT DOES ALLEGIANCE MEAN? WHAT IS ALLEGIANCE? ALLEGIANCE TO PUT YOUR OWN INTERPRETATION TO IT.

"SMITH: Do you feel the Communists are well organized?

"WASHBURNe: THEY WOULD BE BETTER ORGANIZED IF THEY WOULD STOP FIGHTING AMONG THEMSELVES. WHAT WE NEED IS A LEADER.

"SMITH: WHAT ARE YOU, COMMUNIST OR SOCIALIST?

"WASHBURNE: I AM A LEFT-WING SOCIALIST.

"SMITH: WELL, THAT'S BEING A COMMUNIST.

"WASHBURNE: YES, THE SAME THING.

"WASHBURNE: I have to protect myself at the school. I couldn't register Communist.

"SMITH: Well, why didn't you enroll blank?

"WASHBURNE: I have to take a definite stand.

"SMITH: Well, if you're a Communist, you should have enrolled as one, I did. (Smith is a Democrat.)

"WASHBURNE: I couldn't very well, being at school. Talk then shifted back to organization of longshoremen.

"WASHBURNE: I WAS VERY ACTIVE ON THE PACIFIC COAST WITH THE I.W.W. DURING THE WAR.

"SMITH and DRUEHL: Is that so?

"WASHBURNE: Yes, but you fellows wouldn't remember back that far.

"SMITH: DO YOU THINK THERE COULD BE A REVOLUTION IN THIS COUNTRY WITHOUT BLOODSHED?

"WASHBURNE: NO. WE ARE NOT READY FOR A REVOLUTION NOW. WE FIRST MUST HAVE PEOPLE WHO WILL ACT AND NOT SIT BACK AND WAIT FOR THINGS TO HAPPEN. WE MUST HAVE A LEADER."

Professor Washburne was only the most conspicuous victim of the Hearst attack upon Syracuse University "liberals." Other professors were interviewed and somewhat similar insinuations about them were prominently displayed in the Journal. On November 24th the paper reported, "Keen interest aroused throughout Central New York by frank discussion in the JOURNAL of Communistic tendencies among some Syracuse University students and faculty members brought wide approval today from leaders of various Syracuse patriotic societies." It quoted approvingly from statements of the commander of the local American Legion post and from a member of the local American Legion Auxiliary. On November 26th the JOURNAL recommended that eight professors at the university be examined by the Board of Trustees for "Red" leanings.

THE DAILY ORANGE, Syracuse University campus paper, which had been offered remuneration if it would publish an article favorable to the JOURNAL scorned and ridiculed the Hearst attack. Almost without exception other Syracuse papers apparently considering the whole matter as merely a new form of circulation drive carried no comments.

PROFESSOR WASHBURNE'S OWN STORY

THE SOCIAL FRONTIER requested from Professor Washburne a full and frank report of the Hearst attack upon him. It is presented herewith:

"When Hearst's Syracuse JOURNAL started its campaign against the "reds and liberals" in Syracuse University by printing an almost completely false account of conversations between me and two reporters, who masqueraded as prospective students, I enquired about the possibilities of bringing suit for libel, and made some interesting discoveries.

"Among other things, I learned that the JOURNAL could take the amusingly contradictory but safe position that there is nothing disgraceful about being a "red" and therefore even a completely false accusation to that effect is not libelous. Only if I should be discharged from the University avowedly and directly on the basis of the JOURNAL's attack (which, of course, could not happen under an intelligent administration) would I have grounds for action.

"This leaves an attacked individual no recourse but simple denial, which, even when published at all, is likely to be buried, as was mine in the JOURNAL, on an inside page, or negated, as mine was, by editorial comment. Among other things, the JOURNAL remarked editorially that people "usually" make denial when exposed. This, of course, was intended as a reflection upon me and not upon the JOURNAL's "usual" veracity.

"Under such circumstances, having only an opponent's newspaper for a mouthpiece, (the other city newspapers were silent on the matter) argument is worse than futile. In Syracuse it was also unnecessary. For the reaction of most thinking people was in favor of those attacked. The JOURNAL discredited itself by its own disreputable methods of obtaining and handling the story.

"It is true that some of us on the JOURNAL'S editorial board [sic] have received anonymous and, I suppose, irresponsible threats; and it may be true that some who have not yet been attacked are trying to avoid such an occurrence, by concealing their views—are, in short, intimidated. But it seems to me that the main danger is not in any immediate and obviously direct result of the attack, but in what may occur under conditions of public hysteria.

"The red scare which Hearst, according to his own reporters, is trying to drum up is designed to arouse such hysteria. But such a scare cannot be created without recourse to misrepresentation. And misrepresentation can be combated by exposure.

"In my own case the misrepresentation is as obvious as could be desired. It happens that one of the two reported interviews was overheard in its entirety by two witnesses, one of them a high school principal, the other a graduate student, and parts of the other interview were also overheard by from one to three equally reliable people.

"In the first interview I was quoted not only as advising the reporter-"student" to conceal his communistic leanings from the University authorities, but also as agreeing with him that the Russian 'experiment will be repeated here when the government is overthrown.' What actually occurred was so different from this that it is almost inconceivable that the report was intended honestly.

"Here is what the two witnesses say in their signed statement:

I was present during all of the interview. . . . Nothing was said about the overthrow of the United States government or about Mr. Smith's (the reporter) being a communist. In fact, Mr. Smith was very vague about his desires and opinions. . . . Prof. Washburne had difficulty in finding out just what the man wanted from university courses, and finally suggested that it was probably help in clearing up his mind about political and economic matters. Mr. Smith agreed that this was what he wanted . . . . .

'I was working in . . . the office during all of the conversation. . . . I am willing to assert positively that there was no talk about the overthrow of government, no mention of communism, and no talking in whispers."

"The accuracy of the rest of the report was about on a par with this. Some errors were, no doubt, inadvertent (the reporter took no notes) as when I was quoted as referring to the 'Dean of Admissions and to a professor in another college as the 'Dean of the School of Education.'

"This by no means exhausts the list of provable misstatements. I was quoted as saying that I had been closely connected with the I.W.W. on the Pacific Coast during the war, whereas I have never had the remotest connection with them, and, during the entire period of the war, was thousands of miles away from the Pacific Coast, serving with the United States army. I was quoted as saying that the United States Constitution was meaningless (or words to that effect) whereas actually I said I wished it would be more strictly enforced—especially the Bill of Rights. I was quoted as saying that I was very sympathetic with the communist point of view and was deterred from joining the party only by caution, whereas actually I said I was completely out of sympathy with the communists' doctrine of violence and the suppression of civil liberties and democratic procedures. I even went so far, as to leave the two men abruptly in the middle of their meal (for I sensed something wrong) when they, apparently somewhat under the influence of two bottles of wine which they had ordered and finished, began to talk violent nonsense about their plans for a revolution by means of corrupting city police forces and state troopers!

"But it is unnecessary to go into detail. Enough of the major inaccurate and downright provable misstatements of the reporters have been mentioned to indicate that the Hearst newspapers will be quick and willing to use that chief tool of propagandists for hate and violence—the misrepresentation of facts.

"Respectfully submitted,

"JOHN N. WASHBURNE."

Almost simultaneously with the above-summarized Syracuse affair Hearst was launching a similar attack upon faculty members and student organizations reputed to be of liberal or radical tendencies in New York City.

At New York University

On Thanksgiving Day, November 29th, 1934, Professor Sidney Hook of New York University was interviewed by a reporter of the New York AMERICAN who said that he had been sent on this special assignment by the city editor to investigate Professor Hook's radicalism, particularly his connection with the American Workers' Party. The reporter, a former student of Dr. Hook's at Washington Square College, genially admitted that the AMERICAN was waging a campaign against radicalism of every shade and hue in the colleges. He remarked that he had been surprised at this assignment because although he had spent a year in Professor Hook's classes in philosophy he was not aware of Professor Hook's political views. He added that he had attempted to track the professor down for an entire week in order to get an interview. In the course of the conversation he openly admitted that he was not very happy to be engaged at this task. He was afraid, he said, that when he telephoned his story it would be rewritten in a way to damage Professor Hook as much as possible.

But a job was a job, and he had to telephone his story although he would do his best to prevent distortion. Professor Hook then explained his position—beginning with the Declaration of Independence, indicating his conception of the nature of a workers' democracy and his differences with the official Socialists and Communists, and ending with a criticism of Hearst's attack on academic freedom in the colleges. On December 2nd, the New York AMERICAN carried a scare story about the "merger of two groups, so radical that even the Communists have refused to have anything to do with them, into an organization called the Workers' Party of the United States." According to the story, Professor Hook was elected one of the leaders of the new party. Adding one falsehood to another, the writer even invented a special post of national organizer for him. Another N.Y.U. professor, James Burnham, was reported in the same story to have been elected to a prominent post. Among other deliberate fabrications it said: "Acknowledging frankly that their political credo was based on an intention to overthrow the American government by force, the leaders of the new group declared they hoped to foment a revolution in America in a few years."

On December 18th, the New York AMERICAN ran a half-page editorial entitled "Carnegie Money and Communist Propaganda—A New Deal In Disloyalty." The occasion was the publication by the Carnegie Endowment for International Peace of the December issue of its monthly periodical INTERNATIONAL CONCILIATION. This issue contained a translation of Stalin's report to the XVIIth Congress of the Communist Party and an address delivered by Professor Sidney Hook at the Virginia Institute of Politics, July 4, 1934 on "The Dictatorial and Democratic Aspects of Communism," which contained among other things a critical evaluation of the latest phases of Russian development from the Marxian point of view. President Nicholas Murray Butler in the preface called attention to the importance of both pieces for a scientific understanding of the political and social philosophy of communism. The Hearst editorial foamed with alliterative rage. One of its sentences ran: "As if the threadbare twaddle and familiar bunk of the Soviet tyrant and terrorist were not enough, there is appended to his report an article by Dr. Sidney Hook, professor of New York University, who appeared in the news a few days ago (i.e. in the written-to-order columns of the New York AMERICAN) as one of the active figures in the merger of the Communist League in America and the American Workers' Party into an organization whose avowed intention is the overthrow of the American government by force." When asked whether they expected to introduce libel suits against the Hearst Press, Mr. Haskell of the Carnegie Endowment for International Peace and Professor Hook both said that they considered it an honor to be singled out for attack by the Hearst Press.

The most provocative attack on Professors Hook and Burnham came in the form of an editorial Christmas present, Tuesday, December 25th, a day after the metropolitan press carried the story of Hearst's attempt to frame professors at Columbia University. It began again with a reference to the Hearst-AMERICAN press report about the merger of two groups "so radical that even the Communists have refused to have anything to do with them." It repeated the falsehoods carried in the original news item of the New York AMERICAN, and wound up with the following incitement to academic terrorism.

"Well! Gentlemen of the Faculty of New York University, trustees, alumni, students, and everyone else who is a friend of New York University and proud of its history—if the alleged actions of these two professors have been correctly reported, what do you say to it?

"WHAT DO YOU PROPOSE TO DO ABOUT IT?

"Is this old and respected institution of learning to be classified hereafter as a seeding-ground for disloyalty to America and its cherished institutions—as an active center for treasonable plotting for the overthrow of the American Government?"

At Teachers College, Columbia University

On December 14th the following letter was received by Professor George S. Counts of Teachers College, Columbia University.

"Dear Dr. Counts,

"I am thinking of entering Teachers College at the next term.

"Several friends and former instructors have told me that I can get the real stuff about Capitalism, Socialism, and Communism there. They tell me that you and several of your associates are real Liberals and not afraid to give the Liberal side on subjects in your classes.

"That is something I have not been able to get in State universities.

"I hope you can give me a few minutes time soon to outline a study program and help me, decide what instructors and classes to seek.

"Also, are there any Liberal or, even, forthright Communist Organizations or clubs at the college that I might join for open discussions?

"Sincerely yours,

_____."

[This reporter preferred not to have his name used and is hereafter referred to as Mr. X.]

Suspecting the letter to be the work of a stool pigeon, Professor Counts instructed his secretary to reply that he would not be accessible until after the Christmas vacation, when he could be seen at his regular office hours on Wednesday morning. On Tuesday, December 18, two reporters from the Hearst press called on Mr. Clyde Miller, head of the Bureau of Educational Service of Teachers College, and began making inquiries about so-called liberal and radical activities at the institution. One of them, on being questioned, acknowledged himself to be the author of the letter.

Arrangements were made for this man to interview Professor Counts in his office the next morning. The conversation, which follows, was taken down verbatim by a stenographer who was present throughout the interview:

"MR. X began by apologizing for his letter. Said it did not represent his own initiative but was written in compliance with instructions from the city desk. Said he was a newspaperman and that this was his way of earning a livelihood. Decided after writing the letter, however, to call on Dr. Counts as a newspaper man rather than under false pretenses. He went on to explain the reason for the above instructions from the city desk. "Mr. Hearst, he said, is engaged at present in conducting a 'red scare.'" Said the idea of extricating information from alleged liberal and radical institutions, organizations, and individuals, by means of a letter similar to the one written, belongs to Mr. Hearst.

"DR. COUNTS replied that he had no objection whatsoever to making his views known. 'This is one of my objects in life, in fact,' he said. He then asked Mr. X pointedly what he wanted.

"MR. X replied that in the eyes of such organizations as the National Civic Federation Dr. Counts represents the most insidious influence among the intelligentsia today. He then asked Dr. Counts to comment.

"DR. COUNTS asked Mr. X if he was familiar with THE SOCIAL FRONTIER.

"MR. X replied that he had seen copies of the journal. Also that he had seen the Report of the Commission on the Social Studies. Wanted to know if Dr. Counts sanctioned it or wrote it.

"DR. COUNTS replied that he signed the document. 'I did not write it,' he said. 'But in the main I approve it, although I think its argument is confused at places and is on the whole a weak document. I would have made it stronger.'

"MR. X then asked Dr. Counts his opinion of the Ives Bill. 'This bill, as you perhaps know,' he said, 'was practically written by Mr. Hearst.'

"DR. COUNTS: I said what I think about the Ives Bill in the editorial which appeared in the first issue of THE SOCIAL FRONTIER. I don't object to it.

'He then read portions from the editorial and urged MR. X to read the entire article.

"MR. X next wanted to know if Dr. Counts favored revolution for this country.

"DR. COUNTS wanted to know if Mr. X had seen the last issue of THE SOCIAL FRONTIER, in which this question is developed, and then said: 'The real American tradition is that the American people have the right to change their form of government any time that they see fit to do so. And if necessary, by revolutionary means. Of course I don't know what the Fathers had in mind when they used the word revolution. Personally I am entirely opposed to the advocacy of force. In fact, I assume that our problems can be solved through a free dissemination of information and ideas—through educational institutions. If I thought that force is the solution I would not be devoting my life to education. The most un-American thing in American life today is the use of coercive measures designed to regiment the life and thought of the American people. And of the most un-American of Americans.'

"MR. X agreed to the above. He then wanted to know Dr. Counts' position with regard to communism. Whether be approved it because it seemed to spring from the people themselves.

"DR. COUNTS: I have given no approval of communism. There is nothing in my writings to indicate this. I recognize that the development of communism constitutes one of the great events of our age, and that it throws out a real challenge to the so-called democracies. Can we without resorting to the methods of communism solve the economic problem? This challenge cannot be ignored by intelligent men.

"MR. X: It seems to me that in recent developments in Soviet Russia there is curtailment of freedom of thought.

"DR. COUNTS: This of course is known to everybody.

"MR. X: The Soviet leaders say that freedom will be restored after the period of transition is over.

"Dr. Counts: That may happen or not, I don't know. You ask in your letter whether these ideas are being examined at Teachers College. Of course they are. Any college worthy of the name will provide an opportunity for a thorough and objective examination of every important idea moving in the world. That is in keeping with the great university tradition reaching back through the centuries. Universities must fight to preserve this tradition.

"MR. X: I remember that at the University of Missouri the question of Soviet Russia and communism was not permitted to be discussed in the course in political economy.

"DR. COUNTS: No university is worthy of the name which does not provide full opportunity for an examination of all these ideas. If it rejects this responsibility, it is merely a kindergarten.

"MR. X: That is what most universities are. How about social and political demonstrations on the part of students in universities?

"DR. COUNTS: I think such demonstrations are desirable.

"MR. X: So do I.

"DR. COUNTS: I favor permitting students to participate in any demonstration they wish. I think one of the hopeful things is that college students are beginning to think about something besides football and fraternities. Although Mr. Hearst need not be alarmed. College students for the most part are still engrossed in these childish interests.

"MR. X: In fact, it should be viewed with alarm that there is not enough interest in economics and politics.

"DR. COUNTS: Yes, it is unfortunate that there are not more student demonstrations with regard to social and political matters. If the students will not become interested in these matters, the country is certain to drift into catastrophe.

"MR. X: I cannot understand when I speak to young men of my own age how they could be Republicans. One wonders how they can live in this age and escape its ideas. I think what you have said covers the ground pretty well. The fact that you don't get excited and alarmed by student demonstrations and discussions makes a 'red' of you for Mr. Hearst.

"DR. COUNTS: We should have a law requiring every university to give thorough and impartial courses to young people on the philosophies and programs of communism, socialism, and fascism.

"MR. X: You have been in Russia recently?

"DR. COUNTS: No, not recently. I was last there in 1929. I took a Ford car with me then and drove through the European part of the country. And I have not been back since. I hope to return in the near future. I speak about that country with a great deal of hesitation now because I don't know at first hand what has been happening there in recent years.

"MR. X then discussed some of the less important questions pertaining to the roads in Soviet Russia, the village organization, etc. Also related some of his own travel experiences.

"DR. COUNTS: When will you prepare your article?

"MR. X: It will probably be a series of articles, beginning next Monday, taking different institutions in turn.

"DR. COUNTS: I suppose it would be violating Mr. Hearst's standards of ethics if you let me see a copy of your article before it is printed.

"MR. X: Yes, it would be, but I will see what I can do.

"DR. COUNTS: I have no objection to a statement appearing, in the press, provided it is a truthful one, or at lease relatively truthful.

"MR. X: You realize of course that because of my assignment I will have to select the most sensational statements from the interview in order to make out a good case. This is what Mr. Hearst is expecting.

"DR. COUNTS: Of course we shall give Mr. Hearst a good write-up in the next issue of THE SOCIAL FRONTIER. Could you get any information for me?

"MR. X: I have not been on the paper very long, but I should think you would have no difficulty in getting the type of information you want. The Newspaper Guild might furnish you with such information."

This same reporter then proceeded to interview Professor William H. Kilpatrick. The resulting conversation was also taken down verbatim by a stenographer.

After the reporter had asked Professor Kilpatrick a number of questions, whether he believed in studying the Soviet Russian experiment, what he thought about revolution, about the Ives law, and about student demonstrations—matters about which he has never made any effort to conceal his views—Professor Kilpatrick turned to him and said: "Now let me ask you a few questions." The following colloquy resulted:

"DR. KILPATRICK: How do you feel about doing this kind of thing?

"Mr. X: Just about as you think I feel. I don't like it very much. I hope when the Newspaper Guild achieves its complete organization this sort of thing will go.

"DR. KILPATRICK: I have a feeling when I read a Hearst paper that the editorial policy is dishonest, that it is not advocating things because it believes them but because it wants to advocate them for some other reason. Almost every appeal is a demagogic appeal. Does that seem true to you?

"MR. X: You could find instances of it. Many of them in fact. Say last spring, when Hearst decided he wanted the McLeod Bill to go through. We were instructed that we were in favor of the bill and were to go out and make everyone else in favor of it. We were instructed to get one hundred telegrams from various people sent to Congress saying they favored the bill. I don't think I found a single person who knew what the bill was or cared, but we got the telegrams because of the obligations they felt to the paper.

"DR. KILPATRICK: So the telegrams were sent just to carry out the obligation to the paper?

"MR. X: Certainly—another instance was when Mr. Moses came out with the statement that he didn't like the approach to the Tri-Borough Bridge. The next morning we all got instructions that we were to kill that idea—stir up people, get telegrams, etc., to the effect that people didn't want the approach changed. Well, we all knew Hearst had been buying up property around there and wouldn't hear to having the approach changed.

"DR. KILPATRICK : Now tell me, would you not as a newspaper man rather be with a newspaper that was honestly trying to work for the good of the country? Would you not work harder and wouldn't you live a better life? Wouldn't you be on better terms with yourself? Don't you feel ashamed to come and talk to me in this way?

"MR. X: I'm not ashamed for myself but for the situation that makes it necessary to do this in order to keep alive.

"DR. KILPATRICK: You are not ashamed for yourself?

"MR. X: I would rather not do it. Probably I am ashamed, but I won't let myself be. I excuse myself on the basis of expediency.

"DR. KILPATRICK: Wouldn't it be a tremendous relief to you if that whole situation could be got rid of? Don't you think so?

"MR. X: I don't think it, I know it. But after all I have had periods of being out of work. I've been on three papers that folded up unexpectedly and it is pretty tough. I wouldn't like working in a slaughterhouse either, but if that was the only work open, I would probably do it. There's very little choice.

"DR. KILPATRICK: I could do that with a clear conscience. I could at any rate be honest about that.

"MR. X: Certainly your conscience would be clearer. But it's pretty hard to know what to do. We do get pretty sick of the things we're asked to do."

Another reporter interviewed Professor Jesse H Newlon, Director of The Lincoln School of Teachers College, attempting similarly to cross-examine him upon his social and economic views in the hope of gathering material that would readily lend itself to a sensational story in support of the Hearstian thesis that Teachers College is a hotbed of communism. Professor Goodwin B. Watson was unable to grant the reporters an interview but furnished them with a succinct statement summarizing his views on socioeconomic matters. The Hearst reporters freely admitted to Mr. Clyde Miller in the publicity office of the college that Mr. Hearst was planning to conduct similar "investigations" in other educational institutions in the country, and that the city editor was planning a series of about a dozen articles to be run immediately after Christmas in the Journal and the American playing up spectacularly the "evidences" of "Red" activities in the College. Some weeks later it was reliably reported to Mr. Miller that the articles had actually been prepared but that for one reason or another were not published.

The Counter Attack

On December 24, 1934, two days before the articles based upon the interviews were scheduled to begin appearing in the Hearst papers, the following news release was issued from Teachers College:

"American educational leaders, prominent on the faculties of Teachers College, Columbia University, New York University, Union Theological Seminary and other institutions, yesterday sent a request to the McCormack-Dickstein Committee, calling upon it to investigate 'a campaign of terrorism against teachers in American colleges, universities, schools and even private schools.'

"Basing their accusations upon the recent Syracuse University 'Communist expose' secured by two Hearst reporters posing as prospective university students, and by the similar attempt by Hearst representatives to secure information at Teachers College, the educators declare that by such methods the Hearst publications strike at the very roots of the American tradition of freedom of press, speech, and learning.

"'If William Randolph Hearst succeeds in his efforts," said Professor Counts of Teachers College, a signer of the request, 'he will reduce American universities and schools to the ignominious condition of the German schools and universities under Hitler. Is this the beginning of a nation-wide Fascist campaign to destroy our basic American freedoms, or is it just a publicity stunt to increase the circulation to the Hearst newspapers?', Dr. Counts asked. 'The American people have a right to know. The methods so closely parallel those used in Germany under Hitler as to arouse the sharp suspicions of all patriotic Americans.'

"Dr. William H, Kilpatrick, Professor of Education at Teachers College, Columbia University, one of the men questioned by a Hearst reporter, declared:

"'Mr. Hearst's efforts as outlined by the reporter to me would mean the destruction of the school as a preparation for intelligent democratic citizenship. On his basis pupils and students could not be encouraged to think but only made to conform to predetermined positions authoritatively promulgated.

"'In a changing world like ours such a policy could only result in the destruction of intelligent democracy and the enthronement of some demagogic fascism.'

"The request sent to the McCormack-Dickstein Committee reads: "'Recent occurrences at Syracuse University and Columbia University indicate that a campaign of terrorism against teachers in American colleges, universities, schools, and even private schools, is getting under way. Such repressive efforts are not only directly contrary to American democratic tradition but if successful would make it impossible for schools to do their proper work.

"'In a time like this we need every help in getting the people to face the serious problems confronting us. Neither cure of depression nor furthering of the progressive measures of the National administration can go forward without free discussion and inquiry in the universities and schools. This campaign threatens both.

"'We urge upon your Committee an extension of its investigation into this most insidious and un-American attack upon our educational institutions.

"'We append material which substantiates our fear.'

"This request is signed by: Charles A. Beard, former president of the American Historical Association; John Dewey, professor emeritus, Columbia University and honorary president of the National Education Association; William H. Kilpatrick, professor of education, Teachers College; George S. Counts, professor of education, Teachers College and chairman of the Progressive Education Association Committee on Economics and Sociology; Harry Emerson Fosdick, pastor of Riverside Church and member of the faculty of Union Theological Seminary; Howard L. McBain, dean of Graduate Faculties, Columbia University; William C. Bagley, professor of education, Teachers College; George W. Kirchwey, Dean Emeritus, Columbia Law School; E. C. Lindeman, New York School for Social Research; Karl N. Llewellyn, professor of jurisprudence, Columbia University; Howard Nudd, secretary of Public Education Association of New York; John L. Childs, assistant professor of education, Teachers College; Robert K. Speer, professor of education, New York University; Jesse H. Newlon, director of Lincoln School, Teachers College, and former president of the National Education Association; Robert B. Raup, associate professor of education, Teachers College; Joseph K. Hart formerly of Vanderbilt University and associate editor of the SURVEY; Heber Harper, professor of education, Teachers College; Rollo G. Reynolds, principal of Horace Mann School and professor of education, Teachers College; Willard W. Beatty, President of Progressive Education Association; Clyde R. Miller, treasurer, Progressive Education Association; Frederick L. Redefer, executive secretary of Progressive Education Association.'"

Repercussions and Alignments

This release was published widely in daily newspapers in all parts of the country and has resulted in a great deal of sympathetic comment from sources representing all shades of political and economic opinion. The Hearst papers however proceeded to publish frantic editorials urging that "Communist Professors Tell It to Congress." Meanwhile almost daily in the news columns of the Hearst papers were appearing under appropriately sensational titles statements about the cranker of radicalism eating away time-honored American institutions, especially the colleges and public schools, by lords of American patriotism like the Reverend Billy Sunday. One writer has actually demanded that the schools be boycotted! A full two-column editorial under the title "Red Russia's Apostle" appeared in the New York AMERICAN of January 3rd naming Professor Counts as the ringleader of the "Columbia Professors" opposing the Hearst Red crusade and describing him as an apologist for Russia and revolution on the basis of his visit to Russia in 1929 and his book "The Soviet Challenge to America" published in 1931. None of his more recent activities were reported nor was there any reference to the above-quoted interview with a Hearst reporter. A unique feature of this particular editorial was the inclusion of a long list of names of Russians to whom Professor Counts expressed indebtedness for material embodied in the book. These names, nearly all Russian, were printed in heavy black-face type ostensibly as a means of imputing to Professor Counts the social views held by these people.

EDITORIALS AND ARTICLES IN THE PRESS

THE SOCIAL FRONTIER publishes below a few selected documents from among many which have been called to its attention by interested organizations and by readers.

Leading editorials in the New York Post, December 26, 1934

MR. HEARST IMPORTS AN IDEA FROM GERMANY

The country is indebted to the professors of Teachers College, Columbia University, for vigorously opposing William Randolph Hearst's vicious attempt to end free speech in two American colleges by means of a typical Hearstian "red" scare.

Hearst (after coming back from Germany, where he held lengthy conversations with Nazi big-shots) suddenly decided that Teachers College and Syracuse University were "radical breeding centers."

Mr. Hearst has a perfect right to oppose Communism, to attack known revolutionaries advocating overthrow of the Government.

He has no right to try to choke off free discussion of Communism or anything else, to dominate economic inquiry in the universities or to interfere with the sanctity of the classroom. He has no right to paint impartial study as a "plague of radicalism."

Mr. Hearst's palpitating defense of "American institutions" starts by driving a sword home to the heart of the most cherished American institutions of all—free speech, uncensored discussion of public affairs.

It so happens that Mr. Hearst has long been writhing under certain New Deal innovations. He is cut to the quick by the prohibition of consolidated income tax returns, very valuable to the master of many different companies, who can balance one company's loss against another's gain in a joint return. Section 7a, mildly as that has been enforced, has interfered with his 1890 idea of an employer's czaristic power over employees.

It is the recent upthrust of liberalism, the fear that democracy is out to work and produce important reforms that stirs Mr. Hearst's Fascist fire. Mr. Hearst's sudden interest in recession is a reaction that became commonplace among German industrialists.

The Committee on American Activities should hold open hearings, get Hearst on the stand and make him explain what he means by attempting to dictate to the schools, to regiment American youth in the Hearstian pattern, to use terror against free discussion.

And let the professors give their side and meet their accuser face to face.

It is up to Congress to keep the spotlight on this effort to Hitlerize America.

From James McMullin's comments in "The Rational Whirligig," a feature syndicated to newspapers in all parts of the United States, December 29, 1934.

The vendetta, which a group of prominent educators have declared against W. R. Hearst, will be no sham battle. Leaders of the teaching profession are genuinely stirred by the implications of the vigorous campaign which the Hearst papers are about to launch against the "Red menace." They regard it as a thinly veiled attempt to bring about the suppression of all liberal thought in American schools and colleges—and they don't intend to take it lying down.

Editorial in The Pittsburgh Catholic, January 10, 1935

. . . It is important that the effort to correct the evils of our economic and social system be not allowed to carry us into radical excesses, but no confidence can be placed in Mr. Hearst as a defender of the American people against Communism or anything else.

Editorial in The News, Lynchburg, Virginia, January 13, 1935

. . . Hearst has been yelling for months about communism in the United States, about "un-American" activities, about danger from Moscow, about the menace of aliens who do not imbibe the Hearst notions as to what constitutes "Americanism." Especially has he directed his attack at the colleges. These, he declares, are becoming hotbeds of radicalism, of communism, of this, that and the other.

In the process of forwarding his campaign and building up his circulation he has sent spies into colleges.

It was after this that the petition of the college professors for an investigation of Hearst's "un-American" activities was sent to the Mc-Cormack-Dickstein committee.

It is, of course, a neat thrust. The man who has been tearing passion to tatters and shaming the worst of yellow journalists in his pretended devotion to "Americanism" is accused directly of being un-American.

Editorial in The Free Press, Trinidad, Col., January 3, 1935

. . . This is either the beginning of a nation wide Fascist campaign or is a publicity stunt to increase the circulation of the Hearst papers. The American people have a right to know the answer.

The methods so closely parallel those used in Germany under Hitler as to arouse the sharp suspicions of all patriotic Americans.

Editorial in The Press, Bronxville, New York

. . . We do not believe that any amount of propaganda or publicity could ever persuade the people of this country to consider William Randolph Hearst their "savior." Mr. Hearst's demand for investigation of our educational institutions cannot convince us that free discussion of what is going on in the world today is "Communist teaching." Such free discussion not only among children, but among adults as well is necessary if we are going to understand what is happening before our very eyes. No branding of "radical propaganda" can forestall its progress,

The great publisher would do well to forget his recent discussions with Nazi leaders, which may have given him the ambition to become our "dictator" and confine his efforts to the improvement of his newspapers.

Excerpts from an article "Mr. Hearst Sees Red" by Hamilton Basso in the New Republic, January 16, 1935

. . . Perhaps, as has been said before, it is only a coincidence that this vicious attempt to terrorize the teachers in American colleges and universities was made just a short time after Mr. Hearst and Mr. Hitler got together over their cups of tea. Perhaps it is only Mr. Hearst's great, burning, passionate patriotism that prompts him to attack the principles of free speech and free thought and to turn the men who work for him into sneaks and spies. There is no need to point out at this late date what a great patriot Mr. Hearst is. All you have to do is to remember the Maine.

Of course the fact remains that Mr. Hearst has been given a severe case of colic by many of the features of Mr. Roosevelt's New Deal. The idea of having professors in the administration, and liberal professors at that is so repugnant to him that it might easily cause him to attack even the most innocently liberal professors everywhere. It is Mr. Hearst's notion that if it were not for the liberals in the administration there would be no Section 7a and if there were no Section 7a there would be no Dean Jennings case—which Mr. Hearst, who believes in the freedom of the press, is fighting with all the power and influence he can command.

RESOLUTIONS ADOPTED BY VARIOUS ORGANIZATIONS

Resolutions adopted by the Student League for Industrial Democracy in convention at Northwestern University, December 28, 1934.

"In the fight of American students for a peaceful world and against impending Fascism, Enemy Agent No. 1 is the Hearst press. Not unmindful of the CHICAGO TRIBUNE, the LOS ANGELES TIMES and other reactionary organs we must vigorously press our fight against the primary propaganda agents of American Fascism—the newspapers of William Randolph Hearst.

"We are unalterably opposed to international war. The Hearst press incessantly promotes international ill will, suspicion and hatred; it misrepresents the plans and purposes of other peoples; it daily defames the Soviet Union; it has lent aid and comfort to jingo elements urging preparation of the machinery and slaughter for another war; it serves well the munitions manufacturers and prospective war profiteers by advocating what it calls 'preparedness.'

"We are unalterably opposed to Fascism in all nations. By praise of European Fascist governments, and especially by the recent editorial endorsement of Fascism here 'if necessary,' the Hearst press has assumed the leadership of the drive of desperate capitalism to keep going for a while at the expense of those who toil.

"The Hearst press has pretended to be a champion of the American Constitution. In action it has made a scrap of paper of the guarantees of free speech, free press, and free assembly. It has endorsed violence as a means of disrupting the meetings against war or for academic freedom called by students of American colleges. It has incited Fascist-vigilante bands to attack students whose political opinions it did not approve.

"In view of these facts, we call upon American students and faculties to exert every effort to boycott the Hearst press. We call upon college editors and sport writers to withdraw all support from the Hearst International News Service. We call upon students to solicit their families and friends to cancel subscriptions to the Hearst publications. We call upon all students to use their influence in class and church and field to see to it that the American people recognize him for what he is—the errand boy, of the war-makers.

"As we resist war and work for peace; as we resist Fascism and work for a co-operative commonwealth; as we try to perpetuate the revolutionary principles of the Declaration of Independence and resist the encroachments upon the bill of rights, so must we now resist this instigator of violence, promoter of Fascism, agent of reaction—the Hearst press."

Resolution passed at the regular weekly meeting of Methodist preachers of New York Conference, New York East Conference, and Newark, New Jersey Conference, January 7, 1915.

"Whereas certain American educational leaders of New York City have recently asked the Congressional Committee on un-American Activities to investigate what they describe as 'a campaign of terrorism against teachers of American colleges, universities, schools, and even private schools' now being carried on by William Randolph Hearst: and whereas we recognize in this terrorism a particularly vicious and insidious form of propaganda because it masquerades under the guise of a pretended patriotism and because it is aimed not only at college teachers but at the very spirit and practice of free inquiry, discussion, and teaching, whether in the school or in the church.

"Therefore be it resolved: (1) That the New York preacher Meeting unite with the honored educational leaders above mentioned in protesting against this most un-American and malicious campaign and in requesting that it be investigated by Congress through its proper committee; (1) that while we stand for a free press, whether edited by Mr. Hearst or anybody else, we insist as Americans and as preachers on the right of all teachers to pursue their political, social, and economic studies without restraint, to discuss freely all public questions and to express their opinions without being compelled to suffer intimidation and abuse.

"Resolved further that a copy of these resolutions be sent to the Congressional Committee above named, to the editor of the New York Journal, and to the editor of the Syracuse JOURNAL."

Resolutions adopted at the January meeting of the New York University Chapter of the American Association of University Professors.

"Whereas documentary evidence exists indicating that William Randolph Hearst and his newspaper interests are engaged in an attack upon University professors who in the regular performance of their normal duties discuss critically social, economic, and political problems and their educational implications;

"And whereas it is Mr. Hearst's practice to label all such socially concerned professional educators as 'reds' and the institutions which they serve as 'hotbeds of radicalism,'

"And whereas, specifically, his recent attacks upon teachers at Syracuse University, Columbia University, and New York University indicate that a Hearst Newspaper campaign of misrepresentation against teachers in American Colleges, Universities and Schools is under way;

"And whereas such repressive efforts are contrary to teaching and American democratic traditions, and the academic tradition of freedom of research; and if successful would make it impossible for schools to do their proper work;

"Be it resolved that this, the New York University Chapter of the American Association of University Professors, go on record as in accord with the sense of the protest and demands sent to the McCormack-Dickstein committee on December 21 by a group of American educators.

"Be it further resolved that a copy of this resolution with its introduction be sent to Mr. McCormack until January 5 the chairman of the congressional committee investigating un-American activities, with the request that American educators be permitted to appear before his committee (in case its tenure is renewed by the New Congress) in order to present evidence of the un-American activities of the Hearst interests in colleges and universities.

"Be it further resolved that a copy of this resolution be sent to the National officers of the American Association of University Professors and the presidents of the various chapters of the American Association of University Professors with the urgent request that each chapter, and our national body, take similar action, and publish in the BULLETIN these resolutions and all similar ones that other chapters or the national body may adopt."

Resolutions adopted by the Cleveland Teachers' Union January 16, 1935.

"Resolved that the Local 279, American Federation of Teachers, pledge its full support to the faculty members of Teachers College in upholding their right to free and full discussion of controversial social and economic questions both in and out of the lecture halls, and be it further

"Resolved that the Local 279, American Federation of Teachers, pledge itself to help defeat any future attempts to restrict the constitutional rights of teachers.'

News item from the New York Post, January 21, 1935

Fifty professors, meeting for the first session last night of the Anti-Fascist Association of the Staff of City College, demanded a Federal investigation of Hearst newspapers.

The new organization is purely a faculty one. The resolution passed condemned the Hearst newspapers for advocating legislative acts "which would result in the absolute destruction of freedom of thought and discussion by teachers and students."

The teachers added: "The Hearst program would reduce colleges to the ignominious condition of schools and universities of Hitler Germany and Fascist Italy."

AND PER CONTRA

Resolution adopted in January 1935, by the American Coalition, representing 106 patriotic societies throughout the country.

"Resolved, that the American Coalition express its appreciation for the services that are being rendered to the country by the Hon. William Randolph Hearst, personally, and through his extensive chain of newspapers.

"The work which is being accomplished by Mr. Hearst in combating the insidious influences that are seeking to undermine our governmental institutions is most timely and of inestimable value in upholding and sustaining constitutional government in the United States.

"The secretary of the Coalition was directed to forward a copy of the resolution to Mr. Hearst."

THE MATTHEW WOLL INCIDENT

The following letter was sent to Representative McCormack, chairman of the Congressional Committee investigating un-American activities, by Matthew Woll, acting President of the National Civic Federation and Vice President of the American Federation of Labor.

"My dear Mr. McCormack:

"Monday morning's newspapers carried the announcement that twenty educators have sent you a telegram calling your attention to 'a campaign of terrorism against teachers in American colleges, universities, schools and even private schools.' This, of course, refers to recent articles and editorials appearing in the publications of Mr. William Randolph Hearst, which report that certain professors are allegedly engaged in teaching subversive propaganda.

"Such revelations ought not to be dismissed as attempts to "drum up a Red scare nor should we take too seriously the reported statement of Professor George S. Counts of Teachers College, Columbia University, to the effect that 'if William Randolph Hearst succeeds in his efforts, he will reduce American universities and schools to the ignominious condition of German schools and universities under Hitler.' Nevertheless, these allegations and counter-allegation present questions of sufficient interest to the American people to demand a thorough and impartial inquiry.

"I am convinced that if your committee is continued during the next session of Congress, it could do no greater public service than to ascertain precisely what academic freedom is and what are its proper limits. Indeed, I believe that you would find that academic freedom, like other civil liberties of the individual, must be qualified by the rights of others, which are coexistent with it.

"The trustees of colleges must enjoy at least some freedom to employ those who will teach the things they desire to have taught. Students and their parents must have some liberty in the choice of what the student must learn. He should not be compelled to listen to subversive or revolutionary doctrines if he does not wish to do so, simply because he has matriculated and has paid his tuition in the college.

"Mr. Hearst has raised an issue that should be thoroughly threshed out at the earliest possible moment. If the life of your committee is extended by the incoming Congress, the National Civic Federation would appreciate the opportunity of presenting to you further facts to this field of inquiry.

"Very truly yours,

"MATTHEW WOLL, "Acting President, "National Civic Federation."

As a result of the publication of Mr. Woll's letter in the newspapers the following telegram was sent by Mr. Jacob Levitt, Financial Secretary-Treasurer of the Philadelphia Local (No. 192) of the American Federation of Teachers, to William Green, President of the American Federation of Labor:

"THE CONSISTENT EFFORT OF AMERICAN FEDERATION OF TEACHERS TO MAINTAIN ACADEMIC FREEDOM WILL BE SERIOUSLY DISCREDITED UNLESS YOU MAKE PUBLIC DISAVOWAL OF MATTHEW WOLL'S ATTACK ON AMERICAN COLLEGES AS NOT BEING THE STAND OF A.F.L. NOTHING IN MY OPINION WILL MORE EFFECTIVELY HAMPER THE UNIONIZATION OF TEACHERS THAN THE ATTACK BY WOLL IF IT GOES UNCHALLENGED BY YOU."

Dr. Henry R. Linville, President of the Teachers Union of New York City sent the following letter to President Green of the American Federation of Labor.

"Dear Sir:

"I am writing to you to enter a formal protest against the participation of Matthew Woll, a vice-president of the American Federation of Labor, in the 'heresy-hunting' activities of the Hearst newspapers which are being directed against liberal college teachers in some of the great universities. It is true, Mr. Woll now speaks as acting president of the National Civic Federation, an organization active in the state in support of the infamous Lusk school laws, which organized labor itself helped to abolish in 1923.

"However, it is because of Mr. Woll's responsibility as a leader in the labor movement that organized union teachers are forced to bear the brunt of the discredit of his stand in opposition to the spirit of academic freedom in the schools and colleges of this country.

"For several years teachers' unions have been trying to further the organization of the college teachers who are friendly to organized labor. We are obliged to state frankly at this time that the most serious obstacle we have met in this endeavor is the current belief among educators that Mr. Woll represents a reactionary and fascist spirit; and because of his frequent public utterances of that character, such spirit tends to be charged against all labor leadership, no matter how progressive it may actually be. Since Mr. Woll appears to be indifferent to the need of protecting academic freedom in the colleges even in behalf of the interests of organized labor, we believe that it is incumbent on enlightened labor leadership, of which your own attitude toward intolerant fascism is a well-known example, to protect the labor movement from discredit in this emergency.

"I bespeak your deep concern in this matter of making it known to the liberal and progressive elements throughout the country that organized labor stands for freedom of conscience, freedom of inquiry and freedom of speech, not only for the workers in industry, but also for the 'white collar' workers in educational institutions without whose trained intelligence, scholarship and friendly cooperation organized labor may not be able to make effective headway against the social forces aligned in opposition to our movement.

"Fraternally yours,

"HENRY R. LINVILLE."

A similar letter was sent to Mr. Green by the Philadelphia Teachers Union.

Mr. Green's replies to both the Philadelphia and New York City Teachers' Unions were non-committal. Mr. Green suggested that both organizations take the matter up directly with Mr. Woll himself. On January 19th a letter enclosing the correspondence with Mr. Green was sent by the Philadelphia Teachers' Union to Mr. Woll. Up to the present writing no reply has been received. Excerpts from the letter to Mr. Woll follow.

"As fellow trade unionists we urge you to consider the battle we must all fight for the simple civil liberties presumably guaranteed us in the Constitution, but which we must win again in our day-to-day struggles against reaction to the labor movement.

"Academic freedom is not just a phrase to teachers. It is a fundamental right which teachers' unions must persistently fight for in the interests of every teacher who sees his duty to do more than 'educate' by rote.

"We should like to feel that in whatever capacity you speak your aid is given to the trade unions and not to their enemies."

DR. WIRT GOES ALONG WITH HEARST

News item in the New York Sun, January 16, 1935

Dr. William A. Wirt, the Hoosier schoolmaster who sent Congress chasing "red plotters," issued a new warning today. The nation's little red schoolhouses are being used to spread communist propaganda, he said.

Dr. Wirt's attack was aimed broadside at his colleagues in the teaching profession, the National Association of School Superintendents. The superintendents, he charged, are "turning red and using the schools to incite ultraradical sentiment."

Instead of the three r's and Lincoln's Gettysburg address the primer of America's youth soon may be teaching the glories of an overthrow of capitalistic government, he predicted.

After ten months of silence the Gary educator returned to his crusading with the same vigor that he attacked the "brain trust," charging it with plotting to overthrow the Government and put a dictator in the White House.

Dr. Wirt, sitting in the cluttered study of his home, shook his head sadly.

"It looks like these school superintendents," he said, "have pledged themselves to use their schools as propaganda agencies to help in creating an ultra-radical sentiment among our people, which will force the country over the precipice and into the abyss of communism."

He referred to an editorial in the Journal of the National Education Association asking for a redistribution of wealth as a means of recovery. The salaries of fifty prominent executives were listed.

"Every effort seems to be made to appeal to prejudice and inflame class hatred," Dr. Wirt said.

HEARST AT HARVARD

The following excerpt is from a letter in the Correspondence columns of the NEW REPUBLIC of January 30, 1935.

" . . . If any reader is wondering where Mr. Hearst struck next, the answer is Harvard. On January 15, the Boston American, just to add some more fuel to its anti-Red fire, sent James McEnary, a staff member, to investigate secret communistic agitation by the faculty and students. He had a questionnaire ready to submit to reported radicals. Well, I am glad to relate that Harvard got him cold and he left empty-handed. President Conant refused to see him, as did Albert S. Coolidge, lecturer on Chemistry. (Are they making communism in labs these days?) Unsuccessful in his efforts to discover any Red menaces among the faculty, he tried the undergraduates. The head of the Harvard chapter of the National Student's League denied that he knew of any radical professors or any who supported the aims of the N.S.L. The president of the Harvard Liberal Club turned on him with a very pointed denunciation of Hearst and Red-baiters. He hoped that the Hearst organization would not continue to 'throw verbal bombs at papier-mâché radicals with its customary vigor.' The next day THE CRIMSON, the undergraduates dally, published a leading editorial denouncing Hearst newspapers for 'pandering to a nation's prejudices' and warned against giving strength and succor to a fascist Harvard. Needless to add, the Boston American carried no news of its defeat.

"JULIAN S. BACH, JR. "Cambridge, Massachusetts."

Hearst and the Ethics of the Press

In a featured editorial of the New York JOURNAL of January 2 entitled "Seditious Teachers and the Hearst Press" there occurs the following passage:

"The Hearst papers are performing the proudest function of journalism in expressing their rights of free publication to protect the State and the institutions of a free people from danger and damage."

THE SOCIAL FRONTIER invites the teachers of America to judge Mr. Hearst's record, not in terms of the eulogies written by his hired men, but in terms of the Ethical Rules adopted by his peers in the American Society of Newspaper Editors on April 28, 1923. The following extracts seem to be relevant:

"A journalist who uses his power for any selfish or otherwise unworthy purpose is faithless to a high trust.

"Partisanship in editorial comment which knowingly departs from the truth does violence to the best spirit of American journalism; in the news columns it is subversive of a fundamental principle of the profession.

"By every consideration of good faith, a newspaper is constrained to be truthful. It is not to he excused for lack of thoroughness or accuracy within its control, or failure to obtain command of these essential qualities.

"Headlines should be fully warranted by the contents of the articles which they surmount.

"A newspaper should not publish unofficial charges affecting reputation without opportunity given to the accused to be heard; right practice demands the giving of such opportunity in all cases of serious accusation outside judicial proceedings.

"It is the privilege, as it is the duty of a newspaper to make complete correction of its own serious mistakes of fact or opinion whatever their origin."

THE AMERICAN SCHOLAR FACES A SOCIAL CRISIS *

Harold Rugg

I n this remarkably candid and insightful article, Harold Rugg identifies American intellectuals, and in particular college and university professors, as maintainers of the status quo in the United States. According to him, "Their economic-social creed is a synthesis of the concepts of the First Industrial Revolution. Outstanding among these are: scarcity, laissez faire, building for immediate profits, accelerating growth, production for sale, and a hierarchy of social classes in which the entrepreneur and the politician occupy the loftiest positions and the creative person is either ignored or held in contempt."

Rugg rejects the increasing movement in American scholarship toward quantification and measurement. While recognizing the spectacular advances made in areas such as Physics, as a result of the use of quantitative techniques, Rugg maintains that "human nature is mechanism not organism," and that "human traits cannot be reduced to quantitative measures."

Rugg concludes the article with a series of suggestions for the scholar working in Education. He emphasizes that "a period of drastic transition" was underway that demanded scholars "devote themselves to the creative task of the reconstruction of social and personal life."

*   *   *

In every social crisis in American history the scholar has been confronted by the question: Must I take a stand on current issues? Am I obligated to devote some of my energy to the study of the social scene and to participate in programs of action?

FEW SCHOLARS PROTEST—MOST ARE SILENT

Each time the issue has been joined; the body of American scholarship has become a house divided three ways against itself. At one extreme a little minority speaks out, demanding a thorough study of social problems including, where necessary, programs of designed reconstruction. At the other extreme there is an even larger minority, made up of protagonists of the existing social system. These are always vigorous obstructionists who accuse the students of social reconstruction of subversive measures. In between these two is a vast and timid mediocrity which has always kept silent and has thereby buttressed the status quo.

---

* **Source:** *The Social Frontier*, Volume 1, Number 6, 1935, pp. 10–13.

While most of the professed academicians withheld their pens and their tongues, their own students—the free-lances of thought and action outside the universities—stood up for human rights and for social reconstruction. The textbooks hall of fame would be bare indeed had these men kept silent in their respective times: Roger Williams and Thomas Hooker, who were driven out of Massachusetts Bay by the conservative clerical rulers; Samuel Adams, M.A., of Harvard, who preached rebellion as the only possible means of establishing civil and political liberty on the Atlantic seaboard; James Otis, who issued a brave call to independent parliamentary discussion; Patrick Henry, who declared his position on the dread alternatives; the young Jefferson, who documented his bill of particulars against the oppressive business oligarchy of England; the Boston editor, Garrison, who refused to compromise on Negro slavery; Emerson, the serene scholar of Concord, who clarified the slavery issue while—as Wendell Phillips later thundered at the organized Academy— "amid this battle of the giants, scholarship sat dumb for thirty years."

And, coming to our own time for a single concluding example, who among the scholars of today have little to regret about the stand they took in the great crisis of 1914–1918? Do we not think instantly of scholars in and out of academic life who refused to fight the imperialists' war—Angell and Russell interned in England; Rolland exiled from France to Switzerland; Beard, Robinson, and Cattell leaving academic life in America, and Bourne, Frank, Brooks, and their company?

I am not saying that the gowned intelligentsia made no pronouncements of honor in these critical periods. Indeed, from time to time there were brave utterances of integrity from men who strode out of their study halls to condemn vicious platforms, laws, executive acts, judicial decisions, and the terrorists' hysteria of the dominant economic class, but these were conspicuous because they were exceptions. By and large, as Emerson, Phillips, Curtis, and others have reiterated for a full century, the bulk of American scholarship was an accused class. Either by its silence or by its overt acts of obstruction, it has always stood on the side of reaction. Hence in each critical period, advocates of reconstruction have echoed comments similar to Theodore Parker's on the struggle between the North and the South: "If our educated men had done their duty, we should not now be in the ghastly condition we bewail."

These truisms of history set the stage for the drama of our own critical period. One epoch of industrial-democratic culture is moving swiftly into another. Novel problems of design and administration are being thrust upon us. Already an advance-guard of creative thought, largely outside the ranks of academic scholarship, has launched the scientific study of social change. Once again the men of the Academy are called upon to make the great choice. Where shall we stand?

WHY SCHOLARS OBSTRUCT SOCIAL CHANGE

To understand our problem we must explore the question: Why is it that in every decade some of the scholars attempt to block the advance of social trend while the great mass stand aloof and by that very silence which is not really neutrality assent to the obstruction?

Some do so, of course, because of timidity. They are afraid of economics insecurity and of the disapproval of the community. To them this article says nothing.

Others either denounce or withhold their help because they conceive that the study of the social scene is not the proper function of the educational worker. To them the bulk of this article is directed.

The chief reason for the hiatus between the content of American scholarship and the vital problems of the people lies in the fact that the rank and file of American scholars are molded into defenders of the status quo by the dominant social milieu in which they have been brought up, and by the special concepts of their own intellectual climate. Like the stock-brokers and the professionals in general, most of them are members of the upper middle class. They are sons of native stock and are possessors of a small property and of prestige in the community—both of which they earnestly desire to keep. But, true to the American tradition, they are thoroughgoing individualists and practice the concept of freedom to compete and—many of freedom to exploit. Also they are still convinced that, even in the new industrialism, the ladder of opportunity really stretches upward before anyone who conforms, works hard, saves, and invests. Their economic-social creed is a synthesis of the concepts of the First Industrial Revolution. Outstanding among these are: scarcity, laissez faire, building for immediate profits, accelerating growth, production for sale, and a hierarchy of social classes in which the entrepreneur and the politician occupy the loftiest positions and the creative person is either ignored or held in contempt.

Merely naming these characteristic attitudes and ideas suggests the difficulty of lifting ourselves above the mental atmosphere which produced them. It is as though the culture in which we were brought up had clamped blinders around our eyes, restricting the scope of vision to a narrow arc of the total horizon, to a thin sector of the social scene. The inevitable consequence is that either by a fearsome reticence or by overt defense of things as they are most of the scholars become the literary mouth-piece of the dominant economic class, bolter the existing regime, and oppose intelligent control of social change.

THINKING MEN SHOULD ACT

Moreover, the scholar's special intellectual climate is pervaded with false concepts that hamper his struggle to lengthen the radius of his social vision. The first of these fallacies is that thought and actions are mutually antagonistic. It is widely held that the scholar should stand in cold Olympian aloofness from the moving scenes of street and neighborhood. It is not his business to become immersed in the details of market-place and public rostrum. Clear thinking requires quiet seclusion—an isolated hut in the forest, a ranch on the Pampas, a villa above Como; even a Mirabeau prison-cell is proposed for those who venture to gather their materials of education from the contemporary scene of action.

But what is really the case for thought and action? Far from being antagonistic to each other, they are inextricably interdependent. Each supplies the other with its indispensable stuff. As Emerson put it ninety years ago: "Without action thought can never ripen into truth"—and the day's truth, not mere thinking, is the scholar's goal. In his famous address on the American Scholar, in 1837, the most powerful exponent of scholarship struck harshly at those who pretended that one's problems could be solved with an alien content:

"Inaction is cowardice, but there can be no scholar without the heroic mind. The preamble of thought is action. Only so much do I know, as I have lived. Instantly we know whose words are loaded with life, and whose not."

In the three quarters of a century that passed after that utterance, the toilers on the frontier of physiology and psychology have absolutely established the organic character of behavior and the unity of thought and action. Surrounded by infinitely more objective evidence than Emerson had at his command, John Dewey, another quiet but determined scholar, refashioned in psychological terms the former's generalization:

"Means and ends are two names for the same reality. . . . We do not know what we are really after until a course of action is worked out. . . . Security attained by active control is more to be prized than certainty in theory. . . . The chief consideration in achieving concrete security of values lies in the perfecting of methods of action."

Thus neither common sense nor scientific generalization support inaction and aloofness from the social scene among thinking men. The scholar, as Emerson put it, is Man Thinking, not "the parrot of other men's thinking." To think requires data, and data are the very stuff of living. This stuff is not found primarily in the library, although the study of other men's phrasing is a necessary part of the scholar's stock-in-trade. On the contrary, it is gathered in the midst of dramatic fields of social action—in direct contact with the changing data of production and distribution, courts, and assemblies, conference tables and executive offices.

THE FALLACY THAT ANCIENT TRUTH IS BEST

Other false concepts also shunt the scholar into petty blind alleys of research, destroy his integrity, and stunt his contribution. One is that truth can be discovered only in the distant past; that the function of the scholar is to cultivate the fields tilled long ago by the established masters; and that his method of documentation is especially the study of the printed page.

This concept assumes that the truth is something "out there." Some fact of generalization has been established by "history"; scholarship is to "discover" it; that is, to recover it. The problems of scholarship and the valid techniques of documentation were devised by rare mutants of insight long ago. The tasks of contemporary scholarship, then, are to grasp those problems, to master those techniques, and to buttress the knowledge already discovered about them.

This platform of scholarship exhibits a deep contempt for the contemporary. (Witness the unwillingness of most academic historians to give themselves to the study of "recent" history.) It assumes a relation between longevity and the possibility of discovering truth, an assumption that is correct only for the study of long, continuous, and unchanging historical movements. If the purpose of the scholar is to plot the zigzag course of ancient history, then the best available records of that ancient social action are, of course, his best materials. But if his problem is the study of the products of social change in our own times and their projection as alternative pathways to tomorrow, his primary task is to guarantee that his historical materials really fit our times, that they actually portray the trends which precipitated our times, that they unearth the contributing factors and lay bare the true characteristics. That can be done only by measuring social trend against a critical documentation of "our times."

THE FALLACY OF QUANTITATIVE MEASUREMENT

Yet another false concept in the climate gripping the American scholar thwarts his study of Man. This is the fallacy that "I know only what I can describe quantitatively .... whatever exists, exists in some measurable amount." This idea, which has produced many elaborate and useless researches in education and the social sciences, was the inevitable result of the application of the theories of mechanism that achieved pragmatic sanction in the physical sciences to the study of nature-things. These theories worked in the realm of mechanics, for mechanical things are mosaics, not integrations. Each one, whether tool or implement, engine or machine, is equal to the sum of all its parts.

In the nineteenth century the physicists achieved a spectacular success in the documentation of their primary concepts. The scholars of education, enamored of the physicists' perfection of method, their precision of measurement, and the aesthetic charm of the scientific order which was attained, took over their concepts, their outlook on life, and their methods of work. They assumed, for example: that human nature is mechanism, not organism; that personality is the sum of all its traits; that human traits can be reduced to quantitative measures; that particular traits can be held constant; and that changes which are produced in others can be measured by the statistical method of correlation.

But we know now that this was a great fallacy. The nature-thing, Man included, is organism, not mechanism. A chorus of unanimity on the integration principle rises from the students of human behavior. They record that "the individual responds as a whole, totally, not segmentally." Behavior is "organismic," a "process of integration."

The citation of this fallacy illustrates the deadly grip which the prevailing climate has upon our scholarship—the problems which it selects for study, the methods which are employed, and the interpretations and conclusions which are drawn. If this is true in a field in which no social issue must be resolved how much truer it is of the situation confronting scholarship in all of the social sciences!

TO THE AMERICAN SCHOLAR IN EDUCATION

These are conspicuous examples of the harassing pressures upon the scholastic mind and of the fallacies which characterize its life. They set the stage for a brief analysis of the real question which many American scholars today are asking themselves, namely: "How shall I approach the crucial social problems of our times?" My own answer, briefly put, is this:

First: Try as best you can to divest yourself of your fears: fears of loss of job and of economic insecurity generally and fears of what your fellows will say about you. To the extent that you fail to do that you will fail to study the really crucial problems, to explore them to their roots, and to phrase your findings clearly and honestly.

Second: Try to lift yourself by your intellectual boot-straps above the climate that made you what you are. Constantly question the stereotyped social ideas and attitudes which constitute the orienting background of your scholarship, and which guide your selection of research problems, your methods of work, and your conclusions. While regarding your findings as valid scientific hypotheses drawn from data, advocate and practice their utilization in programs of social action.

Third: To do those things will lead you into a difficult and dangerous course of action. If you choose the easier and safer way of conformity, you will, of course, dodge real issues and select innocuous problems as the subject matter of your research. You will describe, tabulate, compute, summarize, and correlate quantitative data with acceptable and respectable "objectivity"—but all to no worthwhile end. You will produce studies that will guarantee you the continued security of a small middle-class economic competence and the approval of others of your company. But your work will make little or no contribution to the building of the great culture which is now within the reach of the American people. And you will have destroyed your own integrity.

Fourth: Especially must you be receptive to the hypothesis that "our times" is a period of drastic transition, covering several decades of time—decades which mark the passing of the first industrial epoch in our history and the emergence of the second one.[1] You must be willing to consider the contention that this is a critical period in American history and that, although a minority of creative minds will continue to apply themselves to physical science and invention and the language arts, most of our thinking men will devote themselves to the creative task of the reconstruction of social and personal life.

Fifth: If you accept that contention you will recognize that the new age now dawning is a period of chaotic confusion and bewilderment. In it the supreme task of the scholar, either in the social sciences or in the arts, is the clarification of ideas and attitudes. For this clarification a new language is imperative, for the old one is no longer appropriate. Let us illustrate:

In the regime of the initial exploitation of virgin continents that has just passed, such characteristic concepts as accelerating expansion, laissez-faire, scarcity, or success via competition were useful, perhaps indispensable. But our regime is a very different one. It is one, first, in which the major struts of the production system have already been erected; second, in which there is no longer any relation between what a worker can produce and the share of the social income that society can pay him as purchasing power; third, in which profits and fixed charges take an undue proportion of the social income; and fourth, in which private ownership and personal competition interrupt the operation of the system and withhold much of it from use. In such a regime, I say, such concepts as expansion, scarcity, laissez-faire, and private ownership and control of basic industries and utilities constitute the vocabulary of a foreign and useless language.

Hence the problems of the coming years simply, cannot be thought through by means of the ideas and attitudes which dominated the mind of the first stage of industrialism. New ideas and principles must be found to fit the new situations and problems. There must be a new orientation, born of the current trends. To devise the needed language of thought and discourse is the major creative task of scholarship in our Great Transition.

Sixth: You may be sure, therefore, that whether you work on the problems of social control (that is, the social sciences) or on those of personal self-realization (that is, the arts) you will be working on the very frontiers of thought and feeling. In these fields the instruments of study are meanings, concepts, generalizations, and attitudes. Yardsticks, either of verbal description or of more exact quantitative measurement, are not available. Emotional bias befogs our vision. Dominant social forces are antagonistic to realistic research. Research methods are undeveloped. You will be working, therefore, in a thrilling but such a devastatingly complex field of scholarship that your work will demand unyielding integrity, and all the documented knowledge, imagination, persistence, and courage at your command.

Seventh: Try to avoid the pitfalls of the intellectual fallacies of the traditional scholar and especially the one that implies that "research" is restricted to any concept, attitude, or area now marked out by conventional academic practice. On the contrary, insist that research is really the discovery of any new meaning or concept the drawing of any new documented generalization (or the confirmation or refutation of any hitherto asserted one), the portrayal of any human trait, attitude or mental pattern, and the building of alternative courses of action out of such materials.

Eighth: To accomplish these ends you must value your own integrity most of all. It is the only sure guarantee of honest and efficient craftsmanship, and this is the supreme goal of the scholar as it is of all true artists. Strive to make every utterance a true replica of your Self that is—to conclude, to make, to speak, to write, what you really think and feel. If your personal philosophy is to constitute an honest program of life, you can utter only what you are.

Ninth, and finally: Bind yourself in adamant solidarity with other Thinking Men of integrity and craftsmanship, for that only, in the long run, will guarantee the economic security and social approval which you crave.

References

1 This hypothesis has been fully documented in many sources in the past few years.

SEEDS OF REVOLT *

The Editorial Board

This editorial recognizes the need for education to be revolutionary. As the editors explain: "education properly conducted in the modern world, is an enemy and not a benign supporter of inherited ways of doing things. Education in its profoundest meaning is revolution." The piece concludes with the argument that elementary school, high school, and college teachers must promote new critical ways of thinking and that "society must learn not to fear the whirlwind."

* * *

It is time that educators, especially the more advanced thinkers on all levels of the profession, begin to make capital out of the patent fact that education properly conducted in the modern world, is an enemy and not a benign supporter of inherited ways of doing things. Education in its profoundest meaning is revolution. Recognition has of course long been afforded this fact in individual life and growth. The changes wrought upon an individual by educative influences between infancy and adulthood are immeasurably great and frequently occur with apparent suddenness. Educators do not aim at bringing the "new" generation into a lockstep with prevailing mores. They have aimed for many years at equipping youth for greater material and cultural conquest than existing society has been able to attain. But these dynamic ideals of the profession have been continuously frustrated by forces other than the school which have tended to idealize the status quo. To the great discredit of the educational profession it must be said that it has signally failed to point out the anomaly between what the schools were attempting and what other educative influences outside the schools were actually accomplishing with youth. Now that a powerful group in America, the business men and financiers, have begun to consider the function of the school, they are not backward in indicating that the ideals of education should be blatant patriotism, blind loyalty, optimistic crowing about the "bright" side of things, "practicality," etc. In primitive times education was unconsciously and necessarily conventional; free intelligence was a detriment and constantly suspect. If the industrial magnates and the bankers have their way in America as they have had in Germany and Italy during late years, we will be deliberately reverting to primitive educational patterns at a time in our history when such reversion becomes a betrayal of all ideal values.

---

* **Source:** *The Social Frontier*, Volume 1, Number 7, 1935, p. 8.

The real spadework in establishing education as the growing edge of society lies ahead of educators, not behind them. The end of free business enterprise as a principle of economic and social organization adequate to this country is at hand. The influences which actually hold ownership title to the structural framework of America—its natural resources and its industrial equipment—deny this and insist that educators have no business "sowing seeds of revolt" in the minds of youth. How will the educator respond to this accusation? Will he deny it? Will he shy away from the issue by uttering a string of ancient platitudes? Or will he boldly assert that genuine education properly and naturally leads to the remaking of human institutions? If the latter, he must seek the backing of the disinherited majority of the productive workers of America who alone stand to gain if education criticizes, evaluates, and attempts to reconstruct everything in the environment which has human significance.

Dare the university say that it has no research department? Dare researchers say that there are regions into which they will not peer? Dare intelligent men and women say that what research has established as truth shall be cast aside if it goes contrary to the authority of established institutions? How long can established institutions withstand toppling traditions? And what shall the elementary school, high school, and college say about all this? Shall they deny it and futilely seek to nurture youth on cold facts and empty ideals? Veritably, teachers must sow the seed and society must learn not to fear the whirlwind.

PROSPECTING FOR THE FUTURE *

William F. Ogburn

illiam F. Ogburn (1886–1959) was among the leading sociologists in the United States during the first half of the twentieth century. He was most well-known for his theory of social change, which he felt was largely technologically driven, but also subject to "cultural lag."

In the article included below, he argues that if "the future is to be different from the past" and we are to live in the future, then we need to educate our children to deal with a future different from the past and present. Ogburn prophetically describes how change will accelerate in the future, and how there is a need in all educational institutions to begin to teach about the future, particularly in the social sciences. Ogburn concludes the article with a discussion of how cultural institutions lag behind technological developments, and how there is a need to be innovative and bold in predicting patterns of future development.

*   *   *

If, (a) the future is to be different from the past, and if (b) we are to [live our] lives in the future, then (c) we ought to educate for a changed future—one different from the present or the past.

The second assumption, that we are to live our lives, not in the past nor in the present, but in the future, there is no occasion to question. The first statement that the future will be different does call for special comment.

THE ACCELERATING RATE OF SOCIAL CHANGE

The future will not, of course, be wholly different from the past. We shall, in this country, continue to speak the English language; and it will, no doubt, be many years before we shall be reading an Esperanto type of language. We shall continue to use the multiplication table. Some cultural forms persist with negligible change from decade to decade.

Certain pattern of human behaviour also have many similarities, no matter what the age. The men that Plutarch describes had their ambitions and intrigues, loves and hates, at the dawn of history, much as we have them today. It is true they fought with spears and arrows, while we fight with guns; but still we fight, in one way or another.

Even though some traits of culture change imperceptibly and even though human behaviour has relatively constant patterns, nevertheless our civilization

---

* **Source:** *The Social Frontier*, Volume 1, Number 7, 1935, pp. 20-22.

is changing. Yesterday we lived on farms, today we live in cities. A generation ago woman's place was in the home, now it is anywhere she wills. Not long ago, the church was active in education, art, healing, government, international affairs as well as in the daily tasks and recreations of individuals; today its role in these activities has been taken over in a large part by other social institutions.

Changes of this type are becoming greater in volume and their rapidity is increasing. The future is likely to be more different from the present than the present is from the past. It is customary to speak of this as an age of transition, as though we were moving in some confusion from a plane of stability to a plateau of calm. The evidence, to the contrary points as far as we can see to an accelerating change, with no stationary period in sight. This means that a larger and larger part of our culture will be different, and hence that a smaller and smaller portion of history will repeat itself.

EDUCATION NEEDS TO PLUMB THE FUTURE

The implications of this logic for education is obvious. The young now in school will live for forty of fifty years in a society that will differ in many respects from what it is now, and even more from the society described in the histories and social sciences dealing with the past. If we are to drive automobiles we do not teach how to handle horses. H. G. Wells says that we ought to have teachers of foresight in our schools. Indeed, he argues that if we have whole departments of history, then we should certainly have whole departments of foresight. No doubt the reader will agree, but he will counter by asking, "Where will you find any one capable of teaching the future?" Will not a proposed chair in foresight go the way of a proposed chair in common sense, for which an endowment was said to have been offered one of our universities? The trustees were unwilling to accept the money (strange as it may seem) because they thought they could find no one to fill the chair. It is supposed to be an axiom that the future is unknown, hence, it is foolish to try to teach the future. But is the problem so hopeless? Scientific research has penetrated beyond thicker veils.

Yet strange to say it is the dead hand of science that holds us back from undertaking this needed preparation of youth. For the scholars leaving the universities are so afraid of being inaccurate, of stating something that isn't reliable, that they dare not venture into so uncertain a realm as the future. Science is all right in its place, but certainly all pedagogy is not science, and should not be dominated by such an over-lord. After all, mathematics not only teaches that two times two is four, but it also teaches the theory of probability.

Scientific research never got anywhere dodging difficulties. So the future is unknown, but whether it will yield its secrets cannot be told until the problem is attacked. Indeed, urgent needs are a well known stimulus to scientific discovery as, for instance, in medical research. The great need of teaching the youth about the future should drive us as teachers (but not scientists) on to forget our scientific reputations and to try to get what we can out of this problem.

The need for knowing something about the future is probably greatest in the social sciences. There is no such demand in literature, in astronomy, in foreign language, in mathematics, or in history. It is peculiarly in the field of social problems that we need to look ahead.

Never before have so many of us been doing so much to solve our social problems. Business depressions are not taken as being so inevitable in their course, as formerly. Indeed, the greater the social change the more the ameliorative effort may be expected, and the further away we get from the fatalism so characteristic of stationary societies. But to make headway against social problems, it is much better to try to figure what they will be in the future, than to study those of the past, such as, say, the slavery issue or the Chartist movement. Workmen's compensation is largely behind us, but health insurance is ahead. States' rights are translated by the communication inventions into problems of centralization and local government. Child labor is being superseded by wider issues of population policy. The problems of democracy are receding before those of collectivism. It does seem obvious that if we wish to make this a better place in which to live then we should concentrate on the problems of the future. But how can we tell what they will be?

A HYPOTHESIS OF CHANGE

In the absence of scientific formulae for prediction, we shall have to fall back on prediction as an art. I should venture to claim, but without scientific proof, that the following hypothesis will be found of value. A very large number of social changes are precipitated by invention and scientific discovery which make their effects felt first on economic institutions, the influence not reaching the other social institutions until a good deal later. Furthermore, inventions require about a quarter of a century, more or less, after they have been made to become widely adopted, and hence modify society. So, one begins with inventions which change, after a number of years, the economic institutions, and, after a still longer lag, other social institutions are modified. This sequence is not the only one, indeed quite the opposite may occur. Not was such a sequence necessarily true in ancient times. But it probably occurs with sufficient frequency to be a useful tool for outlining the coming changes in the social structure. These social problems, while involving a stable biological nature, are in the main precipitated in their new forms by the fact that the different correlated parts of our civilization are changing at unequal rates of speed. Something about these correlations are known as truly as something is known about the sequences and lags. Thus, we know that governmental boundaries are related to transportation inventions. The family is related to industry, as is education also. Science is not unrelated to religion, etc. Changes in one may therefore, be interpreted in terms of changes in another, and problems may be forecast if the idea of lag is appreciated. Furthermore, a study of inventions, the key to the process, will yield large returns. We can readily see that the new electric eye will have wide social effects, as will also the inventions which make artificial climate. The social influences of television can be anticipated somewhat. The electrical inventions will affect the family, and the influences of the automobile and telephone have not ended. Talking books will appear and affect the schools. The future of nationalism cannot be final without a consideration of the communication and transportation inventions. From these illustrations, it can be seen that hypotheses of change may be helpful. Certainly they are better than nothing, even though we must speak of them with qualifications.

There are other rules of the workshop that may be helpful. In the absence of reliable knowledge it is well to realize the dangers of bias in wishful thinking. This danger we recognize in the abstract, but in practice either we are prone to forget it or are incapable of dealing with it. Optimists are more numerous than pessimists, though pessimists are victims of a type of "wishful" thinking also. It is the moralist who has to be especially guarded against. He wants to say what ought to take place. The reformer persuades himself to predict what he wants to occur, thinking thereby it will be made to come to pass through influencing the opinions and actions of others. Prediction for propaganda purposes is a very different thing from prediction for scientific accuracy, and its effectiveness for action is very questionable. Often idealists have been thus let down by trusting in propaganda prediction, to become discouraged and ineffective cynics. But essentially, this practice makes for sloppy work in reliable prediction. It is much better to try to shut the door, so to speak, on our emotions and lock it; then to take the most detached view possible and try to answer the question, "What is likely to happen?" Once this has been done the answer should be written down and kept as free as possible from the distorting influence of bias. When this operation is finished, unlock the emotions, and only then ask the question of what can be done to influence the course of events in the direction we think they ought to move; and proceed to act accordingly.

USEFUL PRACTICES IN PREDICTION

Another useful practice in the art of prediction is to be bold. Most responsible predictors are too conservative. This is not true of course of those who make a living out of being sensational. It is rather the scientist, skilled in caution and trained to suspend judgment, whose guesses are not wild enough. Simon Newcomb, dean of American science, expressed the belief that man would never fly in a machine heavier-than-air, just a few months before two "fool" inventors did the trick at Kitty Hawk, North Carolina. A recent study of the prediction of football scores by sports writers of the newspapers shows that they predicted lower scores than actually occurred. The error is large on the side of conservatism. Timidity is not a great virtue in trying to see the future.

A constructive device for forecasting, which is in wide use, is the projection of trend lines forward a few years. While this procedure is confined to quantitative data, the pattern is roughly applicable to general description. The reliability of this method can be enhanced by a consideration of the factors that make the trend. For instance, to have projected forward the curve of automobile production in 1925 for a decade, would have resulted in quite an over-estimate. Whereas a consideration of true factors contributing to the production trend, would have revealed that the population of the country was such as to indicate a marked stowing up of the demand, because production was getting nearer to the saturation point.

The projection forward of trends suggests that only an estimate of the future conditions can be generally expected at this time. No photographic picture, clear in detail and outline, is to be expected. But the purposes of education can be served by the clues offered by such trends and processes as were indicated in the preceding paragraphs. Other writers may contribute other useful methods. And in time, with attention and effort directed to the problem, it ought to be possible to give the student a pretty good guess as to the social problems which society will be concerned with during his lifetime. It would be very useful if a publisher would bring out a series of serious, but not sensational, books on, say, the future of democracy, the family of tomorrow, what our cities will be like, what's in store for labor, how government and industry will be related, what our population policy should be, and on the future of other parts of our changing social order. But, indeed, there are many things that might be done to educate for the future social order.

TOWARD A NATIONAL SYSTEM OF EDUCATION *

John Dewey

With this article, John Dewey began to regularly contribute to the journal. In this piece he argues that in no other modern country has the control of education been so focused on the local level as it is in the United States of America. Dewey maintains a distinction between "nationalistic" and "national" systems of education. A national system "is an educational system that corresponds to the spirit, the temper, the dominant habits and purposes that hold the people of a country together, so far as they are held together in a working unity of life." A nationalistic system "is imposed by government and maintained by government, though not of necessity in opposition to the will of the people."

The United States system, according to Dewey, is a combination of both systems with an emphasis on local control. According to him: "Some undoubted advantages have accrued to offset the disadvantages of our local and dispersive system. The schools have been closer to the local communities; in many cases local responsibility has been stimulated. There has been, along with great unevenness, a stimulus to experimentation such as a closed centralized system does not afford. Meetings of teachers, emulation, and the spread of ideas by social osmosis, have had to play the part taken by ministries of education in other countries. Mechanical uniformity has not been allowed to exclude wholesome diversity."

Dewey argues that by handing control of curriculum over to teachers, there will be less of tendency for the imposition of political ideologies on the citizenry. Essentially Dewey calls for the free exchange and discussion of ideas as a way of overcoming limited political and social ideologies.

*   *   *

From the standpoint of any European country, except Great Britain, the American public school system is chaos rather than a system. The British system, from the continental standpoint, is even more chaotic than ours, because public education there is superimposed upon schools carried on by religious bodies. Until the arrival of Hitler, there was a good deal of provincial educational autonomy in Germany; the larger divisions of the U.S.S.R. exercise considerable autonomy though of course within the limits of the proletarian-communist scheme. But there is no other country where local control and differentiation are carried as far as in this country.

The historical causes for our peculiar difference are fairly evident. Regions developed in the country before the nation, and localities before regions. Set-

---

* **Source:** *The Social Frontier*, Volume 1, Number 9, 1935, pp. 9–10.

tlers had no choice save to go without schools or themselves to form a school for their own locality, the latter often not being even a village but a collection of farm-homesteads scattered over a considerable territory. The district school and the little red schoolhouse were the answer. As settlers moved westward and out to the frontier, the same conditions prevailed; in addition they naturally followed the precedent with which they were familiar.

Some degree of centralization has followed, by townships, by counties, and by states—but always with the limitations suggested by the word "some." The movement never extended to the nation. The "Office of Education" in Washington is the expression and record of the limitation of the movement. I do not propose to discuss the concrete matter of changing the Office into a Cabinet Department, but rather to say something about a few general principles that seem to me to lie at the basis of a genuinely national system of education.

NATIONAL VERSUS NATIONALISTIC SYSTEMS

In the first place, there is a fundamental difference between a national and a nationalistic system, and we must face the issue of whether we can have one without growing sooner or later into the other. By a nationalistic system, I mean one in which the school system is controlled by the Government in power in the interest of what it takes to be the welfare of its own particular national state, and of the social-economic system the Government is concerned to maintain. The school systems of Japan, Italy, the U.S.S.R., and now Germany, define better what is meant by "nationalistic" education than will any abstract descriptions.

A national system in its distinction from a nationalistic one is not so easy to define. Roughly speaking, it is an educational system that corresponds to the spirit, the temper, the dominant habits and purposes that hold the people of a country together, so far as they are held together in a working unity of life. These terms are all vague, but the vagueness lies in the nature of the situation. In spite of the vagueness, it may be readily demarcated from a nationalistic system. The latter is imposed by government and maintained by government, though not of necessity in opposition to the will of the people. A national system is an outgrowth from the people. It develops from below, rather than is imposed from above. The government intervenes by legislation and administratively, but it follows rather than precedes the more spontaneous and voluntary efforts of the people.

That we do not have a nationalistic system of education in this country is too obvious to require argument. Because of the historic conditions already mentioned, we have a national system only partially and somewhat amorphously. That, as time has passed, local and regional interests have tended to merge, while local boundaries have lost force in comparison with the concerns of the country as a whole, is clear in every field. The educational system could not escape this influence. Unification in economic directions has increased the importance of unity in the ideas and policies that affect national policies. Nevertheless, it was practically inevitable in so large a country and in one with so short a history that the intellectual and moral unification of the different regions of the country should lag behind economic unification.

Some undoubted advantages have accrued to offset the disadvantages of our local and dispersive system. The schools have been closer to the local communities; in many cases local responsibility has been stimulated. There has been, along with great unevenness, a stimulus to experimentation such as a closed centralized system does not afford. Meetings of teachers, emulation, and the spread of ideas by social osmosis, have had to play the part taken by ministries of education in other countries. Mechanical uniformity has not been allowed to exclude wholesome diversity.

NECESSITY SETS A DILEMMA

Yet the necessity in a time of great changes, like the present, of direction in the interest of the people as a whole (unless we are to sink into deeper chaos) is a fact that cannot be escaped. It would however be a great mistake, in my opinion, to think that this urgent need settles the way in which the need should be satisfied. It rather presents a problem. The easy conversion in Europe of centralized systems into agencies of a dominant political regime is a warning. Moreover, local interests and jealousies are still so strong in this country that an administrative national system could not be brought about in this country except through something approaching class coercion of a Fascist variety or a great amount of dangerous propaganda—or both. On the other hand, as I have already said, unless we are to drift into a worse situation than that in which we now find ourselves, a strong unified intelligence and purpose must be built up in support of policies that have a definite trend toward a socialized cooperative democracy. The schools cannot remain outside this task.

THE WAY OUT

Here are the two horns of our dilemma. As far as I can see, the surest as well as safest way out is for teachers themselves to work actively to establish the autonomy of education, rather than to share in direct attempts to establish a national system. By autonomy I do not mean, of course, something separate. Autonomy means rather the right of teachers to determine the subject-matter and methods employed in the schools. This is a right they are far from now

having. Part of the confusion and the social irresponsibility of public education at present springs from the fact that it is controlled in such large measure
by interests that are concerned chiefly with ends that lie outside of the educative field. If the teaching profession can educate itself and the public to the
need of throwing off this incubus, genuinely educative forces will be released
to do their work. In consequence, the freedom and impetus that result will
enable the schools, without a centralized system, to develop a system of truly
national education—by which I mean one animated by policies and methods
that will help create that common purpose without which the nation cannot
achieve unified movement.

What is urged is far from indoctrination in the sense of inculcation of
fixed beliefs. In the first place, this end could not be accomplished without
first indoctrinating teachers into a single body of beliefs, and nothing but Fascist or Communist coercion can bring about even a semblance of such unification. In the second place, any unification of the national will effect by such a
method will have no firm and enduring roots. Dr. Randall has recently made
the following pertinent remarks regarding the use of the method of intelligence in education:

> It is implied that because intelligence does not attain final truth, it reaches no
> conclusion at all. . . . The futile debate about "indoctrination" in education illus-
> trates this strange delusion. If you stimulate inquiry and educate, this leaves the
> student free to adopt any opinion or conclusion he wishes! Therefore it is neces-
> sary to "indoctrinate" him with the ends you have decided upon. As though, in-
> quiry never discovered anything, and investigation never reached conclusions
> that force themselves upon the mind of the investigator!. . . . Inquiry is meaning-
> less unless you discover ideas that put other ideas at a disadvantage.

The bearing of these remarks upon my theme is that they point to the
need of concentration and clarification of the methods of free mutual discussion and communication among teachers—methods that are responsible for
whatever advances have been made in public education in the past. I do not
say this is the final step in the development of a national education, but it is
the first step. Moreover, concentration and clarification involve a good deal.
They involve cutting out repetition of conventionalities, of hullabaloo, and
settling down to basic issues of the relation of education to social direction. If
this can be accomplished, I think the process of self-education of teachers will
educate also the public, and take us on the sure road to the now distant goal
of a truly national education.

Loyalty Oaths—A Threat to Intelligent Teaching *

William H. Kilpatrick

W illiam H. Kilpatrick (1871–1965) was among the most influential progressive educators at Teachers College, and along with George S. Counts, one of the most important figures in the establishment of the field of the Social Foundations of Education. In the following article, he attempts to explain why a national movement for the establishment of loyalty oaths developed in the United States. Kilpatrick concludes that loyalty oaths represent an essentially conservative response to changes in the culture, part of a "vain struggle of the old and outmoded world-view against the inevitable new outlook."

Teachers, according to Kilpatrick must be well-educated and thoughtful individuals who respond consistently to the demands placed upon them by a changing society. According to him: "This means that as long as there is suffering or want among us, and inequality of opportunity or treatment, these good teachers will join with others to seek for better things, for better ways of ordering American life. And, equally, this means for teachers no indoctrination of prior chosen views, but obedience to the highest vision that their study can find, and the teaching of others themselves to seek and follow the highest vision they can get."

Loyalty oaths for teachers, in the end, deny the need for teachers, and in turn students, to think and function critically. Kilpatrick maintains that in a democracy such as the United States, "the people," including teachers, "must control all major decisions, and this means that they must learn through discussion how to judge and weigh . . . a wise education must be founded clearly and inherently on a philosophy of change, and it must prepare young and old ever better to weigh and judge among contending proposals for social improvements. Such a preparation can be got only by practice on actual and unsettled issues. Both young and old among us must learn ever better to criticize our existing American life and its institutions to the end that proper changes can be made, as they are needed." Loyalty oaths "arising out of a panic fear of change," deny this process and thwart the development of a truly democratic culture.

*　*　*

Why loyalty oaths for teachers? What underlies the concerted drive to demand that teachers the nation over shall give oath to support the Constitution? What is the aim and what the fear? Is constitutional government threatened? Is any evil seriously threatened that a loyalty oath would remedy or correct?

---

* **Source:** *The Social Frontier*, Volume 1, Number 9, 1935, pp. 10–15.

THE CONSTITUTION AS ACTUALITY OR SYMBOL

The answers to these questions lie not on the surface of things, but deeper. The impelling fear is almost surely not for the safety of the Constitution or of constitutional government. In fact it is difficult to say just what content is included in loyalty to the Constitution, considering that amendments are possible. And why demand the oath of teachers? Probably not one-tenth of one per cent of American teachers have ever even for one moment wished anything in the way of public policy that the loyalty oaths would deny them. On the contrary, those most concerned for a better social outlook are almost without exception more loyal to the spirit both of the Constitution and of the founding fathers than are proponents of these bills with their wish to stifle freedom of study and discussion. Such considerations compel us to look beneath the surface if we are to understand the moving why of this concerted drive.

Even slight search indicates that it is the Constitution not as actuality but as symbol that is threatened. The supporting movement, it seems safe to say, is not a deliberately planned effort to deal intelligently with a situation—the steps taken are too haphazard and futile for that. Rather is it an outburst of emotion, a near-hysteria. It seems, in fact, exactly the kind of emotional outburst to be expected from unthoughtful persons who feel their accustomed foundations threatened. Thinking in stereotypes, as such persons do, they have seized upon the Constitution as symbol of the threatened status quo and they hope by fixing the one to maintain the other. Hence the loyalty oaths. If this were all, a symbolic remedy for inexorable change, we might smile—or sigh—and pass on to other matters. But unfortunately actual evil is, as usual bound up with the symbolic treatment. On the one hand, the fundamental factor of change is ignored; on the other, the proper work of the school is threatened. The two hang together. We must understand this factor of fundamental change if we are to see and protect the proper work of the school.

CLASSIC BIAS AGAINST CHANGE

What is there to understand about change? Have not change and decay always been with us? What new has happened that popular foundations are threatened? What is there here that can explain the nation-wide fear and emotion?

Change and decay have indeed been universal phenomena of history and, in the past, man has sought to escape at least their more serious manifestations. The dominant philosophies for two thousand years have founded themselves on this quest. But the modern world of science and invention has been forced to accept change no longer as evil or trivial, but rather as normal and fundamental. The fear and emotion we now see in the loyalty oath laws is but the vain struggle of the old and outmoded world-view against the inevitable new outlook. What we witness are the death throes of a dying philosophy. It is this, which explains the emotion and the threat to the schools. If this outmoded theory of no-change can have its way, education will remain static and so fail to prepare the young for the life they must live. A closer examination will help us discover the considerations, motives, and assumptions, which actuate the advocacy of loyalty oaths and the dangers, which inhere in them.

Until recently, as history goes, culture accumulated but slowly; so slowly in fact that the life of each generation repeated that of the preceding with hardly noticeable difference. Changes were noted, to be sure, but not accumulated change; that was too slight. The individual life cycle of birth and growth and death was obvious; also accidents happened, and dynastic overthrows were not infrequent. Such changes all seemed evil, and moreover they went, as it were, back and forth across the stream of life without progressing, that is, with little or no cumulative effect. In fact, the idea of progressive accumulation, popularly called progress, was hardly conceived by any until modern times. Under these by-gone conditions most men feared change lest it get out of bounds. For example, amidst the glory of classical Athens not all was well; social chaos seemed to threaten; and Plato in fear of it proposed his famous republic out of concern for order and security. What here interests us is the philosophic base Plato provided, one founded on the timelessness of truth that seemed to inhere in the propositions of geometry and number theory. Back of all human devices, he taught, there were perfect and everlasting archetypes, or models, "laid up in heaven." It was the duty of man to frame his thoughts, his institutions, and his conduct on the perfect and unchanging models thus provided. If this were done, there could properly be no more change, and order would be perfect and everlasting. At last the evil of change would be overcome.

The hope proved to have a wide appeal. So widely indeed did this philosophy prevail that Christianity, turning aside from its original simplicity, founded its theology upon it. Christianity added to Platonism the notion that God had created these archetypes from "before the foundation of the world" and had revealed them in "the faith once delivered to the saints." In the 13th century the philosopher-theologians restated this outlook in Aristotelian terms. In so doing they gave to the Western world a popular philosophy, which to this day constitutes the basis for those ideas, which most people still accept uncritically. The inmost essence of this popular philosophy lies in its assumption that fundamental ideas, of which concrete objects and events are only imperfect embodiments, cannot change. Many opponents of change among us today unwittingly hark back to Plato and Aristotle. The doctrine that war and the profit motive are forever with us because they inhere in "essential" human nature is a case in point, as also is trust in the alleged necessary and unchanging law of supply and demand. As in Plato's day, so now, the changeless character ascribed to such things as human nature and absolute natural laws serves, to those who profess it, as a welcome bulwark against threatened change. The doctrines are still working as they were designed to work, imbedded as they now are in the uncriticized background of popular philosophy.

EMERGENCE OF A NEW ATTITUDE TOWARD THE DYNAMIC

But modern change has an obviously different characteristic from that previously prevailing. Change nowadays builds on change and so is cumulative. It is clearly more inclusive, it reaches deeper down, and it is far more rapid. In all of this, modern science is the new causal factor. Some three centuries and more ago, man began to test his thought in more careful fashion, and modern science has resulted. Accumulating discoveries beget an ever-increasing volume of discoveries. During the latter half of this modern period the ever-growing science has brought rapid multiplication of inventions, with modern technology as the outcome. Out of science has thus grown a two-fold destruction of old doctrines and positions. On the one hand, science makes men bold in questioning by supplying new methods for directing search and new data from which to question. Beginning with the more intellectual, this questioning has at length reached the populace itself. On the other hand, the inventions of science so remake methods of production and so change our ways of living that old customs are broken down under our very eyes. Never before in history have such far-reaching changes spread themselves so rapidly among men, and the rate of change is ever faster.

If we go back to the beginning of the new science, it was not long before it began to have philosophic and social effects. Copernicus and Galileo upset religious thinking. Descartes was no less than the major prophet of a new order that extended itself to all spheres of human interest. When the Commonwealth overturned the Stuart dynasty in Great Britain, Hobbes defended autocracy not as beforetimes on divine right, but on the basis of the new science. Still later, when autocracy went down before the Revolution of 1688, John Locke defended the results on the same science more humanly conceived. Locke's teachings were united in France with other fruits of the new scientific attitude and the Enlightenment emerged. Henceforth institutions must serve the needs of man, or be consciously changed. It was this new Liberalism that still later furnished the basis for the Declaration of Independence and the Bill of Rights.

CONFLICT OF CLASSIC AND MODERN
ATTITUDES TOWARD CHANGE

The reason for the emotion and fear back of the loyalty oaths is now more apparent. Two philosophies of life are contending. One founds itself on the fact of change. It sees change and becoming as not only universal phenomena, but as essential in life and civilization. This philosophy would accordingly expect change in all institutional arrangements and consciously provide to make the changes better than otherwise they would be. Especially would it provide for the intelligent criticism of life and institutions to the end that further appropriate changes may be intelligently made. The other philosophy founds itself on the older notion that change is fundamentally wrong and evil, and is to be confined as straitly as possible. It will admit change in obvious means, in new machinery for instance, but not in the more fundamental ideas and institutions. These must be kept intact as of old. The crucial difference between the two positions is thus in the attitude toward criticism. The older philosophy fears criticism lest it lead to further change. The newer philosophy demands criticism as the only intelligent safeguard against belated or unwise changes.

We recognize in all history those who will hold to the philosophy-opposed-to-change. They will be the "conservative" groups. Some are merely timorous, preferring the known little they have to any uncertain prospects of the future. Others will know more consciously the interests they wish to conserve. Still others, at least moderately comfortable, will be antiquarian in interest and outlook. For them the past with its ways and thoughts forms an all-engrossing hobby. Many of these latter profess to speak in behalf of our historic patriotism. So the super-patriots among the D.A.R. make much of the American Revolution, but themselves totally belie the revolutionary spirit of the founding fathers.

We equally well recognize our Revolutionary fathers as allying themselves with the new philosophy of change and criticism. John Adams in 1786 quoted with approval the statement that "a revolution of government is the strongest proof that can be given by a people of their virtue and good sense." Thomas Jefferson said in his First Inaugural: "If there be any among us who would wish to dissolve the Union, or to change its Republican form, let them stand undisturbed, as monuments of the safety with which error of opinion may be tolerated, where reason is left free to combat it."

And further, as if to anticipate the present opposition to criticism in our schools, he said of the projected University of Virginia: "This institution will be based upon the illimitable freedom of the human mind. For here we are not afraid to follow truth, wherever it may lead, nor to tolerate error as long as reason is left free to combat it."[1]

INTELLIGENT CRITICISM ESSENTIAL TO DEMOCRACY IN A DYNAMIC WORLD

Let us look a little more closely at the need for providing untrammeled criticism. Any group culture, if adequate, must form one whole, part fitting with part to form an effectual working unity. If then significant change comes in one part of the culture, other appropriate changes must be made in the other parts, or the working balance will be upset and the culture cease to function as a unified whole. Now this is exactly our present state. Because of science and invention our ways of producing have changed greatly and promise to keep on changing even more rapidly. Under such conditions, balanced adjustments are upset. Difficulties of adjustment ensue—must ensue—and problems consequently arise. For the problems thus necessarily arising proposals for solution will be made. As long, then, as men continue to discover and invent, civilization will continue thus to change and we shall continuously have on hand proposals for taking care of the resulting social difficulties. Not all of these proposals can be accepted, for they will contradict each other. Deliberation and choice must thus be a continuing function of any changing civilization.

How shall the choices and decisions be made? Shall they be made by the self-appointed who seek to maintain their own special privileges? Or by the people as a whole? Democracy is committed to the proposition that the decisions must be made by the people, the mass of the people, acting as nearly as possible for the good of all. This way of deciding rejects rule by a minority party as now holds in Russia. It rejects dictators as found in Italy and Germany. It rejects government by a set of experts, as some among us now urge for this country. It rejects government by the possessing groups, as Hamilton advocated and his modern followers in effect still advocate. Democracy rejects all restricted sources of decision and instead relies on the people.

But the people will not decide wisely unless they have the basis of intelligent choice. This looks in two directions, the one immediately urgent and the other fundamentally necessary. The more immediate is free discussion, democracy's way of finding out which new proposal to follow. And this in turn depends on the essential rights of freedom of speech, freedom of press, freedom of assembly. These rights constitute the safeguard of democracy as it seeks through discussion to make valid choices. But the one, the more immediate, the practice of discussion, will go on much better if it is founded on the other—that is on certain underlying attitudes and habits without which discussion too easily becomes demagogic. To deliberate wisely, the citizens must have a certain reasonable breadth of view, the willingness to examine, sufficient knowledge both of the present situation and of its origin to see the current problems in their perspective, and certain habit-skills for analyzing and pursuing ideas that save discussion from being mere word battling and make it fruitful to all concerned.

IMPLICATIONS FOR EDUCATION

These essential underlying attitudes and habits bring then our inquiry to the school. If the citizens are to have the knowledge, the breadth of view, and the habit-skills necessary for fruitful discussion-study, the schools—both higher and lower—must do their part in preparing such citizens. The citizenship curriculum must then base itself adequately upon the fact of inevitable change and the consequent need for its wise direction. What the schools can do lies along two lines, both of which are already familiar to the thoughtful students of change but neither of which is adequately understood by the opposing group.

First as to the university. If it is to face intelligently the fact of change, it must as a research agency live largely in the frontier land of new ideas. It must study any possible suggestion of the new, at least to see whether this proposed new is worthy of further study. It must criticize as thoroughly as possible all live-issue proposals, and it must itself be free to make any new proposal whatsoever that to it seems worthy of further study. In all of this there must be no outside restriction whatsoever, only the internal restrictions of honest and careful study. In spite of some prejudiced opposition to "brain-trusters" it is a fact that university professors increasingly constitute the best single source of the knowledge and criticism necessary for dealing with new ideas, and they must speak as freely as honesty demands. On no other basis can they do their part in fostering criticism. On this basis alone do they best serve civilization. These things follow inevitably from the new factor of accelerating change characteristic of modern times.

Secondly, pupils and students in whatever school must as prospective citizens be learning, each according to his degree of advancement, ever better how to criticize and judge; and this can go on best only as they study controversial issues, the as yet unsettled problems. The instructors, whether in the elementary or secondary school or in the university, are there to help make the process of study and criticisms go on intelligently. They are there to help pupils and students learn to criticize, and not to substitute for such practice in judging any unthinking acceptance of the already formed judgments of the teacher. Most certainly, teachers are not there to hand out orthodoxy, whether old or new, to docile minds. That would be to deny both the fact of a changing world and the process by which learning best goes on.

Let us note here in connection that criticism is a sifting of the more reliable from the less reliable, of the more desirable from the less desirable, of the more promising from the less promising. In particular, the school for whatever age level has the positive duty of helping its pupils or students at their age level to understand and criticize the facts of American life and American institutions. This to the end that change in our institutions may be made intelligently as needed, and not violently because overdue change has been unintelligently or selfishly held back.

It is at this point that the recommendations of the Lusk Report of 1920 are most stupid: "No person who is not eager to combat the theories of social change should be entrusted with the task of fitting the young and old of this state for the responsibilities of citizenship."

This is the clear-cut philosophy of no-change. It would be hard to find a clearer case of partisan opposition to the intelligent study of change. This is exactly the kind of reactionary attitude, which, in the degree that it succeeds, will ultimately lead to violent and unintelligent change.

If, as now becomes necessary, the schools are thus to prepare citizens for the intelligent study of change and proposals for improvement, what kind of teachers will be needed? The answer discloses the lurking danger in the loyalty oaths. If pupils and students are to learn how to study and criticize with reference to wise social choices, and consequent wise changes, clearly, teachers must be of the kind to help such study and criticism best go on. In particular, prospective teachers should come from the flower of our youth, not the culls and left-overs after the capable and daring souls have gone to other fields of work. The teachers we need should be well informed, scholarly, of deep human sympathies, and thoroughly up-to-date as to what the current issues are and why. We must so manage education that these first quality minds and characters will be drawn to teaching as a profession.

INTELLIGENT LOYALTY VERSUS RITUAL OF OATH

What kind of loyalty must teachers show? The answer cuts to the root of one's philosophy of change. These efficient teachers of youth must be loyal not to past formulations or ideas as such, and stop there. That would mean that change is not a significant factor in life and that these teachers are no longer dunking, no longer intellectually alive. Teachers must be loyal, not to what has hitherto been accepted, but to the best that better dunking can now find out. Reliance and allegiance are here put not on any authoritative pronouncement, but on methods of search and whatever these may find. This means that as long as there is suffering or want among us, and inequality of opportunity or treatment, these good teachers will join with others to seek for better things, for better ways of ordering American life. And, equally, this means for teachers no indoctrination of prior chosen views, but obedience to the highest vision that their study can find, and the teaching of others themselves to seek and follow the highest vision they can get.

Our teachers thus in sum must be strong characters, with strong human sympathies, with strong convictions—always held, however, subject to change upon better knowledge or deeper insight. Such teachers cannot be mere yes-men, timid of thought or action where either truth or the public welfare is involved. And all that the rest of us, as citizens and lawmakers, do or say in this connection ought to help select such characters to man our schools and teach our children. And herein is the final condemnation of the loyalty oath laws, that they mean to discourage criticism of our institutions, mean to keep teachers from considering controversial issues, mean to keep the schools from intelligent preparation for change. Such laws are consistent with their origin, they mean opposition to intelligent change.

The loyalty oath laws represent then not an intelligent effort to remedy evils, but the emotional outburst of an unthinking group who with their lips honor the Constitution and the Fathers but, in their hearts, oppose them. The several items in this indictment are easily set down, all illustrative of the philosophy of no-change:

1. The loyalty oath laws are built on the theory that change is either exceptional and trivial or wrong.

2. They are built on the theory that thinking and discussion are fundamentally unreliable, likely to upset and subvert what ought to stand.

3. They inherently assume either that American institutions will not bear scrutiny and criticism, or that they must be maintained even where honest criticism finds that changes should be made.

4. They are built on the theory that schools and colleges exist to hand down on authority an already known orthodoxy which ought to be accepted without serious or impertinent questioning.

5. They are built on the theory that the fathers in 1776 and Abraham Lincoln in 1861 were false prophets in American history. The fathers when they said in the Declaration of Independence: "Governments . . . {derive} their just powers from the consent of the governed, that whenever any form of government becomes destructive of these ends, it is the right of the people to alter or abolish it and to institute new government, laying its foundation on such principles and organizing its powers in such form, as shall to them seem most likely to effect their safety and happiness."

And Abraham Lincoln when he said in his first inaugural: "Whenever they [the American people] grow weary of their existing government they can exercise their constitutional right of amending it, or their revolutionary right to dismember or overthrow it."

6. These loyalty oaths, it seems fair to conclude, are built on the hope and belief that school boards, under the pressure of those who profess the letter of the American tradition but deny its spirit, will allow busybodies to browbeat teachers into avoiding the discussion of current controversial issues.

In summation, the argument stands clear. In the long past, cumulative change was so slow that it could easily be disregarded. In those days a philosophy that denied essential change seemed wise, and it was accordingly formulated and accepted. In modern times, however, change has, because of science and invention, become very rapid and highly cumulative. Life and civilization cannot be intelligently directed except as we learn to expect change and prepare to steer it intelligently. If democracy is to persist — as this writer most earnestly hopes—the people must control all major decisions, and this means that they must learn through discussion how to judge and weigh. But discussion will too often be demagogic if a wise education has not gone before and prepared the minds. Such a wise education must be founded clearly and inherently on a philosophy of change, and it must prepare young and old ever better to weigh and judge among contending proposals for social improvements. Such a preparation can be got only by practice on actual and unsettled issues. Both young and old among us must learn ever better to criticize our existing American life and its institutions to the end that proper changes can be made, as they are needed. This, the loyalty oaths arising out of a panic fear of change, would deny and thwart.

References

1. Letter to Roscoe, Dec. 27, 1820, in H. A. Washington, *Writings of Thomas Jefferson*, Vol. VII, p. 196.

THE CAPTIVE SCHOOL [*]

Granville Hicks

Granville Hicks (1901–1982) was an American Marxist, novelist, editor, literary critic and educator. In this article he argues that capitalism and its assumed superiority has been taken for granted in American education. With the failure brought on by the Depression, however, there is an inherent challenge to the existing system.

Teachers in colleges and universities are recognized by Hicks as being under constant threat by their administrators and boards who almost exclusively represent the interests of the business and the capitalist model. Academic freedom is a necessity. Hicks sees the absolute necessity for teachers, from kindergarten to university, "to use the methods of struggle employed by the labor unions—the strike, picketing, the boycott, and so forth." He calls for the affiliation of teachers with labor unions and the development of a consciously critical and reflective teaching force in the United States. Many of his ideas resonate with the idea of "teachers as intellectuals" posited by critical educational theorists such as Henry Giroux, as well as Donald Schön's idea of "the teacher as reflective practitioner."

* * *

In his commencement address last June at Middlebury College, Silas H. Strawn, former president of the American Bar Association, said:

> One of the guarantees of the Federal Constitution is the freedom of speech. Recently we have heard much about "red" activities in the colleges and universities of the country. I am unable to sympathize with the elastic conscience of those who inveigh against the capitalistic system while on the pay roll of a college or university whose budget, or whose existence, is due to the philanthropic generosity of those whose industry and frugality have enabled them to make an endowment.

After a digression on ingratitude, "the most detestable of all vices," Mr. Strawn continued:

> I believe that Nazi-ism, Fascism, Socialism, and Communism and all other forms of governmental schemes and economic vagaries are proper subjects for study in our schools, but that these subjects should be taught by teachers who are sufficiently wise and experienced to know their fallacies. . . . No one who is not a

---

[*] Source: Granville Hicks, "The Captive School," *The Social Frontier*, Volume 2, Number 1, 1935, pp. 10–12.

thorough believer in the soundness of the fundamental principles of our government should be permitted to teach either political economy, economics, social science, or any other subject.

At about the same time, Acting-President Edwin C. Jarrett of Rensselaer Polytechnic Institute stated to the Institute's alumni:

> We were founded by a capitalist of the old days. We have developed and prospered under the capitalistic regime. The men we have sent forth and who have become industrial leaders have, in their generosity and for the benefit of the youth of the country, richly endowed us. We have trained men eager to work under that system, full of confidence that the doctrine of rugged individualism is the doctrine which, supported by strong self-effort and self-sacrifice, fighting bravely the battle of legitimate competition will bring to them financial independence and protection from adversity. We are proud of those alumni and we are proud of their adherence to the inexorable human laws. I think we should stand four squares to the world and declare our faith. In my opinion as the years pass, time will vindicate just as surely as the past has approved of us. If we are condemned as the last refuge of conservatism, let us glory in it.

Both Mr. Strawn and Mr. Jarrett assert their belief in academic freedom, and there is no reason to think they are insincere. In their minds freedom stops where the basic doctrines of capitalism begin; whatever is said beyond that point is license. That is the attitude of almost all the men who control our educational system, the trustees, the influential — i.e., wealthy alumni, the administrators. Capitalism seems so natural to them, so firmly rooted in what Mr. Jarrett calls "the inexorable human laws," that anyone who criticizes it is to them ipso facto stupid, incompetent, and immoral.

HOW ACADEMIC FREEDOM IS HARNESSED

Anyone can understand the development of such an attitude, but this does not make it easier for those teachers who happen to believe that capitalism should be superseded, nor does it alter in the slightest the desolating effect of capitalist control upon our educational life. Education in America is being strangled by the Jarretts and the Strawns, not because they are engaged in a vicious conspiracy to destroy it, but because they have the power to impose upon the colleges their antiquated and untenable dogmas.

Capitalist control of education is not new, but it has become genuinely dangerous only within relatively recent times. For many decades capitalism was historically valid; that is to say, it served, however inefficiently and with however much suffering, to develop the resources of mankind as well as, at that particular time, they could be developed. The vast majority of Americans, teachers included, accepted the basic doctrines of capitalism, and, if they were critical at all, trusted in various reforms to remedy such evils as existed. It was unnecessary for college presidents and boards of trustees to exercise rigid control over the economic views of their faculties, for the members of these faculties were in fundamental agreement with them. At the same time, if heretics did appear, it was possible to tolerate them, for it was unlikely that they could exercise any significant influence. This is not to say that perfect academic freedom existed, for one can think of expulsions in the nineteenth century for religious or ethical heterodoxy, and certainly since the beginning of the twentieth century it has been unsafe for professors to attack too directly the interests of specific monopolists. But fundamentally the semblance of academic freedom was fairly well preserved simply because there was little inclination to go beyond the limits established in the minds of the Strawns and Jarretts.

Since the World War, however, and especially since the beginning of the depression, it has been extremely difficult to convince anyone that capitalism is a success. To many of us, indeed, it seems perfectly clear that capitalism is no longer historically valid, that it has outlived its usefulness, that it should and must be superseded by a different kind of economic machinery. There are thousands of us who believe that the private ownership of the means of production has become so vastly inefficient that it cannot be tolerated, and there are thousands and thousands who feel at least some degree of skepticism.

This has completely changed the situation in the colleges. Not only are heretics and potential heretics abundant on every faculty; they are actually a danger to capitalism, for they are taken seriously by many of their students and their fellow-citizens. The result is that the Jarretts and the Strawns have become acutely class-conscious. They can no longer view with amused tolerance the economic vagaries of John Jones and Frank Smith; Jones and Smith are a menace to what Jarrett and Strawn believe in all sincerity to be the foundations of civilization. They rally to the defense of civilization; and they have the power.

Unfortunately that power is very great, and they know precisely how to use it. By looking once more at Middlebury College and Rensselaer Polytechnic Institute, we can see how the policies of these men work out in practice. A few months before Mr. Strawn delivered his address, the president of Middlebury sent to all members of the faculty a letter headed "Don't rock the boat." The significant paragraphs are these:

We do not want our students to be thoughtless, nor do we want to tell them what to think. But we do not want them to go off at half cock. Least of all do we want them to go out of class quoting us as anarchists, communists, atheists, free-lovers, as, I regret to say, now and then some student does. In all that is said about capital and labor, public utilities and government ownership thereof, marriage and divorce, social customs, the liquor question and a dozen and one other matter, we cannot be too guarded. It is well to be guarded in what we say at any time, but in this period of tension it is doubly important.

Hardly a year goes by that some foolish student does not misunderstand something that is said and make a certain amount of trouble for the college. Often, in fact generally, the professor is misquoted, but not always. . . . When a man is quoted, as saying something, which is felt, rightly or wrongly, to be disintegrative of what, rightly or wrongly, is believed to be the foundations on which our civilization rests, the defense is difficult. For if the professor did not say the thing he is accused of saying, he conveyed the oppression, and the charge is shifted from his heart to his head. He may not be a knave, but if he can't say what he means in so responsible a position, he is certainly a fool. . . .

The soldier who sleeps at his post in peace times may be lightly punished. The same offense in the presence of the enemy is usually punished with death. In normal times when no one is excited, it is unpleasant to have misunderstandings, but it is endurable. In times like the present it is a different and altogether more serious matter. Individual rights are abridged somewhat. We must keep to the middle of the boat and be constantly on our guard. Least of all are we to encourage others to extreme sentiments or indulge in them ourselves. And we must be respectful to the views of others, even if they are not shared by us. . . . As far as I can, I have protected all my associates when in danger of criticism or misunderstanding. It may not be so easy to do it until things are brighter, and I should feel justified in requesting, in these days as I might not in others, the resignation of any who are unwilling or unable to subordinate their private views to the interests of the College. ... I hope that what I have said will not be regarded as in any way a desire to dictate what you shall think, or to interfere with your private views.

President Moody is an educator, but his trustees are businessmen. Mr. Jarrett is himself a retired businessman. Mr. Jarrett notified me on the tenth of May that, for reasons of economy, my services for next year were not desired. Mr. Jarrett refused to give me any further explanation, refused to see representatives of the American Civil Liberties Union, received various delegations with the utmost rudeness, and maintained throughout, in statements to the press and in letters to individuals, that there was absolutely nothing except retrenchment responsible for my dismissal. Then suddenly, on Commencement Day, he took cognizance of the issue of academic freedom, offered the pronouncement on capitalism already quoted, and added:

The excess of academic freedom must be stigmatized as academic license. We adhere to an unwritten regulation of long standing that there shall be excluded from our classrooms all controversial discussion about politics, religion and sociology. Time devoted to such subjects, when used to arouse and incite, is, if we are to cling to our function as an engineering school, lost time.

It is obvious that Mr. Jarrett's remarks on academic license bear the same relation to his words on capitalism as President Moody's letter bears to Mr. Strawn's address. In both cases it is made perfectly clear that capitalism is not to be attacked. In both cases some attempt is made to keep up a pretence of academic freedom. In both cases teachers are given to understand that the expression of any opinions that are objectionable from the capitalist point of view will bring dismissal.

Middlebury and Rensselaer are not exceptional. What has happened this spring at Columbia, Chicago, and Michigan, President Angell's commencement address, the Turner case at Pittsburgh, and a dozen other public scandals make that clear. Since my dismissal I have had letters from men in at least twenty universities describing the suppression of academic freedom. Middlebury and Rensselaer are representative; if there are colleges in which teachers can, with any degree of security, express a critical attitude towards capitalism, they are the exceptions.

ACADEMIC PRIDE VERSUS ACADEMIC SELF-RESPECT

What is serious in all this is not the expulsion of a few radicals but the effect on the teaching profession as a whole. Imagine what the life of a teacher at Middlebury must be like. Interpret the president's letter in terms of your own classroom experience. It simply makes impossible any candor in the classroom, any frankness between teachers and students, any semblance of intellectual honesty, any atmosphere of truth seeking. It reduces teaching to a dull routine of qualifications, evasions, and downright lies.

I have been told something about the effect of President Moody's letter and Mr. Strawn's speech on the teachers of Middlebury, and I have seen with my own eyes the effect of my dismissal and Mr. Jarrett's remarks on my former colleagues. One example will suffice. This summer a member of the faculty, a person of strong humanitarian sympathies, signed, at my request, a petition for the release of Angelo Herndon. The next day he came to my house in obvious agitation, said he had lain awake all night, and asked to be permitted to blot out his name on the petition.

It is because the Strawns and the Jarretts achieve such results that I have said they are debauching American education. I am not blaming teachers for not wanting to starve, and I realize that the alternatives for most of them are starvation or conformity. But I wonder what will happen to our educational system as the suppression of freedom becomes more and more rigid and the need for criticism becomes more and more apparent. It is bad enough for doctors and mechanics to be deprived of the right of saying what they believe, but, after all, talking is not their business. Teachers have to talk. They have theoretically been dedicated to the discovery and dissemination of truth. And they are told that they will lose their jobs if they breathe a word of what a large number of them are coming to see is the unmistakable truth about our economic system.

The situation can be changed only by the teachers themselves. For a great many reasons it is futile to talk about academic freedom as an abstract right. The question is not how much freedom teachers ought to have but how much they can get. No one likes to be made to choose between self-respect and starvation, but that is the choice that is being forced upon teachers, and will be more and more forced upon them. So long as they continue to argue with trustees about abstract rights, the trustees will continue to rob them of their academic freedom. When they are in a position to demand security, and to enforce their demand, freedom will be theirs.

Today teachers in both public and private schools are threatened in two ways, by the loss of freedom and by the general lowering of American standards of education. The same men who curb criticisms of capitalism are, as a result of the depression, reducing their gifts and fighting against the levying of taxes to pay for education. Some of them are frankly saying that education is a luxury and that this is no time for luxuries. In the full conviction that they are preserving civilization, they are systematically destroying the results in education of what they proudly regard as a century of progress.

Obviously teachers cannot combat these tendencies as isolated individuals. It is not within the province of this article to discuss in detail the types of organization that could effectively resist the dual onslaught, but it is clear that it ought to include all teachers from kindergarten to university, that it will have to use the methods of struggle employed by the labor unions—the strike, picketing, the boycott, and so forth—and that it will be much more powerful if it is affiliated with labor unions. Anyone who knows teachers knows that this is possible only at the expense of some pride-swallowing, but more and more of us are learning that it is better to swallow one's pride than to scrap one's self-respect.

THE NEW DEAL—AN APPRAISAL [*]

Norman Thomas

N orman Thomas (1884–1968) was a leading American socialist and a six-time presidential candidate for the Socialist Party of America. An ordained Presbyterian minister, he was a staunch antimilitarist and conscientious objector. Rejecting revolutionary Marxism, Thomas favored a Christian socialist philosophy. In the following article he outlines the basic characteristics of New Deal politics under the Roosevelt administration, which he sees as "an incongruous combination of state capitalism with the President's own notion of the Brandeis theory of the excellence of small business as against great combinations."

Thomas makes clear the limitations of the New Deal and of the class-based social system of wealth that operates in the United States. He argues that the establishment of the social welfare legislation such as Social Security represents the most significant achievement of the New Deal, but it does not compare in any way in its accomplishments to similar legislation in Great Britain or the Scandanavian countries.

Thomas does not specifically discuss educational issues in the article. Nonetheless, the inclusion of his perspective in the journal represents an extraordinary act on the part of its editors, and an indication of the broad perspectives provided by the journal to its readers.

*   *   *

THE NEW DEAL'S ODD PATTERN

IT IS a somewhat bewildering job to ticket accurately and neatly the New Deal performance. Its own boasted opportunism and lack of philosophy have been still further complicated by Supreme Court decisions, of which that against the N.R.A. was most far-reaching in its immediate effects and still more in its implications. The New Deal, to be sure, is not fascism—not yet! Still more emphatically, William Randolph Hearst, Father Coughlin, the Saturday Evening Post, and Republican propagandists notwithstanding, it is not socialism. While it is difficult to label what we have under the Roosevelt administration, it is not so hard to describe its workings. It seeks to carry on, not by planning for abundance, but by giving something to every group strong enough to command attention—some relief to the unemployed, a subsidy to farmers, a more handsome and less justifiable subsidy to the powerful silver interests, etc., etc. In other words the government is adopting under modern conditions

[*] **Source:** *The Social Frontier*, Volume 2, Number 1, 1935, pp. 12–15.

the ancient plan of the Roman Empire to keep its power by bread and circuses.

If a label is at all necessary to characterize the New Deal it can be asserted with considerable justice that it is an incongruous combination of state capitalism with the President's own notion of the Brandeis theory of the excellence of small business as against great combinations. Nevertheless, whatever opposition the President may have felt against big business was not strong enough to prevent him from continuing the R.F.C. and from bolstering up by its aid and other devices, both banks and railroads, which he left in private hands. That is not socialism—not even David Lawrence's "unconscious socialism."

FUTILITY OF SUBSIDIZING SCARCITY TO ATTAIN PLENTY

Originally the President was dedicated to recovery and reform, but without any clear philosophy concerning the meaning of either or their relation to each other. In consequence, betting whether he would go left or right became a national pastime. There is no reason to doubt the subjective sincerity of his desire to increase the purchasing power of the masses and thus bring them comparative abundance. Actually, however, both N.R.A. and A.A.A., two of the most important features of his New Deal, were based on the economy of scarcity. Oddly enough—from the standpoint of reason but not of capitalist economy— these two measures amount to an effort to restore prosperity by restricting production in a world notoriously lacking in the goods which the age of power-driven machinery might easily produce to satisfy human wants. It is small wonder that they failed. Nor is the third of the three cardinal principles of the New Deal, namely that of "priming the pump," or of spending our way back to prosperity, any more successful in achieving any real or permanent abundance. Instead, it is piling up an enormous debt which, in view of the general political and economic situation now prevailing, will almost certainly lead to inflation of currency or credit and, consequently, further crisis.

The operation of A.A.A. in restricting production is better understood than the equivalent effect of N.R.A. The heartless decapitation of the Blue Eagle by the Supreme Court with nothing else in sight to take its place blinded a great many workers to the actual and potential anti-labor tendencies of the legislation, which became a victim of a judicial oligarchy under an outworn constitution. The workers remembered only that at the beginning N.E.A. had lessened child labor and encouraged organization. But they tended to forget that, especially in the last year of N.R.A.'s life, the intervention of the Federal Government under N.R.A. in every major industry—rubber, steel, automobiles, textiles—had been to the advantage of the employers; that "less than half of all the employees in all industries combined had their hourly wage rate raised as a result of the N.R.A.," while for the great majority of workers the advance in prices actually meant a slight loss in real wages. Nor did workers generally realize that it is they, by accepting shorter hours with no increase in hourly pay, who paid for re-employment, nor that the total number re-employed between the time when N.R.A. went into effect and when it was summarily killed was small. To this the statisticians of the A. F. of L. and of the employers' organization, the National Conference Board, agree, though they disagree as to the precise figures. Meanwhile, from the standpoint of the employers, especially the stronger employers, N.R.A. was a boon. It enabled them to maintain or increase prices by restricting production.

This is no defense of a constitutional system under which the Supreme Court has practically decided that there is no national power to act constructively in a national emergency. Future historians may well rank the N.R.A. and the other anti-New Deal decisions along with the Dred Scott decision as a cause of civil war. This should not, however, blind anyone to the fact that N.R.A. has contributed very little indeed to the improvement of the lot of the under-privileged in America. With respect to the special issue raised by the Supreme Court decisions, it is pertinent to note the Workers' Relief Amendment proposed by Socialists and widely endorsed by labor. There is no immediate political task more important than the adoption of this measure. The enactment of this amendment would explicitly give Congress power to adopt all necessary economic and social legislation for the well being of the workers.

To the failure of the New Deal, with or without N.R.A., to redistribute income, the recent report of Dr. T. J. Kreps, who was chief statistician of the Bureau of Research of N.R.A., bears witness. From 1925 to 1929 labor income rose 20%, while dividends and interest rose 65%. In 1933 labor income declined to 65% of that attained in the years 1923-25. But incomes from dividends and interest managed to maintain themselves at 93% of what they had been ten years before. By the end of 1934 labor had reached 71% of the 1923-25 level, while dividends and interest held their own at 93%. Even Mr. Robert Nathan of the Department of Commerce, tries only to show that labor's share of the greatly decreased national income was greater only by 2% in 1934 than in 1929; only 1.5% greater in 1934 than in 1933—this, taking account of payments for relief work, the great increase of government employees, and including both wages and salary. How little these figures mean, however, in terms of recovery, as well as of reform, is evident when one considers that the present national income—considerably less than that of 1929—has to take care of an increased population. Moreover, Dr. Kreps argues that, comparatively, factory payrolls made less recovery in 1934 over 1933 than did profits.

A review of the other aspects of President Roosevelt's policy only adds to the evidence that the total effect of his administration is not calculated to improve the lot of the exploited sections of our society. The President's recent taxation program, increasing sharply taxes on great incomes and on the estates of the very wealthy that have not or cannot escape by forming family trusts, might mitigate to a degree the inflationary consequences of his effort to spend America's way back to prosperity—but in a small measure at best. It should be noted that this new venture in the realm of taxation was not a part of the President's original New Deal "plan." What is more important is that the notion which this new taxation program has helped implant in some—that the administration has been or, at any rate, is now intent upon a radical redistribution of wealth—is entirely unfounded. The howl set up by big financial interests and their subservient press has obscured the fact that the outstanding achievement of the New Deal in the field of taxation is not "soaking the rich," but soaking the poor, who, as everybody knows, bear a disproportionate burden of every sort of sales tax which becomes part of the price structure. As Mr. Robert Jackson, able counsel for the Treasury Department, points out, 58% of the federal taxes prior to the enactment of the new federal tax were indirect. This leaves out of account the vicious sales taxes to which more than twenty states have resorted, most of them since 1932.

THE PRESIDENT'S SOCIAL INSURANCE PROGRAM

It is in the realm of social security that the most significant achievements of the New Deal are to be found. But even the social welfare legislation, while considerable in amount and meritorious, some of it, shines mostly by comparison with the extraordinary, do-nothing policy of a Hoover. It does not shine by comparison with similar legislation in Great Britain or the Scandinavian countries. The President's famous Security Law is a hodge-podge of dubious constitutionality and of assured inadequacy when viewed in the light of its avowed purpose — social security. Health insurance is left out of the omnibus program. Future old age pensions are to be provided after 1942 entirely by a tax on workers and employers, the latter of whom will be set up constitute a vast problem in investment and an immense temptation to politicians looking for easy money.

The worst thing about the law, however, is that it makes unemployment insurance almost ridiculous. What we have is not a national unemployment insurance law, but only a national tax on employers, 90% of which will be rebated to them to put into state unemployment schemes when such schemes are adopted. Upon the culmination of that happy event we shall have forty-eight different schemes within states whose boundaries do not in the least conform to the boundaries of industrial areas. Benefits will be kept down on the usual pleas that high benefits will drive business out of the states proposing them. The "security" offered to unemployed industrial workers amounts to precisely this: if you are unemployed and if you get a job, and then lose the job, you may get as much as $15 benefit for fifteen weeks, provided your state adopts a sufficiently generous law and provided the federal tax accumulates a sufficient reserve to enable the state to pay it.

Meanwhile your immediate chance of existence depends upon the tender mercies of the President's Work Relief Program, stupendous in total amount but inadequate to satisfy prevailing needs. Moreover the program threatens wage standards won by hardly-fought uphill labor struggles. The program undercuts wage standards and offers to unskilled labor a subsistence standard of livelihood running as low as $19 per month in some Southern states.

One of the most interesting illustrations of the essentially capitalist nature of the New Deal is to be found in its failure to make any significant contribution in the field of public works to re-housing America. This is the one field in which there is both the greatest human need and the most logical chance to make a real contribution towards a revival of industry. Yet in spite of endless talk next to nothing has been done because there is no scheme for re-housing that third of our population, admitted by the government to be outrageously housed, which will not upset our whole capitalist system of land ownership and taxation. It has been reported that in some cases H. O. L. C, or some other government agency, has granted a mortgage on property 15% greater than P.W.A. was willing to pay for it in program of re-housing.

Against this sort of showing the one really socialist enterprise of the New Deal, the Tennessee Valley Authority, is not an adequate makeweight. It may be a comparatively good yardstick, but in the field of electric power we do not so much need a yardstick, as a comprehensive system of social ownership under which alone it is possible to plan adequately for the maximum social use of electricity.

If this is an accurate summary of the New Deal, some reader may be tempted to exclaim, why is the Chamber of Commerce's opposition to President Roosevelt and his program so intense? The question is a fair one, but the answer is easy. American business interests have been the spoiled children of fortune. When they were sinking in the storms of the last days of the Hoover administration they indeed cried out for rescue. But no sooner had President Roosevelt dragged them in where they got at least a temporary respite, than they began to complain because in the process he pulled their hair. While

N.R.A. was in force the President and business had to get along, which they did fairly well. When N.R.A. was knocked out by the Supreme Court decision there was no such reason for friendly relations between the President and big business. Both sought other alliances. The President found himself able to buy the support of farmers, industrial workers, and small investors seeking greater security at a relatively cheap price. Even a fascist dictator has to pay some price to save capitalism. A Republican victory could not and would not repeal outright most of the New Deal legislation. The Coolidge era is gone forever. Emphatically the price required of Mr. Roosevelt did not involve any considerable shift in the distribution of income under the capitalist system and, least of all, the upsetting of that system. Farmers indeed have had their share of the national income increased by the policy of A.A.A. in taxing consumers to subsidize scarcity. There is no other way of construing a policy which pays cotton landlords, for instance, not to produce cotton no matter what happens to tenants and other agricultural workers on land no longer planted—this, at a time when the workers who raise the cotton and make the cotton cloth cannot buy clothing or sheets for their families, and when the total consumption of finished cotton goods for household and domestic purposes is only a little over nine pounds per capita.

CAPITALISM'S INABILITY TO PLAN FOR ABUNDANCE

What I have written concerning the New Deal is critical, but I shall have altogether failed to make my point unless I have made it clear that what I am attacking is not the New Deal as such, but the capitalist system of which it is an expression. Given capitalism, the fanners have as much right to their subsidy under A.A.A. as have manufacturers to tariff subsidies they have so long enjoyed. It is not the fault of the New Deal but of capitalism that it cannot plan for abundance. The great lesson to be learned from the failure of so aggressive and, on the whole, well-meant a program as President Roosevelt's is the failure of capitalism, or to be more accurate, capitalist-nationalism, under any set of reforms that it can tolerate. It is a logical impossibility to plan for abundance for workers under the operation of the profit system, with private ownership of the principal means of production. In a crisis the maintenance of profit depends upon the ability to maintain or restore scarcity. It is a truism that men starve in the midst of potential plenty, but capitalism cannot convert that potential plenty into actuality. Ours is a problem, not of sharing a little more equitably the wealth that we now have, but of producing and then sharing the abundance that we ought to have. This cannot be done while we perpetuate absentee ownership and our fantastically unjust class division of society. Only with this idea as the starting point can we solve the problems of insecurity, exploitation, and war. We must have not a New Deal, but a federation of the cooperative commonwealths of mankind. On the way to it we shall seek to enact those measures which give strength to the workers to ask for more; we shall not, as we love true security, seek to bribe them into longer acquiescence in poverty and insecurity by a few concessions, a few circuses, and an emotional orgy of jingoistic nationalism.

TEACHERS AND THE CLASS STRUGGLE[*]

The Editorial Board

D iscussions of social class and American culture caused concerns among the readers of the journal. In response to these concerns, the editorial board responded with the following article. In doing so, the editorial board argues that: "He who would practise education as an art in social reconstruction must answer to himself the question: what is that society which I aim to change—an aggregation of atomic individuals, an amorphous mass, or a process rendered dynamic by conflicting group needs, interests, and aspirations?" In addition, the question arises as to what forces are at work that "result in a radical transformation of society—'chance,' 'idealism,' 'intelligence,' or the urge of a maladjusted group to establish a life which promises them security, dignity, power, and abundance of living?"

The editorial board maintains nothing more than the aggregation of facts and truth that point to the inherent inequality found within the American capitalist system. Teachers should have as their purpose "teaching the facts of contemporary American life, by pointing to the inequalities and group conflicts therein, and by pointing out that group aspirations and actions are the forces behind historic change." In doing so, the teacher does not need to impose their ideas upon the learner. "All he needs to do is to select significant data from the life of society past and present, and the student will formulate a realistic philosophy of social reconstruction."

The editorial concludes that while most Americans maintain the belief that they live in a classless society, the reality is just the opposite, and the schools and teachers have the obligation to teach otherwise. In doing so, "America will have made considerable headway toward the goal of democratic collectivism."

* * *

In the last issue *The Social Frontier* editorially suggested that the destiny of education, educators, and society in general depended on the outcome of the conflict between those who own and those who create wealth. It was pointed out that teachers are essentially workers—creators of wealth. In consequence, it was held right and proper for teachers to align themselves with labor and to utilize the school in an attempt to bring about a decision, which is favorable to the working population.

That such a recommendation, which carries the ear-marks of an acceptance of class struggle as a fact of contemporary society and as a tactic of social reconstruction, did not meet with the unanimous approval of our readers is

---

[*] **Source:** *The Social Frontier*, Volume 2, Number 2, 1935, p. 39–40.

not in the least surprising. In the inner recesses of their minds most teachers still glory in their "professional" status, even if the bitter experiences of the past five years should have taught them better. The notions that there is a classless "public," of which they are the servants, is still a sufficiently potent prophylactic to protect most pedagogues from the realization of the essential cleavage between the dominant few who control the means of production and the oppressed many who are the pawns in the game for profit conducted by the former.

Chief among the objections to the identification of teachers and school with the interests of life and labor and against the interests of property and profit are:

1. Whether or not there are classes in American society is irrelevant to the work of the school.

2. There is no evidence of class division in American society.

3. Assuming that the interests of capital and labor conflict, it is the business of the school as an agency of society as a whole to transform conflicts into harmony.

4. By its very nature as an educational rather than a propaganda institution, the school cannot effectively strengthen the hand of one class against the other. Relevant objections these, but fairly easy to answer.

To begin with, whether or not there are serious class divisions in American society is a matter of extreme importance to all those who would endow the practice of education with socially reconstructive significance. If education is an art whose goal is the transformation of social life, it must be aware not only of the type of society that is desired, but also of, the structure of society today and of the dynamics of social change. It is not enough for an engineer to know that he wants to build a bridge; he must also be acquainted with the properties of steel and with the laws of mechanics. He who would practise education as an art in social reconstruction must answer to himself the question: what is that society which I aim to change—an aggregation of atomic individuals, an amorphous mass, or a process rendered dynamic by conflicting group needs, interests, and aspirations? Moreover, he must answer a further question: what supplies the drive behind those movements which result in a radical transformation of society—"chance," "idealism," "intelligence," or the urge of a maladjusted group to establish a life which promises them security, dignity, power, and abundance of living? If some of these alternatives are true, teachers in their striving for the new social order would be justified in appealing indiscriminately to the idealism and the intelligence of the slum-dweller, the unemployed, the share-cropper, the banker, the newspaper magnate, and the industrialist. If others are true, he will direct himself mainly to workers in the factory, laboratory, office, and on the farm; he will endeavor to transform their every day resentment and their immediate interests in trifling improvements of their lot into a force capable of transforming a profit-centered into a man-centered society.

The gross inequalities of wealth, income, and power, the disproportionate gains of the wealthy in times of prosperity, the meager gains of the poor during periods of economic upswing and disproportionate sufferings in times of depression, should convince all but the socially myopic of the serious class divisions in American society. Witness some facts and findings:

(1) In 1928, which will be remembered as a year of prosperity, 32,000,000 clerical and manual workers owned on the average $415 in income-yielding wealth. This group constituted 68.5% of all income earners of the community. In the same year 382,500 other individuals, or .8% of all income earners, averaged $343,000 and owned between them 46.1% of the total income-yielding wealth of the country.

(2) On the basis of 1929 income figures, members of the staff of Brookings Institute declare in America's Capacity to Consume: "The 11,653,000 families with incomes less than $1,500 received a total of 10 billion dollars. At the other extreme, the 36,000 families having incomes in excess of $75,000 possessed an aggregate income of 9.8 billion dollars. Thus it appears that 0.1% of the families at the top received practically as much as 48% of the families at the bottom, of the scale."

(3) Federal statistics of income indicate a decline in 1932 incomes from interest and dividends to 66.7% of the 1929 level as compared with the decline in wages to 35%; the aggregate income from interest and dividends in 1930–32 rose considerably above the 1921–22 level, whereas that from wages declined heavily.

(4) Paul H. Douglas, in his Real Wages in the United States, points out that during the period 1900–33 unemployment varied from 6.4% in a year of prosperity to an average of 35.2 for the years of 1930–33.

This is not propaganda material ground out by red agitators, but facts and findings of government officials and economists with a national reputation. Translated into terms of human life these facts mean immense wealth, irresponsible power, ostentatious luxury, for the few; poverty, insecurity, absence of cultural opportunities, slums, insufficient food, and unsatisfactory, or no family life, for the many.

If the interests of the few and of the many could be composed it would, indeed, be praiseworthy for teachers to attempt to work out a harmony. But such a harmony is no more possible now than the comradely relations between the lion and lamb, which will "come to pass in the end of days." The interests of the few who now exercise dominion over the economic destinies of the nation is the realization of a profit on their private investments. In the quest for profits they must maintain a low level of wages, resist effective organization of labor, prevent the flow of capital from "sick" to "healthy" industries, spend large amounts on unproductive competitive advertising, produce low grade goods, and hinder the introduction of technical innovations which might mean increased and improved production. In brief, artificially produced scarcity, waste of social resources, inefficient management, and technological stagnation are necessary for the survival of a profit economy. On the other hand, the true interest of the many—farmers, industrial workers, and professionals—demands the creation of an abundance of goods and services, efficient management of national resources, and constant technological progress.

What harmony between the interests of property and the interests of labor actually amounts to can be determined by the merest glance at the state of affairs in Germany and Italy. It means government by brute force in the interests of financiers and large industrialists, destruction of civil liberties, and probably another world war. Barring this as an altogether undesirable goal to work for, the only choices left for the teacher and the school is either splendid isolation within the territory of vapid moral generalities and the eternal three It's, or participation in the struggle of the working sections of the population to attain mastery over the wealth-producing resources of the nation.

It is realized, of course, that the teacher is not a propagandist. But no more than the true practice of education is required for his social effectiveness. He could contribute considerably to the bending of historical events by teaching the facts of contemporary American life, by pointing to the inequalities and group conflicts therein, and' by pointing out that group aspirations and actions are the forces behind historic change. The teacher need not—should not—fix his opinions upon the student. All he needs to do is to select significant data from the life of society past and present, and the student will formulate a realistic philosophy of social reconstruction. The need now is not for bringing class struggle to an immediate issue, but rather for teaching the masses of farmers and workers about the facts and socially reconstructive possibilities of class divisions and conflicts and the significance of their every day struggles for improved living conditions. Most Americans still believe that they live in a classless society. The school could contribute to the dissipation of that illusion. When that is achieved, America will have made considerable headway toward the goal of democratic collectivism.

THE MEANING OF LIBERALISM [*]

John Dewey

D ewey's comments in this article on the meaning of Liberalism are particularly interesting in the context of contemporary American politics. The term for him represents: "a new interest in the common man and a new sense that the common man, the representative of the great masses of human beings, had possibilities that had been kept under that had not been allowed to develop, because of institutional and political conditions." According to Dewey, Liberalism has been misdirected as a result of the rise of and domination of business, a process which has "given anti-social liberty to the few: has identified rugged individualism with uncontrolled business activity, and has regimented the thought and conduct of multitudes." In this process, "the mass production of the factory and its mass distribution by transportation faculties, has been effectually captured for the benefit of the few." Dewey concludes the article by calling for the development of a new and more democratic model of liberalism.

*   *   *

It is an interesting fact in the history of English words that the word liberal was applied to education even earlier than it was used to denote generosity and bountifulness. A liberal education was the education of a free man. Liberal subjects were those fitted to be pursued by a free man and were opposed to those subjects that were adapted to the training of mechanics. This meant in fact that the liberal arts and a liberal education were confined to persons who occupied a superior social status. They belonged to gentlemen as distinct from the "lower classes." It would be interesting to trace the effect of these ideas upon school education. They influenced schooling even in this country. For the men of this country who prided themselves upon being all free naturally took over for the staple of their subjects, especially in secondary and higher education, just the subjects which in the old country were thought to be suited to preparing gentlemen for their higher walks of life.

However, my present point does not concern this story. The idea of the free and common schools developed among us on the ground that a nation of truly free men and women required schools open to all and hence supported by public taxation. Upon the whole, considerable progress has been made in making schooling accessible to all, though of course it is still true that the opportunity to take advantage of what is theoretically provided for all is seriously

[*] **Source:** *The Social Frontier*, Volume 2, Number 3, 1935, pp. 74–75.

limited by economic status. But what I am here concerned with is the meaning of liberalism itself.

THE SPIRIT AND THE LETTER OF LIBERALISM

The meaning of liberalism has undergone many changes since the word came into vogue not very much more than a century ago. The word came into use to denote a new spirit that grew and spread with the rise of democracy. It implied a new interest in the common man and a new sense that the common man, the representative of the great masses of human beings, had possibilities that had been kept under that had not been allowed to develop, because of institutional and political conditions. This new spirit was liberal in both senses of the word. It was marked by a generous attitude, by sympathy for the underdog, for those who were not given a chance. It was part of a widespread rise of humanitarian philanthropy. It was also liberal in that it aimed at enlarging the scope of free action on the part of those who for ages had had no part in public affairs and no lot in the benefits secured by this participation.

Owing to the conditions that existed in the late eighteenth century and throughout the nineteenth century, liberalism soon, however, took on a limited and technical significance. The class that was most conscious of suffering from restrictions, most active in removing them, and best organized to fight against them consisted of those who were engaged in manufacturing industries and in commerce. On the one hand, the application of steam to production was revolutionizing the production and distribution of goods, opening new avenues to human energy and ambition, and supplying commodities more effectively than was possible under the system of production by hand. On the other hand, there existed a mass of regulations and customs, formed to a large degree in feudal times that hampered and checked the expression of these new energies. Moreover, political power was mainly in the hands of landlords representing older agrarian habits of belief and action.

The liberalism of the industrial class took accordingly the form of political and legal struggle to do away with restrictions upon free manifestation of the newer economic activities. The restrictive and oppressive forces were those embodied in institutions that were readily identified with the government and with the state. Hence the slogan of organized liberalism was, "Let the government keep hands off industry and commerce. Its action in these spheres is preventing the growth of activities that are of the highest value to society. These new industrial activities furnish men with things they need more cheaply and in greater quantities than the old system did or could do. They encourage invention and stimulate progress. They promote energy and thrift by holding out to all the reward of their initiative, skill, and labor. The free exchange of goods binds men and nations together in ties of common interest and brings near the reign of harmony and peace throughout all mankind." Such were the claims.

THE LETTER DESTROYS THE SPIRIT

Given the particular time and place in which the claims were made, they had their own justification. A great burst of energy accompanied the onset of the industrial revolution, and did so in many ways of creative action other than industrial production. But as the new social group won power, their doctrines hardened into the dogma of the freedom of the industrial entrepreneur from any organized social control. Because law and administration had been, at a turning point in history, the foe of the liberation of human energies, it was proclaimed that they were always the enemy of human liberty. The idea of hands off, practically sound under special circumstances was stiffened into the dogma of laissez-faire "individualism." The new economic interests, much better organized than the earlier agrarian class, got an enormous grip upon the social forces.

Because the interests of the dominant economic class became anti-social in some of their consequences, the complete separation of the economic from the political (no government in business), isolated individualism, and the negation of organized social direction were put forward as eternal truths. Meantime, the generous sympathetic spirit characteristic of earlier liberalism was split off and confined to philanthropic movements; when it affected legislation and administration it confined itself to remedial measures for those at marked social disadvantage, leaving intact the system that produced the symptoms dealt with. In this country even these remedial measures were bitterly opposed by the dominant class, although that class would be their final residuary legatee, in as much as these measures would render the inherited system more endurable by the masses.

Consequently, that which began as a movement in the direction of greater liberty for expression of the energies of man and which was put forward as giving every individual new opportunities and powers, has become socially oppressive for the greater number of individuals. It has almost resulted in identifying the power and liberty of the individual with ability to achieve economic success—or, to put it in a nutshell, with ability to make money. Instead of being the means of promoting harmony and interdependence among peoples, it has proved, as it worked out, to be divisive: Let imperialism and war be the evidence.

HOW THE SPIRIT OF LIBERALISM CAN BE REHABILITATED

The idea and ideal of more liberty for individuals and of the release of the potentialities of individuals, the enduring core of the liberal spirit is as sound as ever it was. But the rise of business to a dominant position has, in fact, given anti-social liberty to the few: has identified rugged individualism with uncontrolled business activity, and has regimented the thought and conduct of multitudes. Meantime, the cause that brought about the immense rise in capacity to produce and to distribute, that which made possible the mass production of the factory and its mass distribution by transportation faculties, has been effectually captured for the benefit of the few. The cause of the release of productive energies was the rise of experimental science and its technological application. Physical machinery and trained technical ability have now reached a point where it is all but a commonplace that an era of material abundance and material security for all is possible, laying the material basis for the cultural flowering of human beings.

In consequence, the ends which liberalism has always professed can be attained only as control of the means of production and distribution is taken out of the hands of individuals who exercise powers created socially for narrow individual interests. The ends remain valid. But the means of attaining them demand a radical change in economic institutions and the political arrangements based upon them. These changes are necessary in order that social control of forces and agencies socially created may accrue to the liberation of all individuals associated together in the great undertaking of building a life that expresses and promotes human liberty. At a later time, I shall recur to the bearing of this new liberalism upon the theme of liberal education and free schools mentioned in these opening paragraphs.

THE SOCIAL STUDIES CURRICULUM *

Charles A. Beard

C harles Austin Beard (1874 –1948) was among the most influential historians of the first half of the twentieth century. He is primarily remembered for his *An Economic Interpretation of the Constitution of the United States* (1913) and with his wife, Mary Beard, *The Rise of American Civilization* (1927). In the brief article included below, Beard calls for the development of a new model of the Social Studies curriculum that takes into account that "an epoch is closed" and that something beyond simply facts and historical materials, selected by obscure history professors and educational methods, constructed by pedagogists, is needed.

*   *   *

The few freaks who are accustomed to take a long and wide view of things must now be rather impressed by the interest of professional educators in the social studies curriculum. Indeed, developments in this field may have a significance for the future of the United States that transcends street brawls and Hearst headlines.

THE REIGN OF THE HISTORIAN

A long, long time ago, now remembered only by greyheads, the business of shaping up curricula was left largely to Subject Matter Specialists. And who were they? Usually they were doctors of philosophy in history, political science, economics, or sociology, and professors of some branch of their subject in the great University of Weissnichtwo. Seldom, if ever, had they passed through the gruelling mill in which the classroom teacher had to operate. Generally, also, they were naive persons who had learned something from their professors and were burning up with holy zest to transmit the acquired knowledge and framework to all and sundry. Few, if any, among them ever stopped to inquire: What am I doing when I am selecting a few facts from ten billion available facts and calling my personal aggregation history, economics, political science, or sociology? The major portion of the specialists played their little intellectual game like happy children and imagined that anything they enjoyed was good for the schools. After all, when progress was booming along in that golden age, and "any good man or woman could get a good job," there was

---

* **Source:** *The Social Frontier,* Volume 2, Number 3, 1935, pp. 78-80

not much reason for doing any thinking. Routine worked, or seemed to work. Why disturb it?

In the long ago, a committee of historians framed a program of history for the public schools. Being historians by trade they thought history was a good thing for the schools and, naturally, the more of it the better. So they put a lot of it into the program for the grades, and grabbed nearly four full years in the high schools. They were aware, of course, of the existence of "civics," but that could be disposed of in a few sessions dealing with the Constitution of the United States. Or, to be generous, perhaps six months could be taken away from history for a consideration of civil government and "the duties of citizenship."

Now none of these bold historians who imposed this stereotype on the schools tried to define the term "history." In those simple and easy days, history was history—wars, diplomatic negotiations, presidential administrations, and such things, with a dash of anecdotes, narratives, and geography thrown in for good measure. History was history. It was taught in the universities. Simplify it, boil it down, and hand it to "educators" in desicated form. What a joy it was to live in an age when things were so obvious, positive, and unquestioned!

For many years the historians' stereotype prevailed. Teachers were at first glad to have "something definite." There it was, all laid out in books, chapters, and paragraphs, with questions and tables of dates appended. Dozens of texts were written to fit the stereotype. They were adopted by eager school boards and sold by the millions. To the intellectual interests of historians as such were added the pecuniary interests of authors and the huge vested interests of publishers. Hence, an academic enterprise became entangled with economic enterprise, and a powerful interlocking directorate was enlisted on the side of the history program. De te fibula narratur.

But about the time of the World War unrest broke out. Some of it appeared among the historians, and more among teachers who had the job of getting history into the minds of recalcitrant youth. The World War jarred up a number of things. It let loose revolution and destruction in Europe and sent dangerous ideas booming and banging to the four corners of the earth. How did it happen that the historians who knew so much history had so poorly prepared mankind for enduring more history in such frightful form? Historians were not so sure of themselves after 1918.

School teachers were also disturbed by this outside upheaval. But they had other grounds for discontent. Pupils did not just take to prescribed history like ducks to water. Many of them had to be driven, and even the threat of failure in examinations could not always make them plunge in with zest. Moreover, school teachers did not live in the ivory towers of universities where pay checks came regularly and no questions were asked. They saw face to face the boys and girls who had to study history and, what is more, to withstand the slings and arrows of a bitter struggle for existence in the cold world. So teachers began to ask: What relation do the Wars of the Roses and the sinuosities of Frederick the Great have to the life these boys and girls will soon enter, most of them unsupported by inheritances and trust funds? That was a perplexing question for professors high up in the ivory towers of the great University of Weissnichtwo. In fact, they could not answer it at all. The more they tried, the more school teachers suspected the worth and validity of the history stereotype imposed on them by the adepts.

THE PROFESSOR OF EDUCATION APPEARS ON THE SCENE

After suspicion had spread around a little bit, teachers began to insert some topics bearing on current affairs into the interstices of the curriculum. The professors of secondary education, who like the historians, had to be busy with something, took an interest in the growing schism. The ice was cracking.

But these restless teachers and professors of secondary education, in truth, did not know much about the doings up in the ivory towers of the University of Weissnichtwo. They had not been trained in history, economics, and political science—at least not very much. Most of them had studied that all-embracing and still bewildering subject known as "Education 1 or 2." They were not familiar with the career of Tokugawa Ieyasu or the fierce debate over the marginal utility theory; but they knew something about child psychology and current gossip on politics and public questions. Steadily these teachers and professors of education broke away from the stereotype imposed from above, and sailed out, as innocently as had the historians, on the wide sea of curriculum making.

In the order of time, perhaps, they concentrated on the "method" of the undertaking. Some of them arrived at the blissful and happy state of believing that "the right method" would "turn the trick." It might make even history "interesting." It did not matter much whether the possessor of "the one and only, sure-fire and sure-cure method" knew any history or economics. With the magnet of method the "proper" fragments of history or economics could be picked up and displayed to children. That certainly was a noble and attractive dream. Get the right method and you are spared all the years of drudgery required to find out something about history or economics.

So there were textbooks on methods and their applications to the various social studies. Professors made immense reputations as "great authorities" in educational circles by inventing new methods or, more generally, new names for old methods. Seeing that there was something in this game, historians and other professors of social studies rushed over the line; and approved texts based on the right methods, appeared by the dozens. The sacrificial ardor of publishers was enlisted and a huge vested interest grew up in the new thaumaturgy called method.

LOCAL ANARCHY COMES TO THE FORE

But still unrest continued. Teachers were not satisfied with the assumed values of either history or methodology. They wanted to get nearer to the reality of life in which their boys and girls had to spend their days. No matter what method was used, the history curriculum continued to dissolve. Whole blocks of it were thrown overboard without a sigh and, it seems, without any notable intellectual loss. Between 1920 and 1935, to be brief, the old history stereotype was largely disintegrated. Only a few principal chunks remained intact.

All over the country, teachers, superintendents, and commissions labored at curriculum reconstruction. Towns, cities, and states made new programs, including larger and larger areas of the social studies. In the process, the national stereotype imposed by the historians fell into neglect. Town, city, and state programs, widely differing in content and emphasis, took the place of the old formal unity. Nearly every school and teacher went into the business of making and remaking social studies courses. Now anarchy reigns. Some common principles run through hundreds of programs, to be sure, but they are no longer controlled by any fundamental frame of reference and values. Curricula makers copy from one another and add a multitude of "interesting" fragments all their own.

In the course of this development curriculum making becomes a trade. Specialists went into it, as advisers and consultants, and helped local authorities in their enterprises. Curriculum "laboratories" were founded, and a new vested interest appeared, in the new business. With a considerable equipment of methodological lingo and a considerable knowledge of "what other communities have done," specialists could lend a lot of assistance to local authorities wrestling with the problem of "reconstructing the curriculum."

DAWN OF A NEW INSIGHT

But this age of free-for-all tinkering seems about to draw to a close. Something more fundamental, something more relevant to the great problems of national life, is required by the crisis in thought and economy in which we find ourselves. Local anarchy in curriculum-making has been vivifying and important, but it is not enough. The universities, colleges, and schools, the teaching profession from top to bottom, all public spirited citizens interested in the role of education in society face the task of formulating a social philosophy appropriate to our present situation; for, in the absence of any controlling philosophy or orientation, the selection of materials and the application of methods proceed without guidance, and degenerate into sterile and bewildering fragments and formalities—the signs and symbols of intellectual and moral decay.

To this point in the making of curricula have we been swept by the movement of ideas and interests during the past five or ten years. All about us are signs of recognition, and that is the beginning of wisdom and of renewed effort on a higher plane of purpose and achievement.

Assessment of blame for the past is useless. Only failure to grapple with the challenge before us is blameworthy.

As Croce would say, an epoch is closed. How do we know this? Its formalities no longer satisfy us or correspond to the felt needs of our time. A new epoch is opening. Its precise forms we can only dimly divine. The task of making them falls to us, the living.

THE NEW ARISTOCRACY [*]

The Editorial Board

I n this editorial, the members of the editorial board of the journal quote the nineteenth-century political writer Alexis de Tocqueville about his belief that a "manufacturing" or capitalist aristocracy was emerging in the United States—one which was a potential threat to the "friends of *democracy*." Beard maintains that groups such as the National Association of Manufacturers with their attack on the Roosevelt administration's New Deal and its "programs of social reconstruction," represent a threat of the type that de Tocqueville predicted. The editorial concludes that class-consciousness is alive and well in the United States and that the new aristocracy is a reality.

*   *   *

More than a hundred years ago, in the days of Andrew Jackson and the home-spun democracy, a brilliant young Frenchman crossed the Atlantic to study life and institutions under the American republic. The result was the most pene-trating work on the United States ever penned by a foreigner. The young man was Alexis de Tocqueville and the work was *Democracy in America*. In this work may be found the following remarkable paragraph: "I am of the opinion, upon the whole, that the manufacturing aristocracy which is growing up under our eyes is one of the harshest which ever existed in the world; but, at the same time it is one of the most confined and least dangerous. Nevertheless, the friends of *democracy* should keep their eyes anxiously fixed in this direction; for if ever a permanent inequality of conditions and aristocracy again penetrate into the world, it may be predicted that this is the gate by which they will en-ter."

Many students of de Tocqueville must have thought of this passage in the early part of December when the National Association of Manufacturers, rep-resented by something more than one thousand heads of the great corporate enterprises of the country, met in New York City and girded its loins for a concentrated attack upon the New Deal and all programs of social reconstruc-tion, however mild and innocuous. Under the guise of defending the "Ameri-can system" the manufacturers of the nation passed a three-thousand word resolution in which they placed their privileges beyond the reach of legislative majorities under the sacred guardianship of natural law and inalienable rights. Here is the new aristocracy, the threat to democracy which de Tocqueville foresaw and feared, conscious of itself, demanding solidarity within its ranks,

---

[*] **Source:** *The Social Frontier*, Volume 2, Number 4, 1936, p. 101.

and preparing to marshall practically unlimited power in opposing the march of democracy into the realm of economics.

This action of the manufacturers, moreover, does not stand alone. It seems that the great corporate interests of America—industrial, commercial, and financial—are banding together to mold public opinion, set at naught the will of the people, and hold hack the forces of social change. Mr. Edward F. Hutton, chairman of the board of directors of the General Foods Corporation, let the cat out of the bag in an amazingly forthright article published in the house organ of the public utilities corporations. "Let's gang up," he said. "The business men of the country, the owners of stocks and bonds or any other property, the holders of insurance policies, and the depositors in banks must realize that the only way to prevent regimentation, collectivism, or any other ism [except capitalism?] is for all groups to join together in one great group which will come to the help of any individual group when it is attacked." Although Mr. Hutton attempted a few days later to soften this utterance, he described accurately what business has done in the past and what the National Association of Manufacturers proceeded to do in their meeting in New York City.

The moral of this story, if there be one, is that class consciousness is by no means unknown in America and that it seems to be peculiarly developed in the upper economic ranks of the population, in those very ranks, in fact, where the idea of class consciousness is ordinarily characterized as a foreign importation. We are not in a position to state categorically that Mr. Hutton and the manufacturers have been reading Karl Marx and visiting Moscow, but the evidence certainly justifies the inference. Indeed these gentlemen seem to have stepped right out of the pages of Das Kapital. They constitute the perfect exhibit of the fundamental truth of the Marxian social analysis. They are prepared to defend their privileges, though the heavens fall. Individuals among them may step outside the bounds of their class, but the great majority march to battle for their property. The new aristocracy is here.

Alexis Charles Henri Maurice Clarel de Tocqueville knew his America.

LIBERALISM AND EQUALITY [*]

John Dewey

Dewey points out in this article that the challenge of liberal democracy, and in the end, liberalism is to establish a system of institutions and laws which "secure and establish equality for all." Under the current democratic system in the United States, "machine-industry, controlled by finance-capitalism . . . has resulted in the monopoly of power in the hands of the few to control the opportunities of the wide masses and to limit their free activities in realizing their natural capacities."

According to Dewey, "unrestrained individualistic action in the economic sphere" ultimately leads to the development of a privileged class, one that "is destructive of liberty for the many precisely because it is destructive of genuine equality of opportunity." In a contemporary context, this argument refutes the argument for a laissez-fair system of capitalism—one which Dewey argues is in essential opposition to the fundamental principles inherent in the thought of a Founding Father such as Thomas Jefferson.

* * *

It is constantly urged by one school of social thought that liberty and equality are so incompatible that liberalism is not a possible social philosophy. The argument runs as follows: If liberty is the dominant social and political goal then the natural diversity and inequality of natural endowments will inevitably work out to produce social inequalities. You cannot give free rein to natural capacities, so runs the argument, without producing marked inequality in cultural, economic, and political status as a necessary consequence. On the other hand, if equality is made the goal, there must, the argument continues, be important restrictions put upon the exercise of liberty. The incompatibility of liberty and equality is the rock, it is asserted, upon which liberalism is bound to founder. Consequently, the school of liberalism that identifies liberty with laissez faire claims to be the only logical school of liberalism, and it is willing to tolerate any amount of actual social inequality provided it is the result of the free exercise of natural powers.

LIBERTY AND EQUALITY

The original idea and ideal of democracy combined equality and liberty as coordinate ideals, adding to them, in the slogan of the French Revolution, fraternity as a third coordinate. Both historically and actually the possibility of

---

[*] **Source:** *The Social Frontier*, Volume 2, Number 4, 1936, pp. 105–106.

realization of the democratic ideal is conditioned, therefore, upon the possibility of working out in social practice and social institutions a combination of equality and liberty. As is proved by the present state of democracy in nominally democratic countries (countries that have not openly gone over to dictatorships) the problem is a practical one. No intelligent observer can deny that the existing eclipse of democratic institutions is the product of that kind of liberty which has been striven for and upheld in the name of the maximum economic liberty of the individual.

The formula of early democratic political liberalism was that men are born free and equal. Superficial critics have thought that the formula is peremptorily refuted by the fact that human beings are not born equal in strength and abilities or natural endowments. The formula, however, never assumed that they were. Its meaning is the same as that of the familiar saying that in the grave pauper and millionaire, monarch and serf, are equal: It was a way of saying that political inequality is the product of social institutions; that there is no "natural" inherent difference between those of one social caste, class, or status and those of another caste, class, or status; that such differences are the product of law and social customs. The same principle holds of economic differences; if one individual is born to the possession of property and another is not, the difference is due to social laws regulating inheritance and the possession of property. Translated into terms of concrete action, the formula means that inequalities of natural endowment should operate under laws and institutions that do not place permanent handicaps upon those of lesser gifts; that the inequalities in the distribution of powers, achievements, and goods that occur in society should be strictly proportionate to natural inequalities. In the present social arrangement, opportunities for individuals are determined by the social and family status of individuals; the institutional set-up of human relations provides openings to members of certain classes to the detriment of other classes. The challenge of progressive and liberal democracy can be stated in the familiar war-cry: Institutions and laws should be such as to secure and establish equality for all.

DEMOCRACY AND ECONOMIC EQUALITY

This formula expressed revolt against the existing institutions that automatically limited the opportunities of the mass of individuals. It was this revolt and the aspiration it embodied that was the essence of democratic liberalism in its earlier political and humanitarian manifestations. But the rise of machine-industry, controlled by finance-capitalism, was a force that was not taken into account. It gave liberty of action to those particular natural endowments and individuals that fitted into the new economic picture. Above all, the Industrial

Revolution gave scope to the abilities involved in acquiring property and to the employment of that wealth in further acquisitions. The employment of these specialized acquisitive abilities has resulted in the monopoly of power in the hands of the few to control the opportunities of the wide masses and to limit their free activities in realizing their natural capacities.

In short, the common assertion of the mutual incompatability of equality and liberty rests upon a highly formal and limited concept of liberty. It completely ignores the fact emphasized in the November issue of *The Social Frontier*. It overlooks and rules out the fact that the actual liberties of one human being depend upon the powers of action that existing institutional arrangements accord to other individuals. It conceives of liberty in a completely abstract way. The democratic ideal that unites equality and liberty is, on the other hand, a recognition that actual and concrete liberty of opportunity and action is dependent upon equalization of the political and economic conditions under which individuals are alone free in fact, not in some abstract metaphysical way. The tragic breakdown of democracy is due to the fact that the identification of liberty with the maximum of unrestrained individualistic action in the economic sphere, under the institutions of capitalistic finance, is as fatal to the realization of liberty for all as it is fatal to the realization of equality. It is destructive of liberty for the many precisely because it is destructive of genuine equality of opportunity.

A JEFFERSONIAN ILLUSTRATION

The social philosophy of Thomas Jefferson is regarded as outmoded by many persons because it seems to be based upon the then existing agrarian conditions and to postulate the persistence of the agrarian regime. It is then argued that the rise of industry to a position superior to that of agriculture has destroyed the basis of Jeffersonian democracy. This is a highly superficial view. Jefferson predicted what the effects of the rise of the economics and politics of an industrial regime would be, unless the independence and liberty characteristic of the farmer, under conditions of virtually free land, were conserved. His predictions have been realized. It was not agrarianism per se that he really stood for, but the kind of liberty and equality that the agrarian regime made possible when there was an open frontier. The early Jeffersonians, for example, held that national credit was a national asset and ought to be nationally controlled; they were bitterly opposed to the capture of national credit by private banking institutions. They were even opposed to financing wars by means of bonds and debts where the income accrued to private individuals, maintaining that wars should be paid for during the time they occur through taxation upon the incomes of the wealthy.

I refer to this particular instance merely by way of illustration, and to indicate how far away so-called Jeffersonian democracy has drifted from the original ideas and policies of any democracy whatsoever. The drift of nominal democracy from the conception of life which may properly be characterized as democratic has come about under the influence of a so-called rugged individualism that defines the liberty of individuals in the terms of the inequality bred by existing economic-legal institutions. In so doing, it puts an almost exclusive emphasis upon those natural capacities of individuals that have power to effect pecuniary and materialistic acquisitions. For our existing materialism, with the blight to which it subjects the cultural development of individuals, is the inevitable product of exaggeration of the economic liberty of the few at the expense of the all-around liberty of the many. And, I repeat, this limitation upon genuine liberty is the inevitable product of the inequality that arises and must arise under the operations of institutionally established and supported finance-capitalism.

THE HIGHLANDER FOLK SCHOOL [*]

Myles Horton

The Highlander Folk School was founded in 1932 in Grundy, Tennessee, by the social activists Myles Horton(1905–1990), Don West (1906–1992) and James A. Dombrowski (1897–1983). Horton and West had visited Denmark where they studied its folk schools, which provided centers for adult education and community empowerment. Using this model, they established Highlander as a center for training social activists in the Labor and Civil Rights Movement. Among a few of its most distinguished attendees were Rosa Parks, Martin Luther King Jr., and Andrew Young. In this article, Horton provides an important brief history of the school during the first years after its founding.

*   *   *

I watched my friends leave their mountain homes in response to agents' stories of mill villages, and return a few months later broken in spirit and health. The industrialists, not satisfied with grinding profits out of those who left their homes to take jobs in cotton mill towns, built branch mills in the mountains. There was no escape. In the name of progress, exploitation followed the valleys back into the hills. Moral and physical disintegration was the price that young and old alike were forced to pay for life's necessities. The whip of poverty and lure of shabby mill life combined to make a death trap which sucked in bright-eyed girls in their teens and strong men who loved freedom and the out-of-doors. Some returned to their hillside farms to spend the remainder of their broken lives coughing up lint. But most of the families stayed in the mill villages. They had sold their homes and, unable to get away, were forced to send their children into the mills to help support the family.

Economic conditions were little better back in the mountains. With the coal and timber almost gone, they had turned to farming. But poor land and inexperience produced only enough to make a miserable existence possible. Though trapped, exploitation was not accepted as a necessary part of life. Here in the mountains, should the economic situation become pressing enough, the people could be made to understand that the socialization of property would give them more personal freedom than would ever again be possible under the existing profit system.

The lack of industrial progress and education among the people in the mountains and neighboring mill towns has served as a protection against their acceptance of wage slavery. Workers in the South, especially those not more

[*] **Source:** *The Social Frontier*, Volume 2, Number 4, 1936, pp. 117–118

than two generations removed from the mountains, are willing to fight for the American ideals of "life, liberty, and the pursuit of happiness." Here was an opportunity to direct the American revolutionary tradition towards a cooperative society operated by and for the workers. Ideas of revolt run through many of the songs written by workers, some of which are sung as ballads. Many strike songs are as class-conscious as the writings of Karl Marx, and much simpler.

Having decided to concentrate on the farmers and industrial workers in the southern mountains, the problem arose of how to go about the job. Mountain schools and colleges gave no clue. They were educating people out of their class or giving them vocational training. The people need to be awakened and enlightened as to their place in society as a class, not trained to do better work for the industrialists. The problem of influencing the existing schools to change their aims seemed more difficult than working out a new approach. While working on an educational set-up that would meet people where their interests are and lead them to envision a new society, my attention was drawn to the work of the Danish Folk High Schools which furnish an excellent example of purposive education.

The Highlander Folk School, located on a mountain farm, within five hours' drive of a number of industrial centers, was opened November, 1932, to provide an educational center for southern workers, for the purpose of educating rural and industrial leaders for a new social order. It was not our desire to create another institution, but to develop a natural approach to workers' education. We were fortunate in securing for our advisory committee Reinhold Niebuhr, George S. Counts, Norman Thomas, Mary Van Kleeck, and other outstanding social educators. At first the school was only a large farm house and an idea. It was two months before any students came. During that time we cut wood and worked on the farm. The first resident student was the son of an Alabama coal miner. There was no curriculum. One evening, while visiting a neighbor, we started to discuss psychology. The farmer, his wife, and the resident student wanted to continue the discussion so we met at the school the following evening and held our first class. Soon we had a class of twenty-five, including farmers, miners, unemployed, college graduates, and one minister. Their ages ranged from 18 to 80. No classes were started that were not asked for or that did not grow out of some life situation. A class in cultural geography followed the neighbors' interest in some snapshots taken in Europe. Stories of a miners' strike brought back by teachers who had visited the coal camp at Wilder, Tennessee, raised problems that led to a class in economics. Another class grew out of discussions of the presidential campaign.

Most of the students were neighbors. Only three were full time resident students.

One of the students who came for the special course brought a basket of onions, bacon, and canned fruit to pay her expenses. She had worked in a hosiery mill, but at the time was living way back in the mountains. In an economics class held in the kitchen where the student cook could keep an eye on the stove, the group had been asked to explain a number of theories that they had been studying. One used a small blackboard propped above the sink. A neighbor who had dropped in for the class said he would never forget the illustration of surplus value given by the girl who had brought the basket of food.

"When I was working at the hosiery mill in Chattanooga," she said, "we were told that we would have to take a wage-cut or the mill would go out of business. Of course, we took the cut. About two weeks later I read in the paper that the daughter of the mill owner was sailing for Europe to spend the winter. I suppose it was the surplus value we had produced that paid her way."

There are three phases of our program: residence courses, extension work, and community activities. Workers who show promise of becoming active in the labor movement as organizers or as local leaders are selected as residence students. Last summer we had an enrollment of nineteen regular resident students for a six weeks course. The majority were from the mills, mines, and farms but a few were college graduates interested in workers' education. Courses were given in economies, labor history and tactics, workers' problems, public speaking, dramatics, and labor journalism. In each class an effort was made to stay within the experience of the students.

An example of capitalistic tactics was furnished the students when a gunman hired by the Fentress Coal and Coke Company at Wilder, Tennessee, attempted to dynamite the school. Teachers and students of the Highlander Folk School had helped in a United Mine Workers strike the year before. After threats of death were made to any striker who housed or gave us a meal, we withdrew from Wilder, but arrangements had been made for three students to study in the school. For two weeks, students and teachers guarded the school night and day. It was not necessary to stress the class nature of society to students who had to do guard duty all night for the privilege of studying at a workers' school.

An extension program is carried on throughout the year in connection with unions and farmers' organizations. Some of this work is done by teachers and students who lend assistance to workers during organization campaigns and in strikes. The more systematic work is done through study groups set up by the extension director and by former students. Our activities of this nature keep us in close touch with the labor movement and enable us to help students after they have left school. Most of our new students are recruited through the extension work.

The community activities also continue the year round and are of a cultural as well as educational nature. Piano lessons are provided for anyone in the community. As many as twenty children and young people have been taking music lessons at one time. Old and young take part in dramatics and folk dancing. A few adults attend regular morning classes during our residence courses but all our special lectures are given at night so that a larger number from the community can attend. An average of twenty books are checked out of our library each week by people in the neighborhood. The library also serves dozens of workers' groups throughout the South.

It is the policy of the school to work through the existing organizations whenever possible. Last year the woodcutters in our community struck with the slogan, "It takes a strong back, a sharp ax, and a weak mind to cut bugwood at 75 cents a cord." A Workers' League was organized to carry on the strike. Practically every worker in the community joined, including the staff and students at the school. Repeated failure to get government officials to oppose the wealthy Tennessee Products Corporation we were fighting, taught the entire community that working people must depend upon themselves. They decided to start a cooperative cannery and later a cooperative store. At the request of the community a ten weeks' course in the history and management of cooperatives was given. A small but successful cooperative cannery was operated last summer. Plans for a consumer-producer cooperative to take in most of the community are under way.

The three approaches merge when workers from a union or farm community where we are carrying on extension work come for a residence course and for a time become part of the community. During our short residence courses, farmers and mill workers find that their interests are basically the same. Their problems are discussed with the neighbors, with visiting organizers, and with teachers. New social theories are discussed naturally by the neighbors who drop in for classes or for an evening visit. The students are stimulated and eagerly attend classes where they hope to learn more about these new ideas. They see the need for fundamental social change and become interested in the means for bringing about a new social order. Once students see the economic necessity for organizing and the justice a workers' society alone will make possible, their hearts as well as their heads are won to the cause of labor. Workers' education must furnish heat as well as light, for there is no time to waste.

Our place is with the working class. We must not cut ourselves off from them by proclaiming social theories for which they have not been prepared by experience to understand. We are working primarily with the American Federation of Labor unions. The southern workers have asked for our assistance. National officials of three unions have asked the Highlander Folk School to train organizers and local leaders for them. Education for workers must be financed by organized labor so that they can have full control. At the beginning, this calls for low cost workers' education. The absence of salaries and the supply of food stuff grown on our farm enables us to run the school, exclusive of our extension work, on a yearly budget of $4,800 which maintains a regular teaching staff of six members. It is up to the Highlander Folk School to demonstrate to organized labor in this part of the South that workers' education is necessary.

In an effort to help build a militant labor movement and to give experience to our students, the school moved from Monteagle and is stationed for a week in a mill town near Chattanooga. Teachers and students are scattered in the homes of striking hosiery workers. We meet one hour each day for discussion. The remainder of the time is spent at union meetings or on the picket line. A Washington's Birthday parade, which we helped organize, led by the local High School band, ended as a mass picket line in front of the Daisy Hosiery Mill. Four hundred shots were fired into the unarmed paraders by armed guards inside the mill. Our librarian and four other men and women were shot. As a result of the parade, the three Richmond Hosiery Mills were forced to deal with the union officials. Aside from the educational value to our students, we were able to broaden the outlook of the strikers. The school has been asked to do educational work for the American Federation of Hosiery Workers in Tennessee and neighboring states.

We are becoming accepted as a part of the Southern labor movement. The Highlander Folk School's most important contribution will be to help the workers to envision their role in society and in so doing, make the labor movement the basis for a fundamental social change.

SHALL TEACHERS BE FREE? *

The Editorial Board

In the following editorial, the editors of the journal ask the question of whether or not the schools and the educational system, with their clear class system "can serve as a creative force in bringing a better order into being." Their assumption is that "with very few exceptions, if any, the school has fought on the side of privilege and reaction, serving to stifle protest, to condition boys and girls against basic and significant change, to reduce the role of rational forces in the social process, and thus to prepare the stage for trial by the sword, the machine gun, nitro-glycerine, and poison gas." Teachers are seen as a potentially active force for change, but one that can not necessarily be counted on to act to bring about a more equitable society.

*   *   *

This number of *The Social Frontier* is devoted to the most urgent issue now before American education. Powerful forces, organized on a nationwide scale, are seeking to make the school an instrument of profound reaction. These forces have already succeeded in putting repressive laws on the statute books of twenty-two states and the District of Columbia. They are even boasting of having achieved the dismissal of scores of teachers during the past year. And the volume by Howard K. Beale, which is reviewed on page 194, presents an objective picture of the stultifying conditions under which great numbers of teachers live and work in the United States.

Many teachers and citizens, while conceding the above facts to be true, would take exception to the generalization. They would contend that the supreme issue is one of finance, of keeping the schools open physically, of maintaining the material basis of education. In support of their position they could point to the enlargement of classes, the curtailment of services, and the reduction of teachers' salaries during the past few years. Such tendencies, they would argue, strike at the very root of the public school.

We are prepared to grant the force of this argument. Moreover, we are not disposed to quarrel over a question of precedence. Certainly the friends of education must stand together in the struggle for adequate financial support for the public school. But it is equally necessary that they stand together in the companion struggle for freedom of teaching and learning. It must not be forgotten that autocracies today are quite as ready to support organized education as democracies. All they ask is that the school be employed as an instrument

---

* **Source:** *The Social Frontier*, Volume 2, Number 6, 1936, pp. 163–164.

for molding the mind of the coming generation to the pattern desired—a pattern that will protect privileged classes in their privileges, under a smoke screen of race hatred, national bigotry, and loyalty to the dead bones of ancestors. In America the threat of such autocratic control is already present in such organizations and personalities as the American Liberty League and William Randolph Hearst. The latter has shown himself willing to advocate the support of any kind of education he is permitted to control.

The point to be emphasized is that the question of material support and the question of quality of the educational program cannot be separated. If education were qualitatively the same in all places and ages, then the only problem facing any people would be that of getting enough of this good thing. But since it is actually as diverse in quality as it is in quantity, a rational being must always ask whether a given kind of education is worthy of support at all.

Unfortunately there are many members of the profession who seem to feel that they have no responsibility for the deeper social consequences of their acts. Unwittingly or otherwise, they accept the status of hired men and women. All they ask is that they be paid adequately and be made secure in their positions. They regard themselves as mere instruments in the hands of social forces, to which they give the euphonious name of society, the community, the public, or the state, ready to do whatever they are told to do, even to reverse themselves completely, if given a few days' notice. They are like the lawyer who, for a compensation, is prepared to serve any client or any cause. But history will not render them entirely unaccountable for what they do in the classroom. The teacher cannot, by resort to sophistry, escape responsibility for his acts.

If, as seems certain, American society has entered upon a period of fundamental transition which will be marked by conflict and experimentation, public education faces the most severe test in its history. The question will be decided whether in a society marked by class differences the school can serve as a creative force in bringing a better order into being. The record of the past would seem to answer this question clearly and emphatically in the negative. Certainly with very few exceptions, if any, the school has fought on the side of privilege and reaction, serving to stifle protest, to condition boys and girls against basic and significant change, to reduce the role of rational forces in the social process, and thus to prepare the stage for trial by the sword, the machine gun, nitro-glycerine, and poison gas.

It may be, however, that the example of the past need not be followed in the future. This is a fond hope of both the American people and the American teacher. As a people we have put faith in democratic processes. And among these processes the work of the school is given high rank. For the first time in our history this institution has achieved the position of a major educational agency. Enrolling approximately thirty-million pupils and manned by more than a million teachers it is a powerful factor in shaping the destiny of the nation. Whether it shapes that destiny for good or for ill may well depend upon the fight which the teachers make at this time against the forces of reaction. Freedom of teaching and learning is the most precious thing in education. Let that be destroyed and the school passes out of the picture as a creative influence and becomes a slave of those great property interests which are now endeavoring to stem the tide of social change. From the standpoint of the general welfare there is one thing that is more dangerous than closing the schools—keeping them open as a tool of reaction.

THE SOCIAL SIGNIFICANCE OF ACADEMIC FREEDOM [*]

John Dewey

Dewey argues in this piece that academic freedom involves "the freedom of the school as an agent of education." The academic freedom of students is even more important than the freedom of teachers. In reality, the two are inseparable.   Without freedom of inquiry, teachers and students cannot exercise the "habits of intelligent action" necessary for the orderly development of the society to develop. Dewey concludes the article arguing that: "Every force that operates to limit the freedom of education is a premium put upon ultimate recourse to violence to effect needed change. Every force that tends to liberate educational processes is a premium placed upon intelligent and orderly methods of directing to a more just, equitable, and humane end the social changes that are going on anyway."

*   *   *

I am not especially fond of the phrase academic freedom as far as the adjective academic is concerned. It suggests something that is rather remote and technical. Indeed, it is common to use the word as a term of disparagement. But the reality for which the phrase stands has an importance far beyond any particular expression used to convey it. Freedom of education is the thing at issue—I was about to say at stake. And since education is not a function that goes on in the void, but is carried on by human beings, the freedom of education means, in the concrete, the freedom of students and teachers: the freedom of the school as an agent of education.

THE ATTACK UPON THE FREE SCHOOL

The inclusion of students in the idea of freedom of education is even more important than the inclusion of teachers; at least it would be if it were possible to separate the two. Freedom of teachers is a necessary condition of freedom for students to learn.

I referred in an earlier article to "free schools" as the aim to which the American people are historically committed with a devotion that probably exceeds that given to any other aim in our common life. The full significance of free schools is, however, far from realization in the public mind and in the workings of our educational system. Freedom from payment of fees, support by public taxation, is a necessary condition for schools that are to be free of

---

[*] **Source:** *The Social Frontier*, Volume 2, Number 6, 1936, pp. 165–166.

access to all. This aspect of free schools has been extended to free text-books, free libraries, and, in some public schools, to free dental and medical service and free lunches for those who cannot pay—at least it was so extended until the depression led heavy taxpayers to limit these services. But in final resort, these manifestations of freedom are tributary to freedom of education as the social enterprise in which education forms character and intelligence. There are plenty of restrictions put upon moral and intellectual freedom of education within the school system itself. It is bound, often hidebound, by hampering traditions that originated under conditions alien to the present. These traditions affect subject matter, methods of instruction, discipline, the organization and administration of the schools. These limitations of free education, serious and weighty enough in all conscience, have been the objects of attack by educational reformers at all times. But there is another limitation added to these onerous ones that is especially dangerous at the present time. It is the attempt to close the minds, mouths, and ears of students and teachers alike to all that is not consonant with the practices and beliefs of the privileged class that represents the economic and political status quo.

The question of teachers' oaths is so familiar that I refer to it only by way of illustration. Since our Constitution provides for its own change, though by awkward and cumbrous methods, and since it expressly reserves to the people (as well as to state governments) all rights not conferred upon the Federal Government, and since this reservation of rights to the people includes the right of revolution when conditions become intolerable—as both Jefferson and Lincoln have pointed out—a teacher need have no conscientious scruples in taking an oath of loyalty to the Constitution. But the selection of teachers as the class of persons who must take the oath is socially serious because it is one phase of the general movement calculated to prevent freedom of education in all matters that relate to economic and political conditions and policies.

ACADEMIC FREEDOM—A PARAMOUNT SOCIAL ISSUE

In all the preceding articles in *The Social Frontier* that have dealt with various aspects of liberty, I have pointed out that liberty is a social matter and not just a claim of the private individual. I have argued that freedom is a matter of the distribution of effective power; that, finally, the struggle for liberty is important because of its consequences in effecting; more just, equable, and human relations of men, women, and children to one another. In no phase of social endeavor is the realization of the social content of freedom more important than in the struggle for academic freedom. Everyone who has read the pleas made in the early struggle for universal and free schools in this country knows the emphasis that was put upon education as a necessary condition for creation of the kind of citizenship indispensable to the success of democracy. To-day freedom of teaching and learning on the part of instructors and students is imperatively necessary for that kind of intelligent citizenship that is genuinely free to take part in the social reconstructions without which democracy will die. The question is now whether democracy is a possible form of society when affairs are as complex and economic power is as concentrated as today. Since freedom of mind and freedom of expression are the root of all freedom, to deny freedom in education is a crime against democracy. Because academic freedom is so essentially a social issue, since it is intimately bound up with what the future citizenship of the country is going to do in shaping our political and economic destiny, it is not surprising that those who either give only lip-service or who openly strive to restrict it, should also strive to present it to the public as a matter that concerns teachers only as individuals, and to represent those active in supporting its cause as more or less unbalanced individuals who want more liberty to assert their personal views. There is nothing paradoxical in saying that it is just because of the social significance of liberty of education that it is presented as something that affects only individual teachers.

SOCIAL EFFECTS OF REPRESSIVE LEGISLATION

It cannot be denied that there is at present an unusually large number of young people who find themselves deprived of opportunity in the present situation, who find their legitimate desires and, aspirations so blocked that they have become converts to the idea that social change cannot be effected by democratic methods, but only by violent force. The idea sedulously cultivated in the Hearst press, but not confined to it, that this attitude is the result of teachers' imposition of subversive ideas under the camouflage of academic freedom, is laughable to all those who know the facts about our schools. This attitude is the product of the restrictive and oppressive effect of the present industrial system, aided by a school system, which discounts the value of social intelligence. The feeling that social change of any basic character can be brought about only by violent force is the product of lack of faith in intelligence as a method and this loss of faith is in large measure the product of a schooling, that because of its comparatively un-free condition, has not enabled youth to face intelligently the realities of our social life, political and economic.

There are ultimately but three forces that control society—habit, coercive and violent force, and action directed by intelligence. In fairly normal times, habit and custom are by far the strongest force. A social crisis like the present means that this force has in large measure ceased to operate. The other forces, therefore, come more conspicuously into play. Reactionaries who strive to prevent any change of the old order are possessed of the power that enables them to use brute force in its less overt forms: by coercion, by intimidation, and by various forms of indirect pressure. From lack of understanding of social affairs, a lack of understanding owing to faulty education, as well as to deliberate refusal to learn, reactionaries unintelligently resist change. Those who have suffered from the old order then react by appeal to direct use of force as the only means at their command. Because of the intellectual suppressions experienced in the course of their own education they have little knowledge of means of effecting social changes by any method other than force.

In short, the social significance of academic freedom lies in the fact that without freedom of inquiry and freedom on the part of teachers and students to explore the forces at work in society and the means by which they may be directed, the habits of intelligent action that are necessary to the orderly development of society cannot be created. Training for good citizenship is one thing when conditions are simple and fairly stable. It is quite another thing when conditions are confused, complicated, and unsettled, when class divisions and struggles are imminent. Every force that operates to limit the freedom of education is a premium put upon ultimate recourse to violence to effect needed change. Every force that tends to liberate educational processes is a premium placed upon intelligent and orderly methods of directing to a more just, equitable, and humane end the social changes that are going on anyway.

FREEDOM TO DEVELOP SOCIAL INTELLIGENCE *

William H. Kilpatrick

I n this article, William Heard Kilpatrick argues that the development of social intelligence is essential in a culture and society confronted by change. Academic freedom is needed because of four distinct factors at work in American society: "the fact of rapid and inevitable change in the stream of affairs, the indispensable place of intelligence as a means of steering change, the utility of free discussion or interchange of ideas as a means of building intelligence, and the necessity under our democratic theory that the people themselves decide finally on public policies." Unlike hereditary intelligence, social intelligence can be cultivated and developed through institutions such as schools.

* * *

We can perhaps best answer the questions of the Editors as we see why academic freedom is needed and the part it thus properly plays in a democratic society.

INDISPENSABILITY OF INTELLIGENCE IN AN ERA OF RAPID CHANGE

The basic need of this country for academic freedom seems to lie in the concurrent working of four factors in our situation: the fact of rapid and inevitable change in the stream of affairs, the indispensable place of intelligence as a means of steering change, the utility of free discussion or interchange of ideas as a means of building intelligence, and the necessity under our democratic theory that the people themselves decide finally on public policies. A few words on each of these four may help clarify their significance.

The fact of change need not be argued. Most obviously, rapid changes are taking place and promise to continue. Obvious also is the unevenness of change: some developments outrun others. In this way "cultural lags" arise with a resulting continual stream of social strains and consequent social problems. In order to bring things once more into a proper working balance, change in some areas of civilization necessitates correlative changes in other phases of our social environment.

Intelligence appears our sole resource for dealing with novelty. Neither habit nor tradition suffice. And we can be hopeful as regards the needed intelligence. What man has done in building intelligence along natural science

---

***Source:** *The Social Frontier*, Volume 2, Number 6, 1936, p. 174-175

lines gives us basic hope as to what analogous efforts may do toward building a like adequate social intelligence for dealing with social problems and difficulties. There appears no safe alternative. Social action not based on intelligence is too dangerous to risk. The people must and will decide. They must be prepared to decide wisely.

EDUCATION AS BUILDING OF SOCIAL INTELLIGENCE

But intelligence in thinking is increasingly a social product. The psychology of intelligence testing has misled some into supposing that intelligence is mainly, if not solely, a matter of favorable heredity. This is serious error. Heredity is an essential factor, but environment—particularly one's surrounding culture—is a second essential factor. For one to acquire through shared efforts the distinctions and knowledges culturally available for use is precisely a process of building in one's self a more effective intelligence. And for this the outlook is hopeful. Heredity can be improved at best only very slowly. To improve and disseminate the culture lies far more within our hands. Education thus becomes a powerful means for increasing greatly the effectual intelligence of a people.

Among the agencies for developing expert knowledge and reliable thinking, and so for extending and improving the culture, the university graduate school stands perhaps highest. In order to realize these possibilities, communication and criticism are absolutely essential not only among staff and students within any one university but as well between the one university and others and with the outside world of thought. Such interchange is necessary both to the stimulation of thinking and to the criticism and testing of thought. In other words, the professors must be free not only to report their own thinking at any stage of its development but as well to criticize publicly any other formulation wherever found. On no other basis can the university properly fill its function. This is the original meaning of academic freedom.

But as intimated above, the educational building of intelligence is not limited to making additions to the culture, essential as this is. Schools lower than the university can begin from the very first to help pupils and students to acquire and use the knowledge and thought distinctions already available in the culture. The primary means for thus up building intelligence does not, however, consist in any mere encyclopedic accumulation of facts and subject matter. Rather does it lie in facing actual problematic situations, where new thinking is demanded of the pupil or student and the need inherently arises to make new distinctions and sense new relationships. It is in this inherent use that the culture is properly appropriated. This, let it be said, need not be the indoctrination by teacher or school of prior chosen views or positions. Rather is the learner forced, if the teaching be honest and good, to face the problems for himself and himself to think them through to his own conclusions. Where study is thus carried on under the stimulation and criticism of diverse views among fellows and teachers; with readings specifically directed to the various live options, the resulting learning is the more surely dynamic and intelligence, in fact, the more effectually built.

It is then by the finest interaction between lower and higher schools, and both in close connection with the living current of affairs, that the social intelligence of a people can best be upbuilt. The process itself can be consciously fostered. But, alas, it can also be consciously thwarted. Such thwarting is the situation that creates the problem of this symposium. Some there be among us who deliberately plan to thwart and hinder this process of building a better social intelligence. Whether the aim springs from the mere inertia of ignorance or from a desire to protect special privilege, the steps taken are the same, namely to stop schools from discussing controversial issues.

PROFESSIONAL AUTONOMY FOR TEACHERS

We can now answer perhaps a bit more precisely the Editors' questions.

Academic freedom means the freedom of the teacher in whatever grade of school to help build in his pupils or students the best social intelligence possible in them at that stage of development. Specifically, it also means, since this is a question of the teaching process, that the teacher is the proper judge in respect to what to teach and when and how. It is a just part of professional expertness for him along with his colleagues to settle these matters on the basis of professional considerations, not—be it clear—in behalf of any individualist right of teachers to propagandize their peculiar ideas, but because this is the service that a proper education can render in a democratic society.

Any interference with this proper teaching function constitutes an infringement of academic freedom, whether it come from trustees or school boards or lay public or even from the state itself. It may be legally true that "the king [state] can do no wrong," but morally and socially the state has frequently done wrong things, as for instance in the Tennessee law on evolution.

TACT AND STRATEGY—LIMITATIONS OF
ACADEMIC FREEDOM

There is at least one professional limitation upon an unlimited exercise of this freedom of teaching. Any school, willy-nilly, teaches not only its pupils or students but also its parents and supporting public. This entails the moral obligation to deal educatively in this wider relation. It becomes, then, the obligation of the teaching profession to educate the general public to a better understanding of the social function of academic freedom. To anger is seldom the best educative procedure. In particular times and places the school may then properly withhold somewhat the range of its controversial issues in order that it may the more educatively serve the total population involved. This limitation is a delicate matter and easily abused, but a decent respect for the feelings of others is an obligation not to be lightly disregarded.

INDOCTRINATION VERSUS EDUCATION [*]

Carleton Washburne

C arleton Washburne (1889–1968) was superintendent of schools in Winnetka, Illinois, from 1919 to 1943. He is famous for his development of the Winnetka plan, which drew on John Dewey's Progressive Education models, and emphasized "programmed instruction" in which subjects were divided into "common essentials" and "creative group activities." Common essentials required demonstrated mastery and creative group activities required no strict standards of achievement to advance.

In this article, Washburne tries to clarify the question of indoctrination in the schools. To this end, he defines "indoctrination as the attempt to influence one's pupils in the school to accept one particular solution to a problem where there is difference of opinion among intelligent, thoughtful, informed, and right-minded persons as to what the best solution is." It is not indoctrination, according to Washburne, to show evils or ideals as they actually exist.

Indoctrination in schools is seen as inevitable. Schools, as Pierre Bourdieu later pointed out, reproduce the culture or society of which they are a part. The question, therefore, is "one of what kind of indoctrination we are going to have."

A seeming contradiction is at work. We should indoctrinate students to resist indoctrination. Indoctrination should only occur in the schools with the idea of creating meaningful social intelligence in the child. Thus, "The teacher should, down in his heart, have more desire to develop the child's own thinking than to impose on the child the teacher's viewpoint. If the teacher is fundamentally child-centered in his educational attitude, that is, if he is primarily concerned with education rather than indoctrination, both his conscious and his unconscious influence on the child will be toward free, independent thought."

*   *   *

Before we can intelligently discuss the problem of indoctrination in the schools, we must clearly define our term. Much hazy thinking on the subject is due to a loose use of the word "indoctrinate." Let us then, at least for the purpose of this article, define indoctrination as the attempt to influence one's pupils in the school to accept one particular solution to a problem where there is difference of opinion among intelligent, thoughtful, informed, and right-minded persons as to what the best solution is. Indoctrination, according to this definition, has only to do with controversial issues. It is not indoctrination if we teach a child that flies carry disease, and try to influence him in favor of having his house screened. It is not indoctrination to give child

---

[*] **Source:** *The Social Frontier*, Volume 2, Number 7, 1936, pp. 212–215.

recognition of the value of truthfulness. It is indoctrination to try to convince a child that when he grows up he should refuse to fight in any war, even against armed aggression and invasion, or, conversely, to teach him that no matter whether or not his country is justified in participating in a war, he should immediately enlist his service. It is indoctrination to teach a child that the way out of our present difficulties is through a reversion to rugged individualism, or through fascism, or through socialism, or communism, or any other specified means. It is not indoctrination to show existing evils, which are commonly recognized as evils, or to show ideals, which are commonly accepted as desirable.

I realize that there is room for quibbling as to what "intelligent, thoughtful, informed, and right-minded persons" differ about. One can split hairs in a theoretical discussion as to what subjects are controversial and what ones are not. Practically, however, no one actually conducting schools has a minute's question in his mind as to whether or not an issue brought up for class discussion is controversial. The problem of indoctrination applies only to controversial questions.

THE ARGUMENTS FOR INDOCTRINATION

(1) We must rebuild our social order—or, if we are on the other side of the fence, we must maintain the status quo. Education is necessary for either purpose. One of the fundamental reasons given for public education has been the perpetuation of the particular kind of state, which established it. In this country we say "education is the safeguard of democracy"; in Russia, "education is the third line of defense for communism." Mussolini has recognized education as basic for the carrying forward of fascism, and Hitler is capitalizing on the effectiveness of Imperial Germany's nationalistic education.

Furthermore, the State needs trained citizens. It needs certain like-mindedness among them in order that there may be cohesiveness. It needs certain common ideals. The school is the place where the State can effectively train all its future citizens at a formative period of their lives. A new social order cannot be adequately ushered in or an old order adequately preserved without a trained citizenry.

(2) Education to be realistic and to count in the life of the child must have the same zeal and emotional drive which is called for by the necessity of changing—or preserving—the social order. Schools in which there is no indoctrination tend to be cloisteral, to be out of touch with the live world outside. This fact stands out if one compares an average American school with an average Russian school. In the former, most of the work is abstract, academic, unrelated to the throbbing life going on outside. It is true that the average Ameri-

can school has a sort of watery indoctrination for the preservation of the status quo, but it is too luke warm, too diluted, too un-emotionalized to affect the educational process as a whole. Russia, with its vigorous, frank, and exceedingly effective communist propaganda in the schools, achieves in its education vitality and realism, which we in America have never remotely approached.

(3) Indoctrination is inevitable. The question is merely one of what kind of indoctrination we are going to have. A teacher, by his very nature as a teacher, imposes his views and attitudes on children. This is recognized by Boards of Education, which will not employ a teacher who is known to have ideas widely at variance with those of the community or the School Board. Few American Boards of Education, for example, would knowingly employ a teacher who was a member of the Communist party. No corresponding Board in Russia would employ a believer in capitalism. No German Board would employ a teacher known to be actively opposed to the Nazi regime.

A failure to indoctrinate, moreover, is in itself indoctrination for the status quo or for the point of view held by the parents of the community. Children being continually exposed at home to certain indoctrinating influences and, not receiving any contrary indoctrination in school, are necessarily indoctrinated in the home or community mental pattern.

These arguments are cogent and cannot be ignored. But a closer examination will reveal that the method and aims of indoctrination are opposed to those of education. Moreover, the widespread acceptance of the principle of the use of indoctrination in the schools would defeat the very ends which the advocates of the principle have in mind—building a new society through education.

THE COMPELLING REASONS AGAINST INDOCTRINATION

(1) Indoctrination is unfair to the child. During the period of education he has a right to see all sides of each question, he has a right to have each side clearly and fairly presented, he has a right to expect from the schools the unvarnished truths. He early learns that his parents have certain prejudices. He makes certain allowances for these. But if he cannot count on his teachers' objectivity and honesty, where shall he turn?

(2) Indoctrination is the antithesis of education. Education involves the drawing out of the child, the developing of his own capacities and thought. Indoctrination involves the imposing upon the child of one set of ideas, to the exclusion of his own thought. Education is the freeing of the individual. Indoctrination is the binding of the individual to the views of some group of adults. Education should lead toward growth. Indoctrination stultifies growth.

(3) Anyone who supposes that he has the one and final solution to any problem is inexcusably bigoted and is, therefore, unfit to educate children. Any intelligent person must recognize that however probable he thinks it is that his particular solution to a controversial issue is the best one, there are other persons of equal intelligence who have equal certainty that their solution is right, and that there is always the possibility that either one or both of them may be wrong and that still another solution may be better. The growth of society depends upon our free exploration of all possible avenues of escape from our present evils, of all possible avenues toward our ultimate ideals. Indoctrination shuts off all avenues but one.

(4) The strongest arguments against indoctrination are perhaps the practical ones. If one group can use the schools to indoctrinate the children toward its particular answers to controversial questions, so can another group. After any School Board election the new Board can, if indoctrination is to be allowed, change textbooks, curriculum, and teachers to fit its pet ideas, while after the next School Board election the whole thing may be reversed. The schools become, in a country, which is not yet under a dictatorship, footballs of politics in the worst sense; and, in a country where there is a dictatorship; the way is paved for inculcating the dictator's ideas in all growing young minds.

Those in the educational profession who consciously advocate indoctrination in the schools are almost without exception those who would use it to change the existing social order. Yet from a practical standpoint they would completely defeat their own purpose were they successful in getting an acceptance of the idea that the schools may be used to indoctrinate. For, of necessity, majority opinion favors that which is—were it not so, what is would be changed. If the schools are to be used to indoctrinate, obviously they will be used to indoctrinate toward that which the majority desires. To advocate indoctrination is, therefore, not a way to bring about a new social order but a way to perpetuate the old.

A PROGRAM OF SOCIALLY RECONSTRUCTIVE EDUCATION

How then are we to bring about change? How are we to train children for a new order? How are we to give them the emotional drive they need, both educationally and socially? What are we going to do to make our children ready to face the problems that are going to confront them in an order which, schools or no schools, is changing? Or are the schools simply to sit back passively and teach what man has done, give lessons in the three R's, and trust to the unorganized hit or miss forces of society to do the real job of education? I think there is a solution and that many of the things desired by the advocates of indoctrination can be achieved without corresponding evils.

First of all, we can train our children in social thinking. That is, we can help them to realize that they are integral parts of a social whole. This is not indoctrination because it is not controversial—no one can deny our interdependence. Social thinking can be developed through socialized activities within the schools themselves, through group enterprises or projects where each individual is contributing his own special interest or ability to the success of something in which the whole group is interested. It can be developed through organized games on the playground, provided the director helps the children to become conscious of their interdependence, not only with members of their own team, but with the opposing team.

The active practice of citizenship in a school organized as a democratic community gives the necessary realistic training in group-thinking and social responsibility. Such student responsibility, however, must be real and must deal with things in which the children are actually concerned. It must be directed toward a definite consciousness on the part of the children that they are thinking in terms of the well being of the school as a whole, and toward an awareness of where anti-social acts or inefficiencies do damage to the group as a whole.

And social thinking can be brought about through the treatment of social sciences. From the very beginning of the study of history or geography, children can be made to feel the identity of interests, in the long run, of the members of a community, a state, a nation, and the world at large. One need not cover up some facts and give undue emphasis to others in order to bring about a realization, through the study of history, geography, economics, and sociology, of the fact that the good of the individual is inextricably bound up with the well being of the whole.

But what of emotional drive, since mere intellectual social consciousness lacks motive power? Let the emotional drive come through showing vividly, dramatically, some of the evils that exist, and, in contrast, the potentialities of mankind were its own ideals realized. The ideals of a better society, I admit, cannot be made too specific if one is to avoid indoctrination, yet they too can be given certain vividness. There was, for example, a cartoon recently in the *Chicago Tribune* (of all places!) contrasting the disastrous effects of money spent on one foreign war with what that money would do if put to constructive purposes. A dozen little pictures illustrated the constructive uses to which the money could be put—schools, parks, highways, transportation, old age pensions, etc. A corresponding dozen showed cathedrals and homes destroyed, men hopelessly crippled, cemeteries filled. It is not indoctrination to show that peace and the constructive use of the world's resources are eminently desirable—all agree on this.

Conversely, certain ills are commonly acknowledged. No one questions the harmfulness of the conditions leading to lynch law; no one questions the undesirability of slums, of the insecurity of employment, of gangsterism and racketeering, of the alliance between crime and politics, of political corruption, or of the great gulf that exists between the extremely rich and the extremely poor. Equalitarianism may well be challenged, but the existence of squalor and dire poverty side by side with great wealth is practically never defended.

We can, then, take our children by picture, by story, and by actual excursion into the realities of the evils that exist in our present day society. Our problem is not one of finding enough material to give the children an emotional drive. It is one of mental hygiene—not over-arousing the emotions before the children are able to act on what they feel.

A student trained in social thinking, emotionally activated to work toward the elimination of commonly recognized evils and toward the achievement of commonly held ideals, still needs training in sound thinking as to the means of achieving these ideals. And here is where vigorous discussion of controversial issues needs to be encouraged in the schoolroom. Outside the school, the tendency in discussing controversial issues is for each person to advocate his own particular solution and to try to convince the other persons. In school, the discussion of controversial issues should be rather for the purpose of getting at all the facts on both sides of each question and for the purpose of learning to do logical, scientific thinking. It is true that we act more by emotion than by thought. For that very reason the schools have the responsibility of helping people to realize that while emotion is the motive power, thought is the steering gear. One would get nowhere in a motor less car, but in a car with no steering gear, one rides to destruction.

In the discussion of controversial issues there should be a studious avoidance of reaching conclusions, except where immediate action is possible. There are immediate controversial issues in the school—shall marbles be played for keeps, for example; are Halloween pranks permissible; is snowballing or the use of water pistols on the playground desirable; shall a school corporation in financial difficulties have a lottery to save itself, and so on? These issues should be discussed in exactly the same way as are the larger social issues. But with the immediate ones the children should reach a decision and act upon it. They must get much training in this, lest they become conditioned to a degree of balance like that which caused the donkey to starve when he was equidistant between two piles of hay. But where immediate action is not possible, children should learn to defer decisions. The point that must be gotten across to them through every possible means is that prior to the time of action decision is unwise because it cuts off exploration of other paths, while when the time for action comes, decision must be reached as to which path is most likely to lead toward a desired goal, and vigorous, unhesitating action must immediately follow this decision.

PRACTICALITY OF THE PROGRAM

Is this program practical? I believe that with a reasonable amount of good sense and strategy, it can be carried out in almost any community. There are, it is true, some controversial issues with a definite local setting and these may be so hot that for the moment the teacher will find it necessary to avoid them. A flank attack is sometimes more effective than a frontal one, and there are even moments when it is better to lie low in a dugout than to charge through a barrage. There has to be strategy, and there has to be recognition of the fact that if a community is in a high pitch of emotional excitement on a given issue, it is physiologically impossible to get children to discuss that issue in a calm, dispassionate, scientific way. At such times the issue involved should be avoided, but the principles back of it should be approached through cooler channels. A little skill on the part of the teacher in avoiding unnecessary irritation will give him a very free hand in training the children to think honestly on controversial questions.

But what of the teacher's unconscious influence on the child toward his own viewpoint? The teacher should, down in his heart, have more desire to develop the child's own thinking than to impose on the child the teacher's viewpoint. If the teacher is fundamentally child-centered in his educational attitude, that is, if he is primarily concerned with education rather than indoctrination, both his conscious and his unconscious influence on the child will be toward free, independent thought.

I realize that this program may sound idealistic—that to carry it out perfectly requires ideal teachers and an ideal community. But the program is more practical and attainable than that of having teachers so ideally wise as to know just what pattern children's minds should be cast in, and a community that would permit such casting. Furthermore, it presents a socially and educationally sounder ideal. And it points the direction in which we should move in our practical classroom work.

THE LITTLE RED RIDER [*]

Lionel Heap

I n the following article, Lionel Heap describes the rider placed on the appropriations funding bill for schools in the District of Columbia. It required teachers and other school employees to sign a loyalty oath before they could receive their salaries. The article provides remarkable documentation of the political arguments that were commonly used to justify loyalty oaths in the schools, and gives the reader a unique insight into free speech issues and education during the 1930s.

* * *

A meeting of the Congressional Sub-committee for the District of Columbia was held March 2nd, for the purpose of a hearing on the Sisson bill, repealing the Little Red Rider. This famous Rider, attached to last year's appropriation bill for the District, requires teachers and other school employees to sign a statement before receiving each salary check that they have not taught or advocated communism. Present at the hearing were Congressman Sisson, the Congressional Sub-committee, the school board, schoolteachers, members of the press, and a large group of citizens. Conspicuous among the citizens were gray-haired-and-mustached General Amos A. Fries; Vice-Commander of the American Legion E. Brooks Fetty, a beak-nosed, receding-chinned individual, whose pudgy form suggests that he has done no harder work for a number of years than pester school boards and other respectable citizens; and Attorney George E. Sullivan, who looks the part of a church usher. These three men have led the fight in the District for gag measures and redbaiting.

The hearing opened with a speech by Congressman Maury Maverick favoring repeal of the Rider. Maverick has not the best of delivery, his thought seems obscure; but suddenly a shaft of real worth, crisp and clear, shoots out and redeems all that has gone before. He argued that the school board should be allowed to run its own affairs, criticized the American Legion for not living up to its constitution which declares for free speech, and advised the military (General Fries) to confine itself to its own affairs. He was followed by Congressman Byron N. Scott, an ex-school teacher. He spoke with almost a drawl, emphasizing nothing, the speech seeming to take Scott where it would, rather than Scott dominating it; but it was so fearless, so truth-seeking rather than truth-proclaiming, so simple even, when dealing with complex economic sub-

[*] **Source:** *The Social Frontier*, Volume 2, Number 8, 1936, pp. 254–255.

jects, so human, that no one who heard it will ever forget it. As a sample of its simple force and effectiveness the following may be cited:

When a kid comes to school without his breakfast—a kid whose father has been out of work for three or four years—the teacher cannot indoctrinate that kid with the perfection of the present system, regardless of any oath she may have taken to do so. She gets further with that boy by frankly admitting that the free market as we have known it in the past has broken down.

Congresswoman Virginia Ellis Jenckes, of Indiana, then read a paper opposing repeal of the Red Rider. Exercising the utmost charity, the best that can by said of Mrs. Jenckes is that she represents woman-in-politics at her worst. In a voice, strong for one who later begged to be excused from questioning on the score of ill health, she blasted forth the out-worn trash that communism means Godlessness, the destruction of the home, and nationalization of women. Mrs. Jenckes stated that she had been obliged to remove her daughter from the public schools of the District for fear of contamination. She ended by charging the school board with inefficiency and mishandling of money, and asked the Congressional Committee to reach no conclusion on the Sisson repeal bill until she had time to file a brief. Chairman Kennedy remonstrated at this further delay. Mrs. Jenckes pleaded illness. Representative Ellenbogen, of Pennsylvania, pointed out that it would not be fair to allow the lady representative to file a brief without giving the Board of Education opportunity to file a reply. Representative Sisson began: "Mr. Chairman, I would like to ask the lady member some questions. . . ." But ill Mrs. Jenckes had already risen and was drawing on her coat: "I beg to be excused from answering any questions. I am under doctor's orders." Mrs. Doyle, President of the Board of Education, was on her feet and managed to make Mrs. Jenckes hear, before she left the room: " Mr. Chairman, I charge the Indiana representative with using her Congressional immunity both for publicity purposes and to escape the filing of suits against her by members of this board."

Mrs. Doyle then called upon various principals of the District schools to give their views as to the effect of the Rider upon the teachers and the school system. In two minute talks, these men and women brought out that the Rider had intimidated the teachers and rendered it impossible for them to teach in a natural, effective manner. The speakers pointed out the absurdity of the Rider whose purpose is to combat communism but which actually helps stimulate children to satisfy their curiosity about communism at the Library of Congress.

After the noon recess, Lowell Mellet, Washington editor, spoke in behalf of the Sisson Bill. He said that the Rider had brought disrepute and ridicule upon Congress.

Then the meeting was turned over to the "gag" crowd. Attorney George E. Sullivan was the first to address the Committee. He required two trips to carry all the textbooks, which he proposed to discuss. Dismayed, Chairman Kennedy asked Sullivan how long he planned to talk. "I think I can get through in an hour and a half." No one else had spoken longer than fifteen minutes and most speakers had held themselves to two or three minutes. Apparently the most that he could bring out from his half dozen piles of books was that these books described communism as one of the most important movements in the annals of mankind. He read a statement to the effect that Lenin is the most colossal figure of modern times. Representative Dewey Short, of Missouri, spoke up: "Isn't that true?" "No," thundered Sullivan (or attempted to thunder), then with a graceful wave of his hand, "no mention of Washington, Lincoln—." Short interrupted: "Next to Gandhi I regard Lenin as the most influential man in the past hundred years." Applause from the audience greeted this statement.

Sullivan was asked, when he began to talk, whom he represented. "The Citizens Associations of the District." The interrogation continued: "All of them?" "Yes." During his remarks, slips of paper were sent up to Chairman Kennedy by various citizens' groups advising that Sullivan did not represent them. Kennedy again asked him if he represented all the citizens' associations of the District. He again said "Yes," though in a chastened tone of voice. This was too much. A woman jumped up in the audience and shouted: "Mr. Chairman, that is not the truth. He does not represent my Association."

General Amos Fries followed Sullivan. He began by saying that he believed in free speech, but he made it plain, as he proceeded, that by freedom of speech he meant freedom to say what he, the General, thought proper to say. Sisson asked him savagely at one point, "Who do you think is best qualified to lay down educational courses in the schools—yourself, an ex-army officer, or the educators?" Fries weakly replied that he once taught school for three years. But perhaps the climax in Fries' appearance came in the following episode. Fries produced the Conclusions and Recommendations of the Commission on the Social Studies of which he stated Superintendent of Schools Ballou to be joint author. Ballou stepped up to the Committee's desk and held a short whispered conversation with the Committee. Sisson then asked Fries: "Is it not true that Dr. Ballou declined to sign the report?" "Yes," admitted General Fries." Did you know at the time you called that book to our attention that Dr. Ballou was not a joint author of that book?" "I did," said Fries. "Yet you brought it to our attention as a book of which Dr. Ballou is the joint author." "I did not feel that I had time to go into that question too closely," answered the General.

E. Brooks Fetty, of the American Legion, opened his speech with the re-mark, "I will be very brief," but the size of his manuscript belied this optimistic assurance, and the manuscript proved correct. His complaint against Dr. Bal-lou and the school board turned out to be that they would not, at his behest, consecrate all of school time to patriotic proceedings but insisted on reserving a little time for such un-American subjects as arithmetic, geography, spelling, and history. Finally his remarks became so personal, so impudent that Chair-man Kennedy interrupted: "I know you would not want to appear in the re-cord as saying that. It will be omitted from the record." That ended the March 2nd meeting.

Nothing more clearly illustrates than the Hearst reporting of this meeting, what utterly false news the Hearst press dishes up for its readers. The Wash-ington Herald (March 3rd) contains the following:

Although the committee patiently sat through seven hours of testimony offered by advocates of the Sisson bill. . . . Its members became suddenly im-patient when opponents of the measure were called. Not content with refusing George E. Sullivan . . . and General Amos Fries . . . ample time to present ar-guments, committee members sought to impugn their integrity.

The facts are that not only Sullivan and those following him, but also those preceding him were cautioned to conserve the Committee's time. The proponents of the Sisson bill did so, but the attackers did not.

Liberals may find encouragement in the hearing on the Sisson bill. Of the five members of a committee who may be assumed to represent the general sentiment of Congress as a whole, all but Mrs. Jenckes recognized the unfair-ness and danger of gag laws. The hearings also brought out that ferment is go-ing on in the minds of Congressmen, equivalent to that in the minds of the ordinary citizen, with respect to the future economic and social status of the nation.

There is, however, little ground for sanguine optimism. That the question of putting a positive quietus upon free speech and thought should be a possi-ble subject for debate after one hundred and fifty years of democracy is indeed disquieting. The attack which the various organizations of professional patriots have made and are still making upon the ideals of American education should not be accepted lightly. The attempt to throttle academic freedom and to en-slave the teaching profession has apparently failed in the national legislative body, but it is far from failing in state legislatures. The attempt should be met not with a defense but with an attack. The teachers of America should launch an attack not only upon the teachers oath laws, not only upon every state and national legislator who supports such laws, but they should launch such a vig-orous attack upon the initiators of the gag-law movement that organized mi-norities will be fearsome of a similar undertaking in the future.

DEMOCRACY, EDUCATION, AND THE CLASS STRUGGLE [*]

John L. Childs

R esponding to a previous article in the journal by John Dewey that dealt with social class, John Childs, a professor and well-known progressive educator at Teachers College, establishes the argument that not only is education not neutral, but "that the teacher always deliberately works to produce one type of personal character and social outlook in the young as opposed to other types, which might be developed." Education is never "a bare, neutral process of inquiry and criticism." It necessarily includes socio-moral values.

According to Childs, the teacher in American classrooms must choose between a worker orientation or a capitalist orientation. In the end, this is a class issue. Childs argues that teachers need to orient themselves to the working class and their needs because they "have a common interest, which is not shared by capitalistically minded owners."

Childs also argues that "the chance for a peaceful, orderly transformation of our economy will be increased, not lessened, by an open alliance of professional groups, including educators, with the working class." In doing so, his viewpoint is more radical than Dewey's, and calls for actions more in line with the editorial board of the journal.

*   *   *

In his article last month Professor Dewey called on educators who believe in an experimentalist philosophy to state definitely what they mean by a class orientation for American education.[1] I am happy to respond to his request. In my opinion the relation of educators to the present struggle of classes in the United States constitutes a problem of growing importance. It merits more serious thought from the members of the educational profession than it has as yet received.

Since Professor Dewey raises the question of the bearing of the philosophy of experimentalism on the class struggle, we may appropriately examine the class concept by applying the experimentalist test of meaning to it. According to this philosophy the best approach to the meaning of any conception is to be had by studying the operations—the definite practices—to which the conception leads. Following this principle we may explore the meanings of the class concept for education by asking what practical bearing its adoption has on the work of the educator. In order to arrive at an adequate understanding of the various meanings involved it is necessary to consider the work of the educator in connection with his two most important roles: as a teacher within the

[*] **Source:** *The Social Frontier*, Volume 2, Number 9, 1936, pp. 274–278.

school; as a member of the educational profession, one of the most important functional groups in contemporary American society, enrolling over one million members.

EDUCATION NOT NEUTRAL

Let us first briefly consider the work of the teacher within the school. By its inherent nature education of the young is a moral undertaking. By moral I mean that all education involves a choice of values, and that the teacher always deliberately works to produce one type of personal character and social outlook in the young as opposed to other types, which might be developed. This choice of educational values can be meaningful only as it is based on an intelligent conception of social welfare. In order to possess vitality, this conception of social welfare in turn must take account of concrete changing life conditions. Thus in actual practice education is never reduced to a bare, neutral process of inquiry and criticism. Of necessity it also includes the socio-moral values, which provide the bases upon which criticism finally, rests. Deliberate, democratic education is rightly interested in the development of capacity for critical judgment in the young. But it is also interested in the positive cultivation of the fundamental dispositions and the sense of values through which this process of critical evaluation operates. Whatever educational significance the term "faith in intelligence" may have, therefore, it cannot be soundly interpreted to mean social neutrality.

I suspect that Professor Dewey agrees to this because in his article he states that he is not "urging that teachers be 'neutral'—an impossibility in any case." But if education by its very nature includes social presuppositions, the real contrast can never be between education and a social outlook: it is rather between rival social outlooks. Today the critical issue for American education is what the nature of its social point of view should be.

THE FORCED OPTION—ONE BETWEEN CONFLICTING CLASS ORIENTATIONS

Broadly speaking, two socio-economic orientations are now competing for acceptance in American life. One tends in the direction of the democratic, collective, planned control of production to meet community needs. The other tends to serve primarily the interests of a small class of owners through a controlled form of capitalism, which in effect, if not by intention, involves a restriction of production. It is a mistake to suppose that democracy constitutes a third alternative. The crucial problem for American life is which of these two economic forms democracy is to assume. Some of the important consequences for education and society involved in this choice of orientation were admirably summarized by Professor Dewey in one of his earlier pages in *The Social Frontier*: "Let it he admitted, as is stated in the comments of the editors, that the school must have some social orientation. Let it be admitted that this necessity, 'is implicit in the nature of education, in the personality of the teacher, in the life of the school, in the relation of pupils to pupils and pupils to teachers, in the administrative organization and arrangements, in the very architecture of the school building'—as well as in the subject-matter taught. And when I say, 'admitted,' I do not mean admitted for the sake of argument, but admitted as the fact of the situation, and a fact that cannot be escaped."

Let it be admitted also, and for the same reason, that broadly speaking the teaching profession is now faced with choice between two social orientations. Of these two orientations, one looks to the past, the other to the future. And this is but a part of the story. That which looks to the past, looks also by the necessities of the situation to the interests of a small class having a highly privileged position maintained at the expense of the masses. That which looks to the future is in line with the scientific, technological, and industrial forces of the present, and, what is more, it is in the interest of the freedom, security, and cultural development of the masses. Everything that the editors say about the reality of the contrast between these opposed interests and groups, I believe to be also true. In one-way or another, teachers as a body and individually do and must make a choice between these opposed social orientations and all they practically imply.[2]

As Professor Dewey emphasized in his discussion last month, the terms in a social situation do not uniquely determine the method of dealing with that situation. It is equally important to remember, however, that the character of any concrete historical situation does necessarily condition what can be done. It is mere wishful thinking to suppose that all of the factors in present industrial society are plastic through and through. For those of us who hold the democratic purpose, some of these factors are now so fixed that they exercise a definite limiting effect upon both our social goals and the manner in which we must act to achieve them. By stating that a choice between two orientations now confronts American education, Professor Dewey clearly recognizes the partially coercive character of present interdependent industrial society.

In this situation we discover what I consider to be the most fundamental meaning of the class concept for the work of the educator within the school. The teacher who accepts it chooses deliberately one of the two orientations described in the above statement by Professor Dewey. To be sure, a sense of far-reaching social values and conceptions prompts the teacher to select this orientation. But it is a choice between the orientations of two economic classes nonetheless: that of the owners is rejected; that of the workers is adopted. This workers' orientation, moreover, is regarded by a numerically small, but economically and culturally powerful, class as hostile to the interests for which it is prepared to struggle. It is also evident that the teacher who takes the orientation which "is in line with the scientific, technological, and industrial forces of the present," which "looks to the future," and which "is in the interest of the freedom, security, and cultural development of the masses" encounters the opposition of the property class.

I do not believe the opposition of this class is to be dispelled by calling this workers' orientation a social, rather than a class orientation. The owners are too intelligent and pragmatic to be satisfied in this manner. Their concern is not with names, but with practical consequences. They are fully aware that the teacher who consciously chooses the orientation toward an economy in which production is for community use and not for private profit and personal power no longer serves in the classroom as the apologist for the historic capitalist system. His interpretation of American life is henceforth controlled by a different set of social presuppositions, and this is what the owner class does not want. "Constitutionalism," "loyalty oaths," and similar drives to control the schools are concrete manifestations of this repressive class action.

THE "OPERATIONAL" MEANING OF CLASS ORIENTATION IN THE SCHOOLROOM

From the standpoint of democratic educational procedure, what are the consequences of choosing the orientation of the working class as contrasted with that of the capitalist class? Is there anything in the workers' orientation, which prevents the teacher who accepts it from acting as a genuine educator? On the other hand, is there anything in the capitalist orientation which guarantees that a teacher who holds it will act as a genuine educator? To ask these questions is to answer them. I find nothing in the logic either of the present social situation, or in the nature of the educative process which makes "education a mere matter of inculcation—in short of agitation and propaganda" simply because one takes the workers' orientation as opposed to that of the owners. No educator, be his class orientation that of capitalist or worker, who has respect for intelligence and for the minds of his pupils, will seek merely to indoctrinate the young in the position he personally holds. Neither will he attempt to lead them to conclusions without giving them opportunity to study the data on which these conclusions are based. He will strive to make as objective historical, sociological, and ethical analyses of American culture as possible. He will explore present social conditions and conflicts so that the facts and values involved in them will be uncovered. He will also endeavor to introduce students as adequately as possible to contrasting programs for dealing with these difficulties. In short, if he is an educator fit to be called an educator, he will not permit his general point of view to "cook" his facts, or his examination of interpretations other than his own, or his educational method. His aim will be to develop intelligence, not to impose conclusions.

It is equally certain, however, that his social orientation will enter into what he does. Inevitably the point of view held will condition to some extent the problems which are considered significant and worthy of study, the perspective from which historical events are examined, and the criteria by which social affairs are evaluated. This holds for every educator regardless of his particular social orientation. If we are to judge between these two orientations it can be done only by asking which is the more intelligent in light of actual conditions, and which better articulates the democratic aspirations of the American people. In any event, one of these orientations will condition the work of the teacher. A democratic society, which believes in the social value of criticism, should not condemn an educator merely because his orientation now varies from the historic capitalist outlook.

I hold with Professor Dewey that the teacher is responsible for more than intellectual growth. He also is responsible for "the development of attitudes and convictions." As educator he is interested in the cultivation of the disposition to rely upon intellectual and educational means as opposed to reliance upon sheer force. But educational means are not to be interpreted to imply exclusive reliance upon discussion, conference, and action only by mutual consent. Education is interested to keep conflict on an intellectual and political plane, but it is not concerned to eliminate conflict in all types of situations, It may well be that in a society organized economically so as to result in a conflict between the interests of owners as owners and workers as workers, that the development of intelligence—informed social understanding—will deepen social division. If so, the responsibility for this result should not be placed primarily with the educator, but with the economic and legal arrangements that breed this conflict of interests. The teacher should not be asked to suppress important data about the injustices and weaknesses of the present economic system merely because the dissemination of this information may arouse opposition to the continuance of that system.

LABOR AND THE LARGER INTERESTS
OF THE EDUCATIONAL PROFESSION

The educator's task, moreover, is not limited to what he does in the classroom. He also shares a responsibility for the general welfare of public education in the United States. The class concept has implications for the manner in which this wider responsibility is now to be discharged. American history shows that members of the educational profession played a notable part in the struggle for a free, tax-supported school system. They also pioneered in broadening the curriculum by helping the general lay public to understand the importance of health, recreational, art, and vocational programs in the public school. So have they struggled to keep the schools open intellectually. On many occasions the members of the educational profession have resisted pressure groups who were seeking either to limit the freedom of intellectual inquiry, or to make the schools propagandist tools for special interests. Leadership in struggles of this type is now recognized as an inherent part of the responsibility of the educational profession.

This struggle for academic freedom and adequate support for the public school is also related to the deepening conflict of class interests in American society. The wealthy owning class, which to a very considerable extent educates its children in private schools, is, as a class, more interested in tax economy than in adequate support for the public schools. There is also a connection between the classes whose interest in the maintenance of profit leads it to restrict production and the groups who are seeking to curb intellectual freedom in the schools. Having served for a number of years as a member of the Committee on Academic Freedom of the Civil Liberties Union, I have no doubt about this connection. Even well-meaning patriotic groups are often manipulated by members of this owner class to undertake repressive programs.

In pointing to this positive correlation between the interests of the owning class and efforts to sabotage the work of public education, I do not imply that this correlation is one hundred per cent. Unfortunately many whose economic role places them in the workers' class often share in these repressive drives. It is interesting, however, to note the extent to which labor has made the cause of public education its own cause. This contrast between the attitude of the owner and the worker toward the public school is sharpened by present economic tendencies. Many educational administrators and teaching groups who do not hold the workers' orientation have, nevertheless, been obliged by their practical experiences in city and state struggles for the public school to distinguish between the owning and the working class.

I am not implying that Professor Dewey is unmindful of this connection between the cause of the workers and the cause of public education. For years he served as a leader in the Teachers Union, and often has urged teachers to become members of the organized labor movement of the United States. In one of his earlier pages in *The Social Frontier* he wrote: "   An open alliance of teachers with workers would greatly strengthen the educational as well as the economic position of the teaching body. It is a historic fact that the movement for free public education had one of its most influential sources in the demands of the workers of the country who were engaged in pursuits regarded as non-intellectual. When a school system has been in difficulties it has always drawn its strongest support from this source. . . ."

Organization among teachers is imperatively needed to stem the rising tide of brutal reaction and intimidation. But so many teachers are timid because of "hostages to fortune" that it is foolish to suppose that this organization will be adequate unless it is supported by wider and deeper organization with others, who have a common interest in the reconstruction of the present regime of production for personal gain and personal power.[3]

This statement by Professor Dewey suggests what I consider to be a second important implication of the class concept for education. An "open alliance" with the workers who share with educators "a common interest in the reconstruction of the present regime of production for personal gain and personal power," seems to me to involve more than an orientation in sympathy toward the working class. It suggests to me that educators and the rest of the working class have a common interest, which is not shared by capitalistically minded owners. It should also be emphasized that orientation by the class interest of the workers need not imply that the educator is not controlled by interests other than those which the workers now consciously hold.

But regardless of the particular phrase chosen to describe the relation, I support Professor Dewey's contention that this "open-alliance" of educators and workers is now highly desirable. To the extent that meanings are found in practices here also we apparently mean the same thing. It is significant that educators who minimize the fact of the class struggle, for the most part, oppose the affiliation of the teachers with labor. These educators hold that teachers should stand with the public as a whole, and not identify themselves with a part of the public, not even with as important a part as that of the working class.

EDUCATIONAL NEEDS AS SOCIO-POLITICAL DEMANDS

Finally, educators are citizens. As citizens, they have the right and the responsibility to share in determining through political action what the future of American life is to be. It is important that the educator in his role as citizen should consider the bearing of the conflict of economic classes upon the cause of public education with which he is professionally identified. This is particularly true since the interests of the teacher and the interest of public education are so inextricably bound together. Educational interests such as the following have every right under present conditions of potential abundance to be turned into insistent socio-political demands:

1. A more adequate material support for public education, which would include more and better-equipped buildings and playgrounds, the restoration of many educational services, which have been either curtailed or eliminated since the depression, and the equalization of educational opportunity in the nation by means of federal aid.

2. More and better-trained teachers, adequately paid, who enjoy reasonable economic and academic security.

3. A society so planned and controlled that it can make the maximum social use of the resources of science and technology, and which recognizes that orderly social improvement involves the experimental use of intelligence in all realms. Both as educator and citizen, the teacher who has faith in intelligence must oppose economic practices, which are now resulting in the frustration of science.

4. A society so organized that it can place in socially useful tasks the young who are educated in the schools.

Fundamental educational needs of this sort are not to be met in a society that continues the anarchy of private competition for profit, which curtails production, and which limits the use of science. Neither are the material and cultural conditions for an abundant life for the mass of the people to be had in a society so managed. The educator thus finds an identity between the broader educational need and the democratic social need. To meet these needs a drastic social reconstruction must be undertaken. The necessity for this social reconstruction becomes his controlling hypothesis. He continues to work for many specific reforms, but his deeper interest is in the development of an economic and political movement, which will attain the power to transform the historic economic system of the United States.

His experience also indicates that not all classes in the economic life of the United States are so situated objectively that they will be inclined to favor this fundamental social reconstruction. A small, but economically and politically powerful, class of owners is already taking active measures to forestall it. As this owning class defines its interests and the national need, it believes that capitalism rather than socialized production is the better arrangement. On the other hand, although the great numbers of the population have not as yet consciously accepted the conception of production for use rather than for profit, they are so situated that, as workers, their struggles to care for their needs move them in that direction. Thus, that which is required socially to remove the disabilities of the working class is also that which is required to meet educational and democratic ideals. To this important extent there is an identity between the interests of the educator and the interests of the working class. In this respect the educator is controlled by a class interest.

THE PROGRAM OF A CLASS-ORIENTED, EXPERIMENTALIST EDUCATOR

Confronted with a situation of this sort how does an experimentalist educator who has faith in intelligence and who believes in democracy proceed? In the first place, the fact of a conflict of class interests does not in itself determine his purpose, but obviously if that purpose be to achieve a socialized economy this conflict has profound bearing upon it. It is far too stubborn and important to be ignored.

Secondly, the experimentalist educator will not encourage the preaching of violence and class hatred. His experience teaches him that when passions of this sort are aroused, it is generally chance operating as brute force, and not intelligence, which decides the issue. Under present conditions to pursue such a policy might also lead to a sweeping reaction, which could easily result in some form of fascist control. To the limit of his ability he will seek to develop attitudes and convictions, which are consistent with reliance upon intelligence.

Thirdly, the experimentalist educator will support all movements, which aim to spread information about the changed facts of American life. He will also support all efforts to keep open the avenues of public conference and discussion. He will demand, however, that inquiry be free and that no effort be approved which seeks to conceal or minimize important data in the interest of what is called "good-will."

Fourthly, he will not trust to a "sweet reasonableness" in which "sweetness" in the sense of inaction or weak compromise is more prominent than "reasonable" action to secure socially desirable ends. Nor will he define the democratic way to mean that action is to be taken only by unanimous consent. He will recognize that democracy involves the right of a majority to make its will prevail even if the power of government and law must be utilized to coerce reluctant minorities entrenched in outmoded institutional arrangements. Political democracy is not to be opposed to engaging in-group and class struggles. Historically, democracy has served as a means for resolving social conflicts by peaceful means rather than by violence. It has sought to invent institutions for facilitating and rationalizing this process of struggle. That this right of criticism extends even to the right to transform socio-economic systems when deemed necessary has always been regarded as authentic American democratic doctrine.

Lastly, he will not allow interest in discussion and dissemination of information to keep him from cooperating in the organization of a movement, which seeks to give political power to his ideals. Honest appraisal of conditions convinces him that certain elements of the population are much more likely to respond to this program for socialization than are others. If, as this movement of workers—farm, factory, office, and professional—gathers momentum, he finds that class cleavages in American life grow sharper, he will not thereby be deterred from continuing his work of political and economic organization. Experimentalism holds that thought requires action to complete itself and action in the social field requires organization if it is to be successful.

For the educator interested in developing an organization resolute enough to carry through the needed social reconstruction, the present conflict of classes presents not only a problem, it also presents a resource. Fortunately, most of our populations are workers whose needs, when comprehended in an adequate socio-political program, will prompt them to carry through the social reconstruction, which both intelligence and democratic values now define as desirable. To entertain this end of drastic social reconstruction but to be unwilling to cooperate in developing the means necessary to achieve it is to be guilty of a most non-experimental mode of behavior.

In sum, the program of the experimentalist educator cannot be exclusively a function of his educational method; it must also be a function of the problem situation, which confronts him. In my opinion, the chance for a peaceful, orderly transformation of our economy will be increased, not lessened, by an open alliance of professional groups, including educators, with the working class. I am unable to understand why Professor Dewey assumed in his article that it is necessary to oppose a class orientation to a social point of view. Under present socio-economic conditions it seems to me that the only adequate social point of view for education is one, which includes as an essential part the conception of the class struggle.

References

[1] John Dewey, "Class Struggle and the Democratic Way," in *The Social Frontier*, May 1936.

[2] John Dewey, "The Crucial Role of Intelligence," in *The Social Frontier*, February 1935.

[3] John Dewey, "United We Shall Stand," in *The Social Frontier*, April 1935.

Poems [*]

Wilfred Eberhart

Wilfred Eberhart was a professor of English in the School of Education at Ohio State University. She contributed a number of poems to *The Social Frontier*. Her poem "The School" directly addresses Counts's belief in the importance of teachers being critical and reflective thinkers. "Bessie Howard, B. Sc. in Ed" talks about a love lost. "Arthur Paine, A. B." talks about the possible long-term effect a teacher might have. "Theodore Einsel, B. S." not only addresses the radicalization of a young teacher and his taking action as a politically engaged teacher, but also the reprisals against him.

The School

On my forehead the words are carved in granite:
Education and morality constitute the force and majesty of free government.
Once in a while I think of them
When the x's and y's have all been squared;
And every red-headed sophomore has read
"Omnius Gallia in partes tres divisa est";
And the chromium coffee urns in the cafeteria
Have their four o'clock polish;
And the hammers have stopped tapping and
The saws buzz-buzzing in the basement shops.
There must be a meaning hidden somewhere
In the words that are carved on my forehead.

Bessie Howard, B. Sc. in Ed

Dewey and James, Froebel and Herbart
Are all tangled up for me in my memories of Dave Lewis.
I saw Dave's brown hair and laughing eyes
On every page of every book assigned for Education III.
When Dave went to New York I knew that I would never marry.
There is some phrase about "activity leading to further activity"
That beats through my brain
When the study hall drowses,
And another that has to do with "purposeful living"—
I forget just what.

Source: *The Social Frontier*, Volume 3, Number 10, 1936, p. 16.

Arthur Paine, A. B.

I came to Steelton from the Green Mountains
Where the first Arthur Paine laid down Pilgrim's Progress
To take up arms with Ethan Allen.
They think that I am strange because I know
The first canto of The Faerie Queen by heart
And would rather read Addison and Steele
Than Walter Winchell. Let them.
Six years ago John Matthews was my pupil;
Yesterday I received from the Harvard Press
His monograph on Chaucer: A Clerk Ther Was.

Theodore Einsel, B. S.

My father wanted me to be a doctor.
I read Karl Marx one spring night
In the college library and the world turned upside down.
Last year the American Legion and the D.A.R.
Wanted me fired for what I taught in social science. They could prove nothing beyond
    my saying that War is inevitable under a capitalistic system.
History says that better than I do.
I have seen how the mills turn away the men past
forty,
And how the bread lines stand in the side streets.
Once a girl fainted from hunger when I called on her to recite.
Perhaps Lincoln would understand how I feel.
He hated slavery.

SURVEY OF TEACHERS AND THEIR POLITICAL OPINIONS[*]

Congress of the United States, House of Representatives

Loyalty Oaths were widely introduced in the United States during the Civil War. During Reconstruction, they were required of all people wanting to hold federal, state or local political offices. By the mid-1930s, there was a widespread belief among conservative groups that teachers should be required to take a loyalty oath before they could be employed. In June 1935, Thomas L. Blanton, a Texas congressman and member of the Appropriations Committee, proposed the following loyalty oath for public school teachers. The questionnaire specifically asks whether or not its recipient has read the work of George Counts, Charles Beard and publications such as *The Social Frontier*. It suggests that there was, in fact, a real fear among conservatives that Counts's notion of encouraging teachers to be meaningful social agents was a concern among political conservatives, and not just simply organizations such as the Hearst newspapers.

THOMAS L. BLANTON
17th District, Texas

Member of
Committee on Appropriations

CONGRESS OF THE UNITED STATES
HOUSE OF REPRESENTATIVES
WASHINGTON, D. C.

June 15, 1936.

As Chairman of the Subcommittee handling the District Appropriation Bill, to obviate a hearing and to save you the time and inconvenience of coming before us in person, I request that you kindly give us the following information, filled in by you in the blank spaces provided therefore, and signing same, and return promptly in the inclosed addressed envelope, requiring no postage, namely:

PLEASE STATE: Your present position?_____School?_____ Salary?_____
Do you believe in any of the doctrines of Communism? _____ If so, which? _____;
   Do you approve of Communism being given any favor or support in the schools?_____
Do you believe there is a God?_____ Do you believe in some form of religion? _____
Are you a subscriber to THE SOCIAL FRONTIER? _____; Were you asked to subscribe? _____
   If so, state by whom? _____
Are you a member of the N.E.A.? _____ Since when? _____Who suggested joining? _____
Have you a copy of CONCLUSIONS AND RECOMMENDATIONS? _____; Have you read same?_____
Have you a copy of Count's DARE THE SCHOOL BUILD A NEW SOCIAL ORDER? _____
   Have you read same? _____ Do you approve of same? _____. Do you approve of Dr.
   George S. Counts' writings? _____ Do you approve of Dr. Charles A. Beard's writings? _____
   Have you been to Russia? _____ Did you attend school there?_____
Have you read BOY AND GIRL TRAMPS OF AMERICA by Thomas Minehan?_____ Do you
   approve it?_____ Are you in favor of high school girls reading it?_____ Would you read it
   aloud? _____
Have you read MADE IN RUSSIA? _____. Do you approve of it? _____
Do you approve of SCHOLASTIC as a school magazine for high school students? _____
   Do you know why the School Committee's recommendation to eliminate it from the Washington
   public schools has been held up?_____ If so, why? _____

Very truly yours,

THOMAS L. BLANTON

My answers above are correct.

_____; position: _____

address_____

Teacher Loyalty Oath Form proposed for use in the United States House of Representatives reprinted in *The Social Frontier*.

---

[*] **Source:** Note: This is a facsimile copy of the survey republished by the journal dating June 15, 1936.

Rationality in Education[*]

John Dewey

I n 1936, Robert Maynard Hutchins, the president of the University of Chicago, published a short book entitled *The Higher Learning in America*. Hutchins believed that American higher education was falling into a state of "vocationalism, empiricism and disorder." He proposed the development of a curriculum based around the classics, one which emphasized content rather than context. Dewey's review of Hutchins's book, which was published in two separate issues of the journal (December 1936 and January 1937) provides an alternative perspective, one which emphasizes "the primary place of experience, experimental method, and integral connection with practice in determination of knowledge and the auxiliary role of what is termed Reason and Intellect in the classic tradition." Hutchins responded to Dewey's critique in the February 1937 issue of the journal, and in turn, Dewey responded to Hutchins's comments in the following issue (March 1937). The debate became one of the most important intellectual arguments of the 1930s, and is still being debated today.

*   *   *

It happens that in the last few weeks I have been reading two books, both published this year, one written by an Englishman and one by an American. These books are superficially extraordinarily similar and fundamentally extraordinarily different. The two books are Lancelot Hogben's *The Retreat from Reason* and President Hutchins' *The Higher Learning in America*. Both of them are brief, one consisting of eighty-two pages, the other of one hundred and nineteen pages. Both books present material first given in public addresses. Both deal with basic educational problems in relation to contemporary conditions. Both are troubled deeply about education as it now exists and about contemporary life. Both are concerned with the place of reason and understanding in education and in life, Professor Hogben being profoundly affected by the eclipse of intelligence characteristic of present society and President Hutchins saying that the "most important job that can be performed in the United States is first to establish higher education on a rational basis, and second, to make our people understand it." Both books deserve the most serious attention and study on the part of educators.

---

* **Source:** *The Social Frontier*, Volume 3, Number 12, 1936, pp. 71–73.

THE NATURE OF RATIONALITY

At this point similarity ceases, save that there is some degree of agreement in spirit, if not in words, as to the causes that have occasioned our present ills. The profound difference between the two books, a difference which leads them to opposite conclusions, lies in the conceptions respectively entertained by the two men as to the nature of what both call by the same name – Reason. Mr. Hutchins looks to Plato, Aristotle, and St. Thomas Aquinas in order to discover the nature of Reason and its modes of operation; Mr. Hogben looks to the activities of experimental science as the place in which to discover its real nature. To Mr. Hutchins the sciences represent in the main the unmitigated empiricism which is a great curse of modern life, while to Mr. Hogben the conceptions and methods which Mr. Hutchins takes to be the true and final definition of rationality are obscurantist and fatally reactionary, while their survival in economic theory and other branches of social "science" is the source of intellectual irrelevance of the latter to the fundamental problems of our present culture. Indeed, these disciplines are more than irrelevant and futile. They are literally terrible in their distraction of social intelligence and activity from genuine social problems and from the only methods by which the problems can be met.

This basic difference reflects itself in the authors' treatment of every aspect of education and social culture, both in themselves and in their connection with one another. Of these aspects I select three for special consideration: the constitution of human nature, the relation of theory and action, and the method of the working and development of "reason."

THE ELEMENTS OF HUMAN NATURE

President Hutchins is quite sure that the elements of human nature are fixed and constant. They "are the same in any time and place." One great business of education is "to draw out the elements of our common human nature." "The truth is everywhere the same." Hence, omitting details, "the heart of education will be, if education is rightly understood, the same at any time, in any place, under any political, social, or economic conditions." Mr. Hogben emphasizes equally common elements in human nature. But these elements are *needs*, and therefore the first questions to be considered "are whether the common needs of men as members of the same species, phylum, and type of matter, are at present satisfied, what resources for satisfying them exist, and how far these resources are used." Moreover, the needs in question are growing, not fixed; the needs for food, for protection, for reproduction, for example, are always the same in the abstract, but in the concrete they and the means of satisfying them change their content with every change in science, technology, and social institutions.

KNOWLEDGE AND ACTION

The bearing of this difference upon the relation of theory and social practice is close and direct. President Hutchins feels strongly that the invasion of vocationalism is the great curse of contemporary education. Mr. Hogben would agree as far as by vocational "we usually mean that [which] helps us gain a livelihood irrespective of the social usefulness of the occupation chosen." But the isolation of existing education, taken generally, from connection with social usefulness in distinction from personal pecuniary advancement, is the chief ground of his criticism of that education. The exaltation of knowledge as something too "pure" to be contaminated by contact with human needs and the resources available for satisfying them, he puts on the same level as the prostitution of learning to serve those needs of individuals that are due to the existence of competitive, acquisitive, pecuniary economic-social institutions and ideals – if they can be called ideals. He quotes with approval the saying of Bacon that "the true and lawful goal of science is to endow life with new powers and inventions"; that of Boyle to value "knowledge save as it tends to use," and of Thomas Huxley, "the great end of life is not knowledge but action."

The educational implications of this position contrast with the conclusion which President Hutchins logically draws from his conception of the nature of knowledge and action in their relations to one another. Higher education is to be purified and reformed according to him by complete separation of general and "liberal" education from professional and technical education. The student having exclusively acquired in the liberal college the basic principles of knowledge in a purely theoretical way and having thereby learned "correct thinking," will later proceed to studies that prepare him exclusively for some line of practical activity.[1] Moreover, even in the latter there will be as little connection with "experience" as possible, later practical life supplying the factor of experience, which Aristotle and St. Thomas have already shown to be merely empirical, to be nonrational save as parts of it may be deductively derived from the eternal first principles of rational knowledge.

REASONS AND METHOD OF REASON

Mr. Hogben is himself a scientist of standing as well as a humanist in the only sense in which I can attach meaning to that much abused word. I should give a totally wrong impression if what I have quoted from him indicates that he has a low conception of the value of knowledge and the search for it. On the contrary, the idea of the intimate connection that exists between the very nature of knowledge and such action as is socially useful (rather than socially harmful) carries with it the conclusion that students would obtain more knowledge in a more significant way and have a deeper and more enduring apprehension of the meaning of truth, if the facts and ideas acquired in school had some vital connection with basic social needs, with the resources available for common satisfaction of them, and with an understanding of the forces that now prevent these resources from being used. The methods of getting knowledge are to him best exemplified in the natural sciences and most badly represented in the present methods of the so-called social sciences. He calls, therefore, for more science, taught very differently from the way in which it is now taught; for the necessity of science in the education of those who are to control, directly and indirectly, political life; and for the closest association between the teaching of human history and the course of scientific advance. While he does not discuss the question of "truth," I take it that he would agree that "truth is the same everywhere," though he might well be chary of speaking of the truth. But just because truth is so important, the methods of arriving at it are the things of primary importance in education and in life.

To President Hutchins on the contrary truth only needs to be taught and learned. Somehow or other it is there, and there is something in existence called the Intellect that is ready to apprehend it. *The* truth is embodied in "permanent studies" as distinct from progressive studies. As with the great masters, Plato, Aristotle, and St. Thomas, the eternal and the changing are in sharp opposition to each other. And there is no doubt as to what are the permanent studies with permanent content. They are the three arts, grammar, rhetoric, and logic, which constituted the *trivia* of the university in those medieval days when knowledge was organized and universities *were* universities — though the historian might say that they were most of all professional schools. Then there are the classics, though not necessarily taught in the original language, and mathematics; and "of the mathematical studies chiefly those that use the type of exposition that Euclid employed" — a somewhat curious statement in view of the fact that contemporary logicians recognize the many logical defects in the Euclidean exposition, while working scientists would agree, I think, that of all branches of mathematics it is the one that is of least importance in their pursuits. As for science, "the Physics of Aristotle, which deals with change and motion in nature, is fundamental to the natural sciences and to medicine." In contrast with these permanent studies, what is now called the "scientific spirit" consists in gathering facts indiscriminately and hoping for the best. The basis and keystone of the entire educational arch is metaphysics, which it would appear, though no specimens are given, is also an established system of permanent truths. It is concerned in any case with "things highest by nature, first principles, and first causes."

It is not to be inferred that all "empirical" studies are excluded by President Hutchins. Information, historical and current, may be introduced in the degree that "such data illustrate or confirm principles or assist in their development." But all other studies including the natural and social sciences are to be pursued in "subordination" to the "hierarchy of truths." These empirical studies would proceed, in accord with the classic logic of antiquity and the middle ages, "from first principles to whatever recent observations are significant in understanding them."[2]

THE PROBLEM

In a subsequent article I propose to discuss some of the definitely educational questions raised by the two conflicting conceptions presented in these two books. In this article I have presented a problem in very general outline. I agree with both of the writers in holding that present education is disordered and confused. The problem as to the direction in which we shall seek for order and clarity is the most important question facing education and educators today. Teachers and administrators are not given to asking what the nature of knowledge is, as distinct from the subject-matter that is taken to be known, nor by what methods knowledge is genuinely attained—as distinct from the methods by which the facts and ideas that are taken to be known shall be taught and learned. These two books taken together serve to present the problem in its two aspects with extraordinary clarity. Until educators have faced the problem and made an intelligent choice between the contrasting conceptions represented in these two books, I see no great hope for unified progress in the reorganization of studies and methods in the schools.

References

1. The completeness of the separation set up is indicated by such passages as the following: "I concede the probable necessity in some fields of practical training which the young man or woman should have before being permitted to engage in the independent practice of a profession. Since by definition this training cannot be intellectual, and since by definition a university must be intellectual, this type of specific training for specific jobs cannot be conducted as part of the university's work."
2. Mr. Hogben's idea about such methods may be gathered from the following quotation, which in its context refers to economics as deduced from "rational" first principles: "We can only conclude that economics, as studied in our uni-

versities, is the astrology of the Machine Age; it provides the same kind of intellectual relief as chess, in which success depends entirely on knowing the initial definition of moves and processes of checking, casting, etc. . . . In science the final arbiter is not the self-evidence of the initial statement, nor the facade of flawless logic that conceals it. A scientific law embodies a recipe for doing something, and its final validation rests in the domain of action."

PRESIDENT HUTCHINS' PROPOSALS TO REMAKE HIGHER EDUCATION [*]

John Dewey

In the January 1936 issue, Dewey concludes his review of Robert Maynard Hutchins's *The Higher Learning in America.* The debate between Hutchins and Dewey becomes one of the major discussions of the twentieth century about what should be the nature and purpose of higher education in the United States.

*   *   *

THE EXISTING DISORDER

President Hutchins' book [*The Higher Learning in America*, by Robert Maynard Hutchins. The Yale Press, New Haven, 1936.] consists of two parts. One of them is a critical discussion of the plight of education in this country, with especial reference to colleges and universities. The other is a plan for the thorough remaking of education. This second part is again divided. It opens with an analysis of the meaning of general or liberal education, and is followed by an application of the conclusions reached to reconstruction of education in existing colleges and universities. The criticism of the present situation is trenchant. "The most striking fact about the higher learning in America is the confusion that besets it." The college of liberal arts is partly high school, partly university, partly general, partly special. The university consisting of graduate work for the master's and doctor's degree, and of a group of professional schools, is no better off. The universities are not only non-intellectual but they are anti-intellectual.

There then follows a diagnosis of the disease of "disunity, discord, and disorder." Fundamentally, the ailment proceeds from too ready response of universities to immediate demands of the American public. This public is moved by love of money, and the higher learning responds to anything that promises to bring money to the college and university whether from donors, student-fees, or state legislatures. The result is that these institutions become public service-stations; and as there is no special tide in public opinion and sentiment, but only a criss-cross of currents, the kind of service that is to be rendered shifts with every change in public whim and interest. Love of money results in demand for large numbers of students, and the presence of large numbers renders training even more indiscriminate in order to meet the demands of united heterogeneous groups.

[*] **Source:** *The Social Frontier*, Volume 3, Number 22, 1937, pp. 103–104.

Another symptom of our quick response to immediate and often passing public desires is seen in the effect upon higher education of the popular notion of democracy. This notion, although confused, encourages the belief that everybody should have the same chance of getting higher education, and everybody should have just the kind of education he happens to want. As against this view, President Hutchins holds that the responsibility of the public for providing education ends properly at the sophomore year of college, and after that point education should be given only to those who have demonstrated special capacity. (Incidentally, the author attributes to the false popular idea of democracy the existing perverse system of control of higher institutions by boards of trustees.)

The third major cause of our educational disorder is the erroneous notion of progress. Everything is supposed to be getting better, the future will be better yet. Why not then break with the past? Since in fact the "progress" that has taken place is mainly in material things and techniques, information, more and more and more data, become the demand; and higher learning is swamped by an empiricism that drowns the intellect. Somewhat strangely, the natural sciences are regarded by Mr. Hutchins as the cause and the mirror of this empiricism.

THE REMEDY

One may venture to summarize the evils in relation to their source by saying that they are an excessive regard for practicality, and practicality of a very immediate sort. The essence of the remedy accordingly, is emancipation of higher learning from this practicality, and its devotion to the cultivation of intellectuality for its own sake.

Many readers will share my opinion that Mr. Hutchins has shrewdly pointed out many evils attending the aimlessness of our present educational scheme, and will join in his desire that higher institutions become "centers of creative thought." So strong will be their sympathies that they may overlook the essence of the remedy, namely, his conception of the nature of intellectuality or rationality. This conception is characterized by two dominant traits. The first, as I pointed out in an article in the December number of this journal, is belief in the existence of fixed and eternal authoritative principles as truths that are not to be questioned. "Real unity can be achieved only by a hierarchy of truths which shows us which are fundamental and which are subsidiary." The hierarchy must be already there, or else it could not show us. The other point is not so explicitly stated. But it does not require much reading between the lines to see the remedy proposed rests upon a belief that since evils have come from surrender to shifting currents of public sentiment, the remedy is to be found in the greatest possible aloofness of higher learning from contemporary social life. This conception is explicitly seen in the constant divorce set up between intellect and practice, and between intellect and "experience."

I shall not stop to inquire whether such a divorce, if it is established, will be conducive to creative intellectual work, inviting as is the topic. I content myself with pointing out that—admitting that many present ills come from surrender of educational institutions to immediate social pressures—the facts are open to another interpretation with respect to educational policy. The policy of aloofness amounts fundamentally to acceptance of a popular American slogan, "Safety first." It would seem, on the other hand, as if the facts stated about the evil effects of our love of money should invite attention on the part of institutions devoted to love of truth for its own sake to the economic institutions that have produced this overweening love, and to their social consequences in other matters than the temper of educational institutions; and attention to the means available for changing this state of things. The immediate effect of such attention would probably be withdrawal of donations of money. But for an institution supposedly devoted to truth, a policy of complete withdrawal, however safe, hardly seems the way out. I have given but one illustration. I hope it may suggest a principle widely applicable. Escape from present evil contemporary social tendencies may require something more than escape. It may demand study of social needs and social potentialities of enduring time span. President Hutchins' discussion is noteworthy for complete absence of any reference to this alternative method of educational reconstruction. It is conceivable that educational reconstruction cannot be accomplished without a social reconstruction in which higher education has a part to play.

AUTHORITY AND TRUTH

There are indications that Mr. Hutchins would not take kindly to labeling the other phase of this remedial plan "authoritarian." But any scheme based on the existence of ultimate first principles, with their dependent hierarchy of subsidiary principles, does not escape authoritarianism by calling the principles "truths." I would not intimate that the author has any sympathy with fascism. But basically his idea as to the proper course to be taken is akin to the distrust of freedom and the consequent appeal to some fixed authority that is now overrunning the world. There is implicit in every assertion of fixed and eternal first truths the necessity for some human authority to decide, in this world of conflicts, just what these truths are and how they shall be taught. This problem is conveniently ignored. Doubtless much may be said for selecting Aristotle and St. Thomas as competent promulgators of first truths. But it took the authority of a powerful ecclesiastic organization to secure their wide recognition. Others may prefer Hegel, or Karl Marx, or even Mussolini as the seers of first truths; and there are those who prefer Nazism. As far as I can see, President Hutchins has completely evaded the problem of who is to determine the definite truths that constitute the hierarchy.

In view of the emphasis given by our author to the subject of logic, it is pertinent to raise the question of how far institutions can become centers of creative thought, if in their management it is assumed that fundamental truths and the hierarchy of truth are already known. The assumption that merely by learning pre-existent truths, students will become even students, much less capable of independent creative thought, is one that demands considerable logical inquiry. President Hutchins' contempt for science as merely empirical perhaps accounts for his complete acceptance of the doctrine of formal discipline. But it is difficult to account for complete neglect of the place of the natural sciences in his educational scheme (apart from possible limitations of his own education) save on the score of a feeling, perhaps subconscious, that their recognition is so hostile to the whole scheme of prescribed antecedent first truths that it would be fatal to the educational plan he proposes to give them an important place. Considering, however, that their rise has already created a revolution in the old logic, and that they now afford the best existing patterns of controlled inquiry in search for truth, there will be others besides myself who will conclude that President Hutchins' policy of reform by withdrawal from everything that smacks of modernity and contemporaneousness is not after all the road to the kind of intellectuality that will remedy the evils he so vividly depicts.

The constant appeal of President Hutchins to Plato, Aristotle, and St. Thomas urgently calls for a very different interpretation from that which is given it. Their work is significant precisely because it does not represent withdrawal from the science and social affairs of their own times. On the contrary, each of them represents a genuine and profound attempt to discover and present in organized form the meaning of the science and the institutions that existed in their historic periods. The real conclusion to be drawn is that the task of higher learning at present is to accomplish a similar work for the confused and disordered conditions of our own day. The sciences have changed enormously since these men performed their task, both in logical method and in results. We live in a different social medium. It is astounding that anyone should suppose that a return to the conceptions and methods of these writers would do for the present situation what they did for the Greek and Medieval eras. The cure for surrender of higher learning to immediate and transitory pressures is not monastic seclusion. Higher learning can become intellectually vital only by coming to that close grip with our contemporary science and contemporary social affairs which Plato, Aristotle, and St. Thomas exemplify in their respective ways.

THE CRISIS IN CONTEMPORARY GRAMMAR, RHETORIC, AND MR. DEWEY *

Robert M. Hutchins

utchins' responds in this article to Dewey's critique of *The Higher Learning in America* in a legalistic and technical manner, one which Dewey describes as adopting " the method of legal forensics." The debate between them is essentially one in which the conservative "canon" is opposed to the pragmatist's "progressive" response to the real world. As mentioned earlier, it is an ongoing debate, and like matters of faith not likely to be resolved in the future.

*   *   *

Mr. John Dewey has devoted much of two recent articles in *The Social Frontier* to my book, *The Higher Learning in America*. The editors of The Social Frontier have asked me to reply to Mr. Dewey. This I am unable to do, in any real sense, for Mr. Dewey has stated my position in such a way as to lead me to think that I cannot write, and has stated his own in such a way as to make me suspect that I cannot read.

Mr. Dewey says (1) that I look to Plato, Aristotle, and Aquinas; (2) that I am anti-scientific; (3) that I am for withdrawing from the world; and (4) that I am authoritarian.

(1) "Mr. Hutchins looks to Plato, Aristotle, and Aquinas. . . ."

(a) Mr. Hutchins also looks to Sir R. W. Livingstone, p. 25; Dean C. H. Wilkinson, p. 54; Newman, p. 63; Shorey, p. 64; Whewell, p. 73; Locke, p. 76; Nicholas Murray Butler, p. 80; De Tocqueville, p. 90; Judge Learned Hand, p. 92; Kant, p. 99; and Lenin, p. 105.

(b) If I had not already done so in an earlier book, I should have looked to Mr. Dewey. In *No Friendly Voice*, p. 39, I said, "Mr. C. I. Lewis had written that 'Professor Dewey seems to view such abstractionism in science as a defect—something unnecessary—but always regrettable.' Mr. Dewey replied: 'I fear that on occasion I may so have written as to give this impression. I am glad therefore to have the opportunity of saying that this is not my actual position. Abstraction is the heart of thought; there is no other way ... to control and enrich concrete experience except through an intermediate flight of thought with conceptions, relata, abstractions. . . . I wish to agree also with Mr. Lewis that the need of the social sciences at present is precisely such abstractions as will get their unwieldy elephants into box-cars that will move on rails arrived at by

* **Source:** *The Social Frontier*, Volume 3, Number 23, 1937, p. 137–139.

other abstractions. What is to be regretted is, to my mind, the tendency of many inquirers in the field of human affairs to be over-awed by the abstractions of the physical sciences and hence to fail to develop the conceptions or abstractions appropriate to their own subject-matter.'"

c) If he had made it earlier I should also have looked to Mr. Dewey's address before the Progressive Education Association, November 13, 1936, in which he said, according to the New York *Herald-Tribune*, "Even social studies suffer greatly from that dead hand of worship of information that still grips the schools."

(d) In the second of his articles in *The Social Frontier* Mr. Dewey refers to Plato, Aristotle, and Aquinas and their work as significant, genuine, profound, etc. He says: "Higher learning can become intellectually vital only by coming to that close grip with our contemporary science and contemporary social affairs which Plato, Aristotle and St. Thomas exemplify in their respective ways."

If we are to perform in our own day the work that Plato, Aristotle, and Aquinas performed in theirs, should we not know what they did and how they did it? My position as to the significance of these writers is precisely that (if I understand it) of Mr. Dewey. What they did was to restudy, rework, and revitalize the intellectual tradition they inherited for the purpose of understanding the contemporary world. We must do the same.

(2) "President Hutchins' contempt for science as merely empirical . . . complete neglect of the place of the natural sciences in his educational scheme. . . ."

(a) The faculty of natural science is one-third of the university I propose in *The Higher Learning in America*, Chapter IV.

(b) At least one-third of the great books of the western world proposed as the basis of general education in Chapter III are in the natural sciences. Mathematics and logic, two disciplines put forth as central in general education in Chapter III, are important to the understanding of natural science and intimately related to it.

(c) Chapter II criticizes engineering schools for their remoteness from departments of natural science and congratulates the newer medical schools on their close association with them.

(d) "I yield to no one in my admiration for and belief in the accumulation of data, the collection of facts, and the advance of the empirical sciences," p. 89.

(e) Pp. 89–94 seem to me to make clear that I am arguing against a misconception of natural science, namely that it is merely collections of data, not against natural science as it actually is.

(3) "The remedy [proposed by Mr. Hutchins] is to be found in the greatest possible aloofness of higher learning from contemporary social life. This con-

ception is explicitly seen in the constant divorce set up between intellect and 'experience'. . . .

It is conceivable that educational reconstruction cannot be accomplished without a social reconstruction in which higher education has a part to play."

(a) "I agree, of course, that any plan of general education must be such as to educate the student for intelligent action." *The Higher Learning in America*, p. 67.

(b) "I know, of course, that thinking cannot proceed divorced from the facts and from experience." Ibid, p. 90.

(c) "We may say in behalf of the Marxists that they at least realize that there is no advance in the speculative realm which does not have practical consequences, and no change in the practical realm which need not be speculatively analyzed." Ibid, p. 91.

(d) "If we can secure a real university in this country and a real program of general education upon which its work can rest, it may be that the character of our civilization may slowly change. It may be that we can outgrow the love of money, that we can get a saner conception of democracy, and that we can even understand the purposes of education. It may be that we can abandon our false notions of progress and utility and that we can come to prefer intelligible organization to the chaos that we mistake for liberty. It is because these things may be that education is important. Upon education our country must pin its hopes of true progress, which involves scientific and technological advance, but under the direction of reason; of true prosperity, which includes external goods but does not overlook those of the soul; and of true liberty, which can exist only in society, and in a society rationally ordered." Ibid, pp. 118–119.

(e) One-third of the university I propose (Ibid, Chapter IV) is the faculty of social science. What does Mr. Dewey think that faculty will study?

(f) At least one-third of the books proposed for study in general education (Ibid, Chapter III) are in the social sciences and history. The discussion of contemporary problems would of course be an integral part of the discussion of these books.

(g) If I am a follower of Aristotle and Aquinas, I must be in Mr. Dewey's view a very poor one: "Lack of experience diminishes our power of taking a comprehensive view of the admitted facts. Hence those who dwell in intimate association with nature and its phenomena grow more and more able to formulate, as the foundation of their theories, principles such as to admit of a wide and coherent development; while those whom devotion to abstract discussions has rendered unobservant of the facts are too ready to dogmatize on the basis of a few observations." Aristotle, *De Generatione et Corruptione*, 1, 2, 316a 5–12.

"The truth in practical matters is discerned from the facts of life." Aristotle, *Ethics*, 1–179a.

"Knowledge in natural science must be terminated at sense in order that we may judge concerning natural things in the manner according to which sense demonstrates them . . . and he who neglects sense in natural questions falls into error." Aquinas, *De Trinitate Boetii*, Q. 6, Art. 2.

"For me human intellect is measured by things, so that a human concept is not true by reason of itself, but by reason of its being consonant with things, since an opinion is true or false according as it answers to the reality." Aquinas, *Summa Theologica*. Part I of Part II, Q. 93, Art. 1, Reply Obj. 3.

(4) "Fixed and eternal authoritative principles [are regarded by Mr. Hutchins] as truths that are not to be questioned. . . . But any scheme based on the existence of ultimate first principles, with their dependent hierarchy of subsidiary principles, does not escape authoritarianism by calling the principles 'truths.' I would not intimate that the author has any sympathy with fascism. But basically his idea . . . is akin to the distrust of freedom and the consequent appeal to some fixed authority that is now overrunning the world. There is implicit in every assertion of fixed and eternal first truths the necessity for some human authority to decide . . . just what these truths are and how they shall be taught. This problem is conveniently ignored. . . ."

(a) The words "fixed" and "eternal" are Mr. Dewey's; I do not apply them to principles or truths in my book.

(b) There is no suggestion anywhere in the book that principles are not to be questioned. On the contrary, "Research in the sense of the development, elaboration, and refinement of principles together with the collection and use of empirical materials to aid in these processes is one of the highest activities of a university and one in which all its professors should be engaged." *The Higher Learning in America*, p. 90.

(c) "I am not here arguing for any specific theological or metaphysical system. I am insisting that consciously or unconsciously we are always trying to get one. I suggest that we shall get a better one if we recognize explicitly the need for one and try to get the most rational one we can. We are, as a matter of fact, living today by the haphazard, accidental, shifting shreds of a theology and metaphysics to which we cling because we must cling to something." Ibid, p. 105.

(d) Today the faculties decide what the curriculum shall be. These human authorities would continue to do so.

(e) Is Mr. Dewey saying that there should not be a faculty of metaphysics? If so, is it because there is no such thing as metaphysics or because there are no metaphysicians? Would a university, which had a faculty of philosophy, be more or less authoritarian than one which had not and in which only the natural and social sciences were studied and taught?

(f) Mr. Dewey's dexterous intimation that I am a fascist in result if not in intention (made more dexterous by his remark that he is making no such intimation) suggests the desirability of the educational reforms I have proposed. A graduate of my hypothetical university writing for his fellow-alumni would know that such observations were rhetoric and that they would be received as such. As a matter of fact, fascism is a consequence of the absence of philosophy. It is possible only in the context of the disorganization of analysis and the disruption of the intellectual tradition and intellectual discipline through the pressure of immediate practical concerns.

In *Reconstruction in Philosophy*, p. 24, Mr. Dewey says, "Common frankness requires that it be stated that this account of the origin of philosophies claiming to deal with absolute Being in a systematic way has been given with malice pretense. It seems to me that this genetic method of approach is a more effective way of undermining this type of philosophic theorizing than any attempt at logical refutation could be."

One effect of the education I propose might be that a philosopher who had received it would be willing to consider arguments. He would not assume that his appeal must be to the prejudices of his audience.

Mr. Dewey has suggested that only a defective education can account for some of my views. I am moved to inquire whether the explanation of some of his may not be that he thinks he is still fighting nineteenth-century German philosophy.

THE HIGHER LEARNING IN AMERICA *

John Dewey

In this article Dewey responds to Hutchins's critique of his review of *The Higher Learning in America*. In doing so, he rejects the idea of a "hierarchy of truths" in human knowledge and the belief of the preeminence of the Classics as a source of knowledge. This is not to say that the Classics are not worth knowing for Dewey, only that the Canon is ultimately undemocratic and insufficient. Of course, for Dewey the question remains unanswered (one asked by Spenser seventy-five years earlier): "What knowledge is of most worth?"

*   *   *

President Hutchins' book, *The Higher Learning in America*, seems to me to be a work of great significance. I thought it such because, in addition to vigorous exposition of the present confused state of education in this country, it raised, as I supposed, a basic issue—one not often explicitly brought forward and one which is so basic in the philosophy of education that it needs to be stated and discussed. I heartily welcomed the book because I thought that in raising that issue it would clarify educational discussion. This issue as I read the book, was the inherent nature of knowledge and intelligence in relation to the locus of authority in matters intellectual. I understand President Hutchins to hold that there is a power or faculty of Reason or Intellect (in the sense in which these words have been understood by great figures in the history of philosophy) which is capable of grasping first and ultimate truths that are the measure and criterion of all inferior forms of knowledge, namely, those which have to do with empirical matters, in which knowledge of both the physical world and practical affairs is included. I understood him to hold that only on the basis of a hierarchical order determined on the basis of these truths could order be brought out of present disorder—"a hierarchy of truths" which "shows us which are fundamental and which subsidiary."

LEGAL FORENSICS

That this view is, to put it mildly, a highly respected one is sufficiently proved by the great names in the history of thought that have supported it. It is still held, I imagine, in theory, by many educators who do not act upon it in their educational practices. In accepting and expounding it clearly and vigorously, as

---

* **Source:** *The Social Frontier*, Volume 3, Number 24, March 1937, pp. 167–69.

I supposed, President Hutchins' book focused upon the issue of the place of experience, practical matters, and experimental scientific method in the constitution of authentic knowledge, and consequently in the organization of the subject matter of higher education. His discussion clarified, I thought, this issue, by making it incumbent upon those who did not accept the classic traditional theory to state *an* alternative conception upon which their ideas regarding the way out of present educational confusion are founded. I say an alternative, but I believe that there is but one ultimate alternative; namely, the primary place of experience, experimental method, and integral connection with practice in determination of knowledge and the auxiliary role of what is termed Reason and Intellect in the classic tradition. In that spirit I wrote my two articles to which President Hutchins has kindly replied.

Unfortunately, however, I do not find that President Hutchins has discussed what I thought to be the main issue, and while it is clear that he regards my articles as irrelevant to his position, I cannot find in his reply any indication that he either repudiates the position I attributed to him or is willing to defend it. His reply seems to me rather to adopt the method of legal forensics. There are many quotations from his own book, from the writings of others and from my articles. But for reasons which I shall attempt to state, they do not touch the issue.

EVIDENCES OF A REAL ISSUE

(1) I begin with an instance of what is meant by the latter sentences. Mr. Hutchins quotes from me the statement that he "looks to Plato, Aristotle, and Aquinas." He replies by naming eleven other authors from whom he quotes with approval. It is quite true that he quotes in his book from the eleven authors mentioned. But most of the passages he cites are irrelevant to the issue regarding the problem of knowledge, and it was with reference to this that I said Mr. Hutchins looked to the three authorities mentioned. I certainly was not reflecting in any way upon the breadth of Mr. Hutchins' reading or his ability to support his views upon incidental matters (with many of which I am in agreement) by appropriate citations.[1] What bearing, other than a purely rhetorical one, does the fact that they were cited upon incidental matters have to do with either my articles or with a relevant reply to them?

(2) Statements which I made regarding Mr. Hutchins' disparaging view of experience, natural science, and connection with practice, in relation to knowledge and higher education, are countered by quotation of passages from Aristotle, St. Thomas, and himself in which the necessity of sense and experience is recognized. Of course, the two philosophers mentioned recognized the

necessity of sense and experience in the *inferior* grade of knowledge found in physical science and moral affairs. It is, however, precisely because both of the latter are connected with sense and experience that they are inferior in rank to pure rational knowledge of ultimate first principles and truths, which has nothing to do with sense and experience. Since the passages cited are strictly in accord with the position I attributed to Mr. Hutchins, in what way is their citation a factor in a relevant reply to what I said? The quotations Mr. Hutchins makes from his own book regarding his admiration for "accumulation of data, the collection of facts, and the advance of the empirical sciences," and about the importance of association of the natural sciences with the work of medical and engineering schools fall in the same category. Upon the ground of the doctrine as to knowledge I attributed to him, of course these things are necessary *in their place*. The question raised was the question of their subordinate and inferior place in comparison with pure rational and "metaphysical" knowledge.

President Hutchins quoted in his book[2] (and I had supposed with endorsement) the system of intellectual virtues that correspond with the hierarchical rank of various grades of knowledge in Aristotle and Aquinas. These are the three speculative virtues: (a) of intuitive knowledge; (b) of scientific demonstration (and *demonstration* is always purely rational in a sense which excludes experience and reference to practice in Aristotle and St. Thomas); (c) and of intuitive reason of "things highest by nature, first principles and first causes" – the metaphysical. The two virtues of the practical intellect, which are added, are, on the other hand, concerned with making and doing, and they belong in the lower order of things – things which change and fall in the scope of "experience" instead of "reason." Unless I completely misunderstood the text in supposing that Mr. Hutchins was approving this view, the quotations he makes regarding the importance of sense, experience, and natural science in relation to the inferior kind of knowledge support the correctness of the view I attributed to him, instead of militating against what I said.

WHERE DOES MR. HUTCHINS STAND?

(3) Mr. Hutchins quotes from me a passage in which I attributed to him the conception that ultimate and first truths are "fixed and eternal." He replies that he did not apply these terms to principles or truths in his book. This statement is correct. But Plato, Aristotle, and St. Thomas regarded them as such. Unless Mr. Hutchins follows them in this respect, his quotations from them regarding knowledge and first truths have no point. Moreover, their fixed and eternal character is quite consistent with the passage Mr. Hutchins

quotes from his own book in which he speaks of the need for research and of empirical materials in "development, elaboration, and refinement of principles." Of course, neither Aristotle nor St. Thomas held that rational intuition of eternal and fixed first truths takes place, in the case of human beings, as distinct from divine, without prior experience and reflection. But once they are thus led up to, the scaffolding of experience and reflection falls away, and they are known in their inherent purity as fixed and eternal. There is nothing in President Hutchins' *reply* to indicate that he does not accept that view — nor yet to indicate that he accepts it. The issue as to respective places of experimental method and "rational intuition" in institution of truths is the issue I was raising, and I can only again express my regret that Mr. Hutchins did not regard it as fit to touch upon. This issue is certainly fundamental with respect to the final ground for regarding the natural sciences important in education. The passage he quotes from his book to the effect that our country must pin its hope for progress upon education "which involves scientific and technological advance" does not decide his view upon this issue. For he adds "*under the direction of reason.*" If he means that the advance must be conducted intelligently, no one can disagree. But the phrase "under the direction of reason" in view of other passages in his text is open most naturally to the interpretation by which reason in independence from experience and the method of the natural sciences is given superior status and the latter are given subordinate rank.

METAPHYSICS IN THE UNIVERSITY

(4) President Hutchins asks whether I am saying "that there should not be a faculty of metaphysics" and whether "a university which had a faculty of philosophy" would "be more or less authoritaritarian than one which had not?" My answer depends in part upon what is meant by a *faculty* of metaphisics and philosophy, and in part upon whether philosophy is identified with metaphysics in the sense of a search for ultimate first principles known by Reason which transcends experience, and which when found afford the criterion for ordering other truths, assigning to them their proper subordinate grade in the hierarchy. Having been for forty-five years a member of *departments* of philosophy, I naturally believe that every university should have one. I do not, indeed, know any university of any standing that does not have one. But it is difficult to believe that Mr. Hutchins attaches the primary importance which he does attach to the place and role of a "faculty of metaphyics" in the reform of higher education to something which already exists as a matter of course. If, then, as is already clearly implied, a faculty of metaphysics means one that ex-

ists in splendid isolation from other departments as a separate faculty, and which attempts to discover ultimate first truths that are to be adopted by other faculties as a condition of their own proper intellectual organization, I do not believe in such a faculty. I do believe that a university which was organized on this basis could not help being more authoritarian than others not so constituted.[3] Mr. Hutchins' conception of metaphysics was represent, I supposed by the following passages: "It is in the light of metaphysics that the social sciences, dealing with man and man, and the physical sciences dealing with man and nature, take shape and illuminate one another. In metaphysics we are seeking the causes of the things that are. It is the highest science, the first science, and as first, universal. It considers being as being, both what it is and the attributes which belong to it as being. The aim of higher education is wisdom. Wisdom is knowledge of principles and causes. Metaphysics deals with the highest principles and causes. Therefore metaphysics is the highest wisdom."[4]

If this statement does not imply a hierarchy in the order of truths and the subordination of physical and social knowledge to first truths which are attained and guaranteed by a method which is unlike and superior to the methods of the natural and social sciences, I am unable to read the English language. It is with respect to the entertainment of such a doctrine that I said that President Hutchins "looked to" Plato, Aristotle, and St. Thomas; and, unless these first and highest truths are in themes fixed and eternal, however temporal may be the processes by which we come into possession of them, common logic indicates that they cannot perform the authoritative regulative function ascribed to them. For otherwise they are of the same experimental and hypothetical order as that which they are supposed to control.

The tone and substance of President Hutchins' reply would lead one to suppose that after all he was not raising or meaning to raise any fundamental issue. I must ask his forgiveness if I took his book too seriously.

References

1. Quotations from Newman and Whewell are, however, definitely in the Aristotelian tradition and in so far support what was meant when I said that Mr. Hutchins "looked to" the philosophers named. The quotation from Kant, moreover, is given as an endorsement of the necessity of a priori principles as the foundation of morals.
2. *The Higher Learning in America*, p. 63.
3. This statement does not mean that it might not be advantageous to have *some* institution so conducted, just as the School of Higher Studies is almost

exclusively a faculty of physics and mathematics. I am speaking, as President Hutchins is speaking of the general plan of university re-organization.

4. *The Higher Learning in America*, pp. 97–8.

EDUCATION AND SOCIAL CHANGE[*]

John Dewey

In this article Dewey establishes that while schools reflect the existing social order, this order is neither fixed nor uniform. Change is multifaceted and often confusing. He goes on to outline three possible courses for educators: (1) They can act so as to perpetuate the confusion, (2) They can adapt to new technologies and information, or; (3) They can assume a conservative position and "strive to make the schools a force in maintaining the old order intact against the impact of new forces."

Ironically, Dewey points out that conservatives who are often critical of the schools do not recognize they are a direct outgrowth and reflection of the existing culture. He then asks: "What movement of social forces, economic, political, religious, cultural, shall the school take to be controlling in its aims and methods, and with which forces shall the school align itself?"

Dewey establishes the idea that in a country such as the United States, democracy should be the frame of reference for learning. While our understanding of democracy may be limited, that does not mean that we should not actively pursue it as the "chief" theme in the schools and our educational system.

Dewey concludes, in much the same way that Horace Mann did one hundred years before him, that the schools are potentially the great engine of democracy. As he explains: "Our public school system was founded in the name of equality of opportunity for all, independent of birth, economic status, race, creed, or color. The school cannot by itself alone create or embody this idea. But the least it can do is to create individuals who understand the concrete meaning of the idea with their minds, who cherish it warmly in their hearts, and who are equipped to battle in its behalf in their actions." This should be the mission of the public schools, one that complements the democratic traditions of community and mutual purpose and interest as a society.

*   *   *

Upon certain aspects of my theme there is nothing new to be said. Attention has been continually called of late to the fact that society is in process of change, and that the schools tend to lag behind. We are all familiar with the pleas that are urged to bring education in the schools into closer relation with the forces that are producing social change and with the needs that arise from these changes. Probably no question has received so much attention in educational discussion during the last few years as the problem of integration of the

---

[*] **Source;** *The Social Frontier,* Volume 3, Number 26, 1937, pp. 235–238

schools with social life. Upon these general matters, I could hardly do more than reiterate what has often been said.

Nevertheless, there is as yet little consensus of opinion as to what the schools can do in relation to the forces of social change and how they should do it. There are those who assert in effect that the schools must simply reflect social changes that have already occurred, as best they may. Some would go so far as to make the work of schools virtually parasitic. Others hold that the schools should take an active part in directing social change, and share in the construction of a new social order. Even among the latter there is, however, marked difference of attitude. Some think the schools should assume this directive role by means of indoctrination; others oppose this method. Even if there were more unity of thought than exists, there would still be the practical problem of overcoming institutional inertia so as to realize in fact an agreed-upon program.

There is, accordingly, no need to justify further discussion of the problem of the relation of education to social change. I shall do what I can, then, to indicate the factors that seem to me to enter into the problem, together with some of the reasons that prove that the, schools do have a role—and an important one—in production of social change.

SCHOOLS REFLECT THE SOCIAL ORDER

One factor inherent in the situation is that schools do follow and reflect the social "order" that exists, I do not make this statement as a grudging admission, nor yet in order to argue that they should not do so. I make it rather as a statement of a conditioning factor which supports the conclusion that the schools thereby do take part in the determination of a future social order; and that, accordingly, the problem is not whether the schools should participate in the production of a future society (since they do so anyway) but whether they should do it blindly and irresponsibly or with the maximum possible of courageous intelligence and responsibility.

The grounds that lead me to make this statement are as follows: The existing state of society, which the schools reflect, is not something fixed and uniform. The idea that such is the case is a self-imposed hallucination. Social conditions are not only in process of change, but the changes going on are in different directions, so different as to produce social confusion and conflict. There is no single and clear-cut pattern that pervades and holds together in a unified way the social conditions and forces that operate. It would be easy to cite highly respectable authorities who have stated, as matter of historic fact and not on account of some doctrinal conclusion to be drawn, that social conditions in all that affects the relations of human beings to one another have changed more in the last one hundred and fifty years than in all previous time, and that the process of change is still going on. It requires a good deal of either ignorance or intellectual naiveté to suppose that these changes have all been tending to one coherent social outcome. The plaint of the conservative about the imperiling of old and time-tried values and truths, and the efforts of reactionaries to stem the tide of changes that occur, is sufficient evidence, if evidence be needed to the contrary.

Of course the schools have mirrored the social changes that take place. The efforts of Horace Mann and others a century ago to establish a public, free, common school system were a reflection primarily of the social conditions that followed the war by the colonies for political independence and the establishment of republican institutions. The evidential force of this outstanding instance would be confirmed in detail if we went through the list of changes that have taken place in (1) the kind of schools that have been established, (2) the new courses that have been introduced, (3) the shifts in subject-matter that have occurred, and (4) the changes in methods of instruction and discipline that have occurred in intervening years. The notion that the educational system has been static is too absurd for notice; it has been and still is in a state of flux.

The fact that it is possible to argue about the desirability of many of the changes that have occurred, and to give valid reasons for deploring aspects of the flux, is not relevant to the main point. For the stronger the arguments brought forth on these points, and the greater the amount of evidence produced to show that the educational system is in a state of disorder and confusion, the greater is the proof that the schools have responded to, and have reflected, social conditions which are themselves in a state of confusion and conflict.

INCONSISTENT CONSERVATISM

Do those who hold the idea that the schools should not attempt to give direction to social change accept complacently the confusion that exists, because the schools have followed in the track of one social change after another? They certainly do not, although the logic of their position demands it. For the most part they are severe critics of the existing state of education. They are as a rule opposed to the studies called modern and the methods called progressive. They tend to favor return to older types of studies and to strenuous "disciplinary" methods. What does this attitude mean? Does it not show that its advocates in reality adopt the position that the schools can do something to affect positively and constructively social conditions? For they hold in effect that the school should discriminate with respect to the social forces that play upon it;

that instead of accepting the latter in toto, education should select and organize in a given direction. The adherents of this view can hardly believe that the effect of selection and organization will stop at the doors of schoolrooms. They must expect some ordering and healing influence to be exerted sooner or later upon the structure and movement of life outside. What they are really doing when they deny directive social effect to education is to express their opposition to some of the directions social change is actually taking, and their choice of other social forces as those with which education should throw in its lot so as to promote as far as may be their victory in .the strife of forces. They are conservatives in education because they are socially conservative and vice-versa.

ALTERNATIVE COURSES

This is as it should be in the interest of clearness and consistency of thought and action. If these conservatives in education were more aware of what is involved in their position, and franker in stating its implications, they would help bring out the real issue. It is not whether the schools shall or shall not influence the course of future social life, but in what direction they shall do so and how. In some fashion or other, the schools will influence social life anyway. But they can exercise such influence in different ways and to different ends, and the important thing is to become conscious of these different ways and ends, so that an intelligent choice may be made, and so that if opposed choices are made, the further conflict may at least be carried on with understanding of what is at stake, and not in the dark.

There are three possible directions of choice. Educators may act so as to perpetuate the present confusion and possibly increase it. That will be the result of drift, and under present conditions to drift is in the end to make a choice. Or they may select the newer scientific, technological, and cultural forces that are producing change in the old order; may estimate the direction in which they are moving and their outcome if they are given freer play, and see what can be done to make the schools their ally. Or, educators may become intelligently conservative and strive to make the schools a force in maintaining the old order intact against the impact of new forces.

If the second course is chosen—as of course I believe it should be—the problem will be other than merely that of accelerating the rate of the change that is going on. The problem will be to develop the insight and understanding that will enable the youth who go forth from the schools to take part in the great work of construction and organization that will have to be done, and to equip them with the attitudes and habits of action that will make their understanding and insight practically effective.

DRIFT OR INTELLIGENT CHOICE?

There is much that can be said for an intelligent conservatism. I do not know anything that can be said for perpetuation of a wavering, uncertain, confused condition of social life and education. Nevertheless, the easiest thing is to refrain from fundamental thinking and let things go on drifting. Upon the basis of any other policy than drift—which after all is a policy, though a blind one— every special issue and problem, whether that of selection and organization of subject-matter of study, of methods of teaching, of school buildings and equipment, of school administration, is a special phase of the inclusive and fundamental problem: What movement of social forces, economic, political, religious, cultural, shall the school take to be controlling in its aims and methods, and with which forces shall the school align itself?

Failure to discuss educational problems from this point of view but intensifies the existing confusion. Apart from this background, and outside of this perspective, educational questions have to be settled ad hoc and are speedily unsettled. What is suggested does not mean that the schools shall throw themselves into the political and economic arena and take sides with some party there. I am not talking about parties; I am talking about social forces and their movement. In spite of absolute claims that are made for this party or that, it is altogether probable that existing parties and sects themselves suffer from existing confusions and conflicts, so that the understanding, the ideas, and attitudes that control their policies, need re-education and re-orientation. I know that there are some who think that the implications of what I have said point to abstinence and futility; that they negate the stand first taken. But I am surprised when educators adopt this position, for it shows a profound lack of faith in their own calling. It assumes that education as education has nothing or next to nothing to contribute; that formation of understanding and disposition counts for nothing; that only immediate overt action counts and that it can count equally whether or not it has been modified by education.

NEUTRALITY AIDS REACTION

Before leaving this aspect of the subject, I wish to recur to the Utopian nature of the idea that the schools can be completely neutral. This idea sets up an end incapable of accomplishment. So far as it is acted upon, it has a definite social effect, but that effect is, as I have said, perpetuation of disorder and increase of blind because unintelligent conflict. Practically, moreover, the weight of such action falls upon the reactionary side. Perhaps the most effective way of re-enforcing reaction under the name of neutrality consists in keeping the oncoming generation ignorant of the conditions in which they live and the issues they have to face. This effect is the more pronounced because it is subtle and indirect; because neither teachers nor those taught are aware of what they are doing and what is being done to them. Clarity can develop only in the extent to which there is frank acknowledgment of the basic issue: Where shall the social emphasis of school life and work fall, and what are the educational policies, which correspond to this emphasis?

REVOLUTIONARY RADICALS BELIEVE
EDUCATION IMPOTENT

So far I have spoken of those who assert, in terms of the views of a conservative group, the doctrine of complete impotence of education. But it is an old story that politics makes strange bedfellows. There is another group which holds the schools are completely impotent; that they so necessarily reflect the dominant economic and political regime, that they are committed, root and branch, to its support. This conclusion is based upon the belief that the organization of a given society is fixed by the control exercised by a particular economic class, so that the school, like every other social institution, is of necessity the subservient tool of a dominant class. This viewpoint takes literally the doctrine that the school can only reflect the existing social order. Hence the conclusion in effect that it is a waste of energy and time to bother with the schools. The only way, according to advocates of this theory, to change education in any important respect is first to overthrow the existing class-order of society and transfer power to another class. Then the needed change in education will follow automatically and will be genuine and thoroughgoing.

This point of view serves to call attention to another factor in the general issue being discussed. I shall not here take up in detail the basic premise of this school of social thought, namely the doctrine of domination of social organization by a single rather solidly-unified class; a domination so complete and pervasive that it can be thrown off only by the violent revolutionary action of another distinct unified class. It will be gathered, however, from what has been said that I believe the existing situation is so composite and so marked by conflicting criss-cross tendencies that this premise represents an exaggeration of actual conditions so extreme as to be a caricature. Yet I do recognize that so far as any general characterization of the situation can be made, it is on the basis of a conflict of older and newer forces—forces cultural, religious, scientific, philosophic, economic, and political.

But suppose it is admitted for the sake of argument that a social revolution is going on, and that it will culminate in a transfer of power affected by violent action. The notion that schools are completely impotent under existing conditions then has disastrous consequences. The schools, according to the theory, are engaged in shaping as far as in them lies a mentality, a type of belief, desire, and purpose that is consonant with the present class-capitalist system. It is evident that if such be the case, any revolution that is brought about is going to be badly compromised and even undermined. It will carry with it the seeds, the vital seeds, of counter-revolutions. There is no basis whatever, save doctrinaire absolutism, for the belief that a complete economic change will produce of itself the mental, moral and cultural changes that are necessary for its enduring success. The fact is practically recognized by the school of thought under discussion in that part of their doctrine which asserts that no genuine revolution can occur until the old system has passed away in everything but external political power, while within its shell a new economic system has grown to maturity. What is ignored is that the new system cannot grow to maturity without an accompanying widespread change of habits of belief, desire, and purpose.

IS INDOCTRINATION THE WAY OUT?

It is unrealistic, in my opinion, to suppose that the schools can be a main agency in producing the intellectual and moral changes, the changes in attitudes and disposition of thought and purpose, which are necessary for the creation of a new social order. Any such view ignores the constant operation of powerful forces outside the school, which shape mind and character. It ignores the fact that school education is but one educational agency out of many, and at the best is in some respects a minor educational force. Nevertheless, while the school is not a sufficient condition, it is a necessary condition of forming the understanding and the dispositions that are required to maintain a genuinely changed social order. No social change is more than external unless it is attended by and rooted in the attitudes of those who bring it about and of those who are affected by it in a genuine sense, social change is accidental unless it has also a psychological and moral foundation. For it is then at the mercy of currents that veer and shift. The utmost that can be meant by those who hold that schools are impotent is that education in the form of systematic indoctrination can only come about when some government is sufficiently established to make schools undertake the task of single-minded inculcation in a single direction.

The discussion has thus reached the point in which it is advisable to say a few words about indoctrination. The word is not free from ambiguity. One definition of the dictionary makes it a synonym for teaching. In order that there may be a definite point to consider, I shall take indoctrination to mean the systematic use of every possible means to impress upon the minds of pupils a particular set of political and economic views to the exclusion of every other.

This meaning is suggested by the word "inculcation," whose original signification was "to stamp in with the heel." This signification is too physical to be carried over literally. But the idea of stamping in is involved, and upon occasion does include physical measures. I shall discuss this view only as far as to state, in the first place, that indoctrination so conceived is something very different from education, for the latter involves, as I understand it, the active participation of students in reaching conclusions and forming attributes. Even in the case of something as settled and agreed upon as the multiplication table, I should say if it is taught educatively, and not as a form of animal training, the active participation, the interest, reflection, and understanding of those taught are necessary.

The upholders of indoctrination rest their adherence to the theory in part upon the fact that there is a great deal of indoctrination now going on in the schools, especially with reference to narrow nationalism under the name of patriotism, and with reference to the dominant economic regime. These facts unfortunately are facts. But they do not prove that the right course is to seize upon the method of indoctrination and reverse its objective.

DEMOCRACY AS A FRAME OP REFERENCE

A much stronger argument is that unless education has some frame of reference it is bound to be aimless, lacking a unified objective. The necessity for a frame of reference must be admitted. There exists in this country such a unified frame. It is called democracy. I do not claim for a moment that the significance of democracy as a mode of life is so settled that there can be no disagreement as to its significance. The moment we leave glittering generalities and come to concrete details, there is great divergence. I certainly do not mean either that our political institutions as they have come to be, our parties, legislatures, laws, and courts constitute a model upon which a clear idea of democracy can be based. But there is a tradition and an idea which we can put in opposition to the very much that is undemocratic in our institutions. The idea and ideal involve at least the necessity of personal and voluntary participation in reaching decisions and executing them—in so far it is the contrary of the idea of indoctrination. And I, for one, am profoundly skeptical of the notion that because we now have a rather poor embodiment of democracy we can ultimately produce a genuine democracy by sweeping away what we have left of one.

The positive point, however, is that the democratic ideal, in its human significance, provides us with a frame of reference. The frame is not filled in, either in society at large or in its significance for education. I am not implying that it is so clear and definite that we can look at it as a traveler can look at a map and tell where to go from hour to hour. Rather the point I would make is that the problem of education in its relation to direction of social change is all one with the problem of finding out what democracy means in its total range of concrete applications; economic, domestic, international, religious, cultural, economic, and political.

I cannot wish for anything better to happen for, and in, our schools than that this problem should become the chief theme for consideration until we have attained clarity concerning the concrete significance of democracy—which like everything concrete means its application in living action, individual and collective. The trouble, at least one great trouble, is that we have taken democracy for granted; we have thought and acted as if our forefathers had founded it once for all. We have forgotten that it has to be enacted anew in every generation, in every year and day, in the living relations of person to person in all social forms and institutions. Forgetting this, we have allowed our economic and hence our political institutions to drift away from democracy; we have been negligent even in creating a school that should be the constant nurse of democracy.

I conclude by saying that there is at least one thing in which the idea of democracy is not dim, however far short we have come from striving to make it reality. Our public school system was founded in the name of equality of opportunity for all, independent of birth, economic status, race, creed, or color. The school cannot by itself alone create or embody this idea. But the least it can do is to create individuals who understand the concrete meaning of the idea with their minds, who cherish it warmly in their hearts, and who are equipped to battle in its behalf in their actions.

Democracy also means voluntary choice, based on an intelligence that is the outcome of free association and communication with others. It means a way of living together in which mutual and free consultation rule instead of force, and in which cooperation instead of brutal competition is the law of life; a social order in which all the forces that make for friendship, beauty, and knowledge are cherished in order that each individual may become what he, and he alone, is capable of becoming. These things at least give a point of departure for the filling in of the democratic idea and aim as a frame of reference. If a sufficient number of educators devote themselves to striving courageously and with full sincerity to find the answers to the concrete questions which the idea and the aim put to us, I believe that the question of the relation of the schools to direction of social change will cease to be a question, and will become a moving answer in action.

FOOTNOTE[1]*

Carl Bode

Carl Bode completed his doctorate at Northwestern University in 1941. After serving in the military, he spent his professional career as a professor of American Literature at the University of Maryland. An expert on H. L. Mencken, Henry David Thoreau and Ralph Waldo Emerson, the following poem suggests that simply pursuing an academic life—no matter how laudable—by itself is unrealistic in the type of world that was coming into being by the late 1930s.

*   *   *

[1]Ours is a life of dusk and monastic quiet;
Amid the library stacks we graduate students,
Carefully avoiding the outside world's riot,
Prepare to exemplify scholastic prudence.

We toil in the dim irreligious light of
The library—few other places are dimmer,
And even those we tend to lose sight of:
For us there is not the glow not even the glimmer.
Yet here we receive employment and nourishment—
This labor is the best thing that ever befell us,
We are sure; but we really need no encouragement,
Except that a tremor seems now to tell us

That outside the library windows huge forms are moving
And on their armor a bloody steam condenses.
But let us, not looking out, go on improving,
Seek scholastic light, and verify our references.

***Source:** *The Social Frontier*, Volume 4, Number 32, 1938, p. 151.

QUESTION AND ANSWER[*]

Leon Trotsky

Among the most extraordinary articles to appear in *The Social Frontier* is Leon Trotsky's discussion of whether or not the Soviet government under Stalin still follows the principles of the Russian Revolution.

Trotsky (1879–1940) was one of the leaders of the October Revolution—second only to Lenin. Expelled from the Communist Party by Stalin and his followers and deported from Russia, he had been invited to come to the United States toward the end of 1939 to testify before the Dies Committee. When it was discovered that he would testify in support of a global Communist revolution, he was denied a visa to enter the United States. Trotsky went to Mexico where he was attacked with an ice axe by an undercover Russian agent. He died a few days later from his wounds.

In this article Trotsky argues that the revolution under Stalin has failed and is diametrically opposed to the true principles of Bolshevism. He asserts that: "We can say without risk of mistake that in the history of humanity there has never been a government so deceitful and hypocritical as the present Soviet bureaucracy." Trotsky argues that the oppression of women under the Stalinist regime represents a denial of the principles underlying the October Revolution. As he explains: "Woman's position serves as the clearest and most convincing index for the evaluation of a social regime and of state policy. The October revolution inscribed on its banner the emancipation of woman and created the most progressive legislation on marriage and family that has ever existed in history. Naturally this did not mean that a 'happy life' had come all at once for the Soviet woman. The real liberation of woman is inconceivable without a general rise in economy and culture, without the destruction of the petty-bourgeois family economy, without the introduction of socialized kitchens and education. But meanwhile the bureaucracy, guided by its conservative instincts, has taken fright at the 'destruction' of the family. It has begun to sing panegyrics to the family dinner and the family wash—i. e., to the family enslavement of the woman. To crown everything it has reestablished criminal punishment for abortion, thus officially returning woman to the status of a beast of burden." As objectionable as the denial of women's rights was the suppression of freedom in artistic and cultural thought. Trotsky concludes the article by arguing that a political revolution is inevitable, and calls for a return to the principles of the October Revolution—one that represent a true and valid model of socialism.

[*]**Source:** *The Social Frontier*, Volume 4, Number 34, 1938, pp. 211–214.

DOES THE SOVIET GOVERNMENT STILL ADHERE TO PRINCIPLES SET DOWN TWENTY YEARS AGO?

In order to answer correctly the question posed at the head of this article it is necessary from the very outset to establish the disparity between the basic conquest of the October revolution, the nationalization of property, and the policies of the present government. The revolutionary form of property and the Thermidorian, i.e., reactionary policies, stand in contradiction to each other. But up to now these policies have not yet been able, have not yet ventured, or have not yet succeeded in over-throwing the revolutionary form of property. The line of the present government is diametrically opposed to the program, of Bolshevism. But since the institutions founded by the revolution still exist, the bureaucracy is constrained in outward appearance to apt its line to the old principles of Bolshevism; it continues to swear by the commandments of October, by the interests of the proletariat, and calls the Soviet regime nothing less than socialist. We can say without risk of mistake that in the history of humanity there has never been a government so deceitful and hypocritical as the present Soviet bureaucracy.

PRODUCTION, SOCIALISM, AND DEMOCRACY

The safeguarding of the state property in the means of production has enormous progressive importance in itself, since with the aid of planned economy it permits the attainment of a rapid development of the productive forces. True, the economic statistics of the bureaucracy do not merit confidence they systematically exaggerate the successes and conceal the failures. Nevertheless, it is impossible to deny the fact that even now the forces of production in the Soviet Union are developing at a tempo such as no other country in the world has ever experienced or is experiencing now. Those who refuse to see this side of the question and identify the Soviet regime with fascism, as does Max Eastman, for instance, pour out the baby with the dirty bath water, as the German saying goes. The development of the productive forces is the fundamental factor in human civilization. Without increasing the power of man over nature it is impossible even to think of the annihilation of the power of man over man. Socialism cannot be erected on backwardness and destitution. In the last twenty years in the Soviet Union the technical premise for socialism has made an enormous stride forward. However, this is due least of all to the bureaucracy. On the contrary the ruling caste has become the greatest brake upon the development of the productive forces. Socialist economy, in its very essence, must be guided by the interests of the producers and by the needs of the consumers. These interests and needs can find their expression only through the intermediation of expanded democracy for producers and consumers. Democracy is not in this case a mere abstract principle. It is the only conceivable mechanism for the preparation and realization of a socialist system of economy.

BUREAUCRATS NOW DOMINANT

The present ruling clique has replaced democracy in the soviet, party, trade union, and cooperative by the command of functionaries. But even if the bureaucracy consisted entirely of geniuses, it would not possibly be capable of assuring from its offices the necessary proportion to all branches of economy—i.e., the necessary correlation between production and consumption. What in the language of Stalin's "justice" is termed "sabotage" is, in reality, the unfortunate consequence of the bureaucratic methods of command. The manifestations of disproportion, of waste, of blundering, growing more and more, threaten to sap the very foundations of planned economy. The bureaucracy invariably seeks a "culprit." This, in most cases, is the hidden meaning of the Soviet trials against "saboteurs."

Explaining the present regime by Stalin's personal "lust for power" is too superficial. Stalin is not just an individual but the symbol of a caste. Power is not something insubstantial. Power gives the possibility of disposing of material values and of appropriating them. Naturally complete equality cannot be achieved at one stroke. At the present stage certain differentiations in wages are dictated in the interest of increasing the productivity of labor. However, the question of decisive importance for the evaluation of the nature of society is whether society is developing toward equality or toward privilege. The answer to this question leaves no room whatever for any doubts. The differentiation in society has long since passed the limits of economic necessity. The material privileges of the bureaucracy grow like an avalanche. Frightened by its isolation from the masses, the bureaucracy is trying to create a new worker and collective farm aristocracy under the banner of Stakhanovism.

The distribution of the national income defines, in its turn, the political regime. The ruling caste cannot permit democracy for producers and consumers for the very simple reason that it robs them both unmercifully. It can be assumed with assurance that the bureaucracy devours no less than half of the sum total of national consumption, counting, naturally, not only lodging, food, clothing, means of transportation and communication, but also the use of institutions of learning, the press, literature, sports, motion pictures, radio, theatres, museums, etc. We can therefore say with full justification that although the bureaucracy is still constrained to adapt itself to the institutions and traditions of the October revolution, its policies, expressing its own interests, are directly opposed to the interests of the people and of socialism, This fundamental contradiction can be verified in all the other realms of social existence, such as the state, the army, the family, the school, culture, science, the arts, etc.

STATE AND ARMY

From the point of view of Marxism, the state is the apparatus for the domination of one class over another. The dictatorship of the proletariat is only a temporary institution, required by the toilers in order to have done with the resistance of the exploiters and to end exploitation. In a society without classes, the state, as an apparatus of coercion, would gradually wither away and be replaced by the free self-administration of the producers and consumers. But what do we see in reality? Twenty years after the revolution the Soviet state has become the most centralized, the most despotic, and the most bloody apparatus of violence and coercion. The evolution of the Soviet state proceeds, therefore, in complete contradiction to the fundamental principles of the Bolshevik program. The reason for this lies in the fact that society, as has already been said, is developing not toward socialism but toward the regeneration of social contradictions. If the process goes much further on this road, it will lead inevitably to the regeneration of classes, to the liquidation of planned economy, and to the restoration of capitalist property. In this case the state will inevitably become fascist.

The October revolution proclaimed as one of its tasks the dissolving of the army into the people. It proposed to build the armed forces on the militia principle. Only such an army organization, making the people the armed master of its own fate, corresponds to the nature of a socialist society. The transition from a standing army of the barrack type to an army of militia was systematically prepared during the first decade. But from the moment that the bureaucracy completely crushed every manifestation of independence on the part of the working class, it has openly transformed the army into an instrument of its own domination. The militia system has been completely abolished. The two million strong army is now, surely, a standing army. The caste of officers with generals and marshals at the top has been re-established. From an instrument of socialist defense the army has become an instrument for the defense of the privileges of the bureaucracy. However, things did not stop here. The struggle between Stalin's narrow clique and the most authoritative and talented military commanders, truly devoted to the interests of defense, has led to the beheading of the Red Army.

RETROGRESSION OF WOMEN AND "CULTURE"

Woman's position serves as the clearest and most convincing index for the evaluation of a social regime and of state policy. The October revolution inscribed on its banner the emancipation of woman and created the most progressive legislation on marriage and family that has ever existed in history. Naturally this did not mean that a "happy life" had come all at once for the Soviet woman. The real liberation of woman is inconceivable without a general rise in economy and culture, without the destruction of the petty-bourgeois family economy, without the introduction of socialized kitchens and education. But meanwhile the bureaucracy, guided by its conservative instincts, has taken fright at the "destruction" of the family. It has begun to sing panegyrics to the family dinner and the family wash—i. e., to the family enslavement of the woman. To crown everything it has reestablished criminal punishment for abortion, thus officially returning woman to the status of a beast of burden. Thus, in complete contradiction to the ABC of communism, the ruling caste has restored the most backward, the most reactionary unit of class society, the petty-bourgeois family.

But the situation is no better in the realm of culture. The growth of the productive forces was preparing the material prerequisites for a new culture. The development of culture, however, is impossible without criticism, without mistakes and groping, without independent creation in a word, without the awakening of personality. But the bureaucracy does not tolerate independent thinking in any creative field. And, in its way, it is right; if criticism aroused in the arts or pedagogy, it will inevitably direct itself against the bureaucracy, against its privileges, its ignorance and its arbitrariness. This explains the fact that the "purge" which began in the party; afterwards penetrated into all branches of social life without exception. The GPU "purges" poets, astronomers, pedagogues, and musicians under the label of "Trotskyism" and the best heads fall under the Mauser. Is it conceivable under such conditions to talk of "socialist" culture?

In the realm of simple literacy the successes are indubitable. Tens of millions have learned how to read and write. But parallel with this, they have been deprived of the right of expressing their opinions and interests in print. The press serves only the bureaucracy. The so-called "socialist" poets have the right of writing only hymns to Stalin. The same privilege is granted to writers of prose. The population is obliged to read these hymns. Exactly the same thing is happening in the motion pictures, radio, the theater, etc. Recently a new prize history textbook was introduced in the schools. It can be said without exaggeration that this textbook contains nothing but falsifications the purpose of which is to justify the despotism of the bureaucracy and the personal absolutism of Stalin. Even the history textbooks of the Catholic Church, published with the approval of the Vatican, are models of scientific conscientiousness compared with the Stalinized textbooks of the U. S. S. R. Tens of millions of children's heads are contaminated and poisoned by this dishonest literature.

OTHER SYMPTOMS OF REACTION

The October revolution proclaimed the right of every nation not only to independent cultural development but even to a separate state existence. The bureaucracy has in reality transformed the Soviet Union into a new prison of the peoples. True, the national language and the national school continue to exist; in this field the most powerful despotism can no longer turn back the wheel of development he language of the various nationalities is not an for their independent development but an or-of bureaucratic domineering over them. The governments of the national republics, are of course, appointed by Moscow, or stated more correctly, by Stalin. But what a striking fact, that thirty of these governments suddenly appear to be "enemies of the people" and agents of foreign powers! Behind this accusation which sounds too gross and preposterous given from the lips of Stalin and Vyshinsky, is really concealed the fact that even though appointees of the Kremlin, once in the national republics, the functionaries fall under the influence of local conditions and moods and generally become infected with the opposition spirit against the stifling centralism of Moscow. They begin to dream and to talk about the removal of the "beloved leader" and the unloosening of the vise. That is the real reason for the recent decapitation of all the national republics of the U.S.S.R. It is difficult to find in history an example of reaction in which has not been tainted by anti-Semitism. Its peculiar historic law is now completely concerned in the Soviet Union as well. In his interested, though not profound book, "Assignment in Eutopia," Eugene Lyons, who spent long years in Moscow, shows how the bureaucracy systematically, though in covert form, exploited anti-Semitic prejudices in order to strengthen its domination. And how should it be otherwise? Bureaucratic centralism is inconceivable without chauvinism, and anti-Semitism always offers the line of least resistance for chautism.

In foreign policy a turn no less radical than that in internal policy has occurred in these last twenty years. It is only through inertia or for some hidden motive that bourgeois reaction continues to denounce Stalin as the inspirer of world revolution; in reality the Kremlin has become one of the bulwarks of the conservative order. The period when the Moscow government tied the fate of the Soviet republic to the fate of the international proletariat and the oppressed peoples of the East is left far behind. Good or bad, the policy of the

"People's Front" is but the traditional policy of Menshevism against which Lenin fought all his life. It signifies the abandoning of proletarian revolution in favor of conservative bourgeois democracy. The ruling Moscow caste has but one wish—to live in peace with all the ruling classes.

EXECUTIONS AND ELECTIONS

The contradictions between the October revolution and the Thermidorian bureaucracy found their most tragic expression in the extermination of the old generation of Bolsheviks. Vyshinsky, Yezhov, Troyanovsky, Maisky, agents of the Comintern and of the GPU, journalists of the type of Duranty and Louis Fischer, lawyers of the type of Pritt, will not deceive world public opinion. Not a single rational human being believes any longer that hundreds of old revolutionists, leaders of the underground Bolshevik party, directors of the Civil War, revolutionary Soviet diplomats, commanders of the Red Army, heads of thirty national Soviet republics, all at one stroke, as if by command, became agents of fascism. The New York or "Dewey" Commission of Inquiry consisting of irreproachable and impartial people announced after nine months of work that the Moscow trials were the most gigantic falsification in human history. It is no longer now a question of proving that Zinoviev, Ka-menev, Smirnov, Piatakov, Serebriakov, Sokolnikov, Radek, Rakovsky, Krestinsky, Tuchachevsky, and hundreds of others fell the victims of a frame-up.* This has been proved. The question now consists in explaining how and why the Kremlin clique could venture such a monstrous frame-up. The answer to this flows from all that has been said. In its struggle for power and income the bureaucracy was forced to strike down and to destroy those groups that are bound up with the past, those who know and who remember the program of the October Revolution, those who are sincerely devoted to the tasks of socialism. The extermination of the old Bolsheviks and of socialist elements of the middle and younger generation is the necessary link in the anti-October reaction. That is why the former white-guard Vyshinsky appears in the trials as prosecutor. That is why the U. S. S. R. is represented at Washington by the former white-guard Troyanovsky and in London by the former minister of Kolchak, Maisky, etc. The right people are found to occupy the right places.

Hardly anyone will let himself be deceived by the comedy of the latest Moscow elections. Hitler and Goebbels have more than once contrived the same thing and by the very same methods. It is sufficient to read what the Soviet press itself wrote on Hitler's plebiscites to understand the secret of Stalin's "successes." Totalitarian parliamentary experiences prove only that if one destroys all parties, including one's own, stifles the trade-unions, subordinates the press, radio, and the motion pictures, either to the Gestapo or the GPU, gives work and bread only to the submissive and silent ones, and places a revolver against the head of every voter, it is possible to achieve "unanimous" elections. But this unanimity is neither eternal nor stable. The traditions of the October revolution have disappeared from the official stage but they continue to live in the memory of the masses. Beneath the cover of judicial and electoral frame-ups, the contradictions continue to deepen and cannot but lead to an explosion. The reactionary bureaucracy must and will be overthrown. A political revolution in the U. S. S. R. is inevitable. It will signify the liberation of the elements of the new society from the usurping bureaucracy. Only under this condition can the U. S. S. R. develop toward socialism.

* [Written on January 3, before the March, 1938, executions. Presumably the names of Bukbarin, Rykov, and others prominent in the "Who's Who" of the U.S.S.R. would have been added by the author.—Editors, *The Social Frontier*.]

THE DIES COMMITTEE AND TRUE AMERICANISM*

The Editorial Board (William Heard Kilpatrick)

In May 1938, the House Committee on Un-American Activities was established under the chairmanship of Martin Dies, Jr. (1900–1972), a democratic representative from Texas. Subsequently known as the Dies Committee, it focused most of its attention on Nazi and Ku Klux Klan activities. In this editorial, published by the the the journal's editorial board, but evidently written by William Heard Kilpatrick, the mission and purpose of the Dies Committee (which was to evolve into the infamous House un-American Activities Committee) is challenged. Kilpatrick asks: "What is true Americanism?" He distinguishes between un-American activities and un-American opinions—opinions and advocacy being principles guaranteed by the Bill of Rights.

Kilpatrick directly attacks the smear tactics employed by Chairman Dies, and makes clear that the actions of the committee largely represent entrenched politically and socially class-based groups. He maintains that "We cannot expect undemocratic means to produce democratic results."

*   *   *

The Dies Commitee was appointed "to investigate un-American activities." As its work draws to a close, a variety of questions arise. Has the Committee adequately conceived "un-American activities?" Has its work helped the American people to understand what is involved, or have the Committee methods tended rather to mislead and confuse thinking on the subject? And, finally, what about the Committee's methods of investigation and inquiry: has the Committee itself obeyed the finer demands of true Americanism?

As to what constitutes true Americanism and where to draw the line cutting off "un-American activities," it will perhaps suffice to begin, as did the Dies Committee, with certain outstanding instances of un-American activities. Examining these in order we can build up, piece-by-piece, working definitions of Americanism and un-American activities to fit the facts. In the light of these we can then judge, first whether the Committee's inquiry has not omitted at least one significant type of un-American activity and, second, whether the Committee itself, by the methods it used, has or has not violated true American demands for fair play and orderly processes.

Before going further, it should be said that what is here written is the writer's own and does not commit his colleagues of the Editorial Board. He has consulted with such of them as were available and has profited by their

* **Source:** *Frontiers of Democracy*, Volume 6, Number 50, 1940, pp. 102–104.

suggestions; he regrets that he has not had the criticisms and suggestions of all. But the responsibility for what is written is his alone. It may be added that one purpose of writing is to help clarify the liberal position as over against the dogmatists of both the left and right. The essence of liberalism, as here understood, is final reliance upon conscious study, shared study of the developing situation, with willingness to follow the argument—this to tell us what to think and do in all matters so ever. How such liberalism joins with democracy to help define Americanism and un-American activities will appear as we go.

There is so much popular misconception on one matter essential to our discussion that we must consider it as preparation for what follows. It was un-American activities, not un-American opinions, that the Dies Committee was appointed to investigate. The distinction is capital. By the Bill of Rights opinion is free, and not only opinion but advocacy. How changes are to be effected, that is activity and becomes therefore the concern of others. But any person or group is properly free to propose and advocate any change in our government or other institutions, however radical or sweeping.

The statement just made may appear to certain among us as unduly "radical" and "un-American." There are many Americans so anxious to protect certain cherished political doctrines and social institutions that they would, if permitted, declare it un-American and even illegal to criticize either doctrines or institutions, still more so to advocate any change in connection. But such an attitude is directly contrary both to American history and to American law. THOMAS JEFFERSON, for example, in his first inaugural, upheld freedom of speech even for those "who would wish to dissolve this union, or to change its republican form," MR. JUSTICE HOLMES speaking to the same point said, "If there is any principle of the Constitution that more imperatively calls for attachment than any other, it is the principle of free thought—not free thought for those who agree with us but freedom for the thought we hate." (Italics supplied).

Since these things are so, the definition of "un-American activities" cannot lie in the content or character of the changes sought, but in the manner either of advocacy or of effecting the changes. Whether the change sought is good or bad, that is to be settled by discussion and voting—and ultimately by trial. But any activity that interferes with orderly discussion and voting, that is wrong and is properly to be declared un-American. With this as a beginning, we may now ask specifically what, if any, groups there are at work in American life that deserve to be held up to public view as engaged in un-American activities. It appears that five such groups can be named.

1. First with reference to the fundamental principle of equality of treatment,—any group, of whatever colored shirt or other alignment, right or left,

lay or clerical, that works to sow hatred of group against group is by so doing denying true Americanism. And this is so no matter what may be the alleged grounds of hatred, whether racial or religious or difference of economic status or anything else. For it is of the essence of American democracy not only that all shall receive equality of treatment but that everything done shall be conducted on a basis of respect for personality as such. Any among us who knowingly and willingly sow group hatred ought to be exposed to public view.

2. Any group that admits varying standards of honesty and truthfulness: dependable truth and honesty for use among themselves, deceit and dishonesty for use with others, all such deserve to be uncloaked and exhibited for what they are to the American public that others may know how to appraise their words and deeds, and besides may know the futility of trying to act in organized capacity with them.

It is essential to the democratic process that any group or association shall govern itself by shared decisions based on free discussion. Both for the carrying on of such discussion and for the consequent cooperative action, it is necessary that people, as they deal with each other, should be able not only to understand each other in the same sense but to be able to put trust in what is said. In this way a common honesty and truthfulness become a sine qua non to social interaction. Any who refuse it thereby unfit themselves for proper social intercourse.

3. Any group of people who acknowledge in their jeans allegiance outside the American scene so as to act and speak according to directions given them from without, and who, hiding this allegiance, act under cover to make their dictated aims prevail here in this country: all such directly infringe the essential principles of shared discussion and consequent shared decision and cooperative action which constitute democracy. In fact, two democratic principles are here violated: one the principle of shared discussion already considered, the other the duty of each individual to think and act for himself. Any citizen may consult and be advised, but a successful democracy demands that each one do his own thinking, that each one be and act a person in his own right. This seems the most essential difference between democracy and the totalitarian dictatorships abroad.

From a further and more immediately practical point of view, our people have already seen the dangers of hidden connections and have by law required newspapers to make public their ownership and political parties to disclose their larger contributors. This is a safeguarding extension of the principle of shared discussion. Part of the appraisal of any policy is to know by whom it is advocated so that we may the better judge why it is advocated.

In these various ways is external allegiance an utter denial of true Americanism,

4. Any group whose method of action is to sow dissension and otherwise bring disruption in legitimately functioning social organizations with the intent of exploiting such disruption for hidden purposes: any such group and any such action deserve to be made public in order that all concerned may be warned accordingly, specifically that the organizations thus attacked may the better protect themselves.

It requires no argument to show that such efforts at dissension and disruption constitute a further infringement of the principles of shared discussion and cooperative action and of respect for personality. The members of a democracy have a right to be protected, if possible, against such disruptive efforts.

5. There is a further group, one not investigated by he Dies Committee but still clearly guilty of un-American practices. This group includes all those who, being strongly, perhaps selfishly, wedded to things as they are, so act as to hamper the free study and discussion of the existing social institutions. If there is one social danger greater than any other it is that a people will hold on to institutional forms after they have so ceased to be useful as to become oppressive. Violent revolutions have their roots just here. Among us now certain unwise people consciously try to prevent the free discussion of ailing institutions, whether through public forums or in our schools and colleges. MAYOR HAGUE was but a vulgar representative of many such all over the land, vigilantes in spirit and often so in fact. Certain so-called patriotic groups thus disgrace their country, as do certain reactionary businessmen. All such efforts are pointedly anti-democratic and thus un-American. That the Dies Committee saw nothing of this kind of un-Americanism raises various questions as to bias.

When we turn from these various un-American groups to the Dies Committee itself and consider the way in which it has functioned, questions earlier raised take on greater seriousness. We are compelled to question the acts and procedures of the Committee. But before considering these in detail, it is fitting to note, first, that the Committee seems to have been more careful of proprieties since its reorganization than before; and, second, that not all the members stand on the same footing as to propriety of conduct. MR. DIES himself and MR. THOMAS seem more questionable in respect of their acts, and Mr. Voorhis more to be commended for the standards he has sought to maintain.

In the light of all the foregoing and of the data thus far attainable as to Committee action, the following conclusions seem reasonably warranted:

1. The Committee, especially as led by Mr. Dies, deserves condemnation for the reckless and inefficient way in which its investigations and hearings have been conducted and reported.

In general, the Committee has willingly, if not willfully, so conducted its management as to "smear" many public men and movements—unwarrantably on the evidence—with various taints. It must be called un-American thus to spread distrust of named individuals without allowing full opportunity at explanation and rebuttal and otherwise taking every care to get at the exact truth. Hearsay evidence should not indict, still less convict.

2. Specifically the Committee deserves condemnation for the way in which it made public the Washington mailing list of the American League of Peace and Democracy. Apart from every other consideration, every informed person knows how such mailing lists are made up. Thus to smear all these people with the taint of Communism is a gross violation of right, in fact an outrage.

3. The publicity efforts of MR. J. PARNELL THOMAS, member of the Committee from New Jersey, to fasten Communism upon prominent officials in Washington, is a clear instance of the hurtful results of wrong Committee action. First the Committee investigates carelessly, and then one of its members exploits the results for partisan effect.

4. A most recent instance of unwarranted publicity is that given by Chairman Dies to the highly questionable report made by the Committee's aide, one J. B. MATTHEWS, against certain consumer groups. It is common knowledge that Matthews has here a private grudge to satisfy. For Chairman Dies to receive this as a report to the Committee and give it as such to the press when not even the other Committee members had seen it—not to mention the fact that the accused had had no opportunity to deny or explain—for such things to happen calls seriously in question the fitness of MR. DIES to direct the work of the Committee. Certainly such procedures violate the safeguards, which a decent respect for the persons concerned would throw about Committee practice. If the term un-Americanism fits anywhere, it does here and to such acts.

The true Americanism we wish to uphold is sensitive to the rights and feelings of all concerned. It will demand the faithful observance of the democratic processes of free discussion and shared decisions and acts without which a desirable social life is impossible; and it will demand this of all groups both left and right. It will particularly respect the spirit of justice and orderly processes in those areas not covered by specific laws, as for instance in the management of Congressional Committees where the ordinary laws of evidence are not legally binding.

It may not be amiss finally to say that most of these un-American practices have their root in economic distress and inequalities. We shall never have true Americanism in any full sense until we can remedy the unjust inequalities of an outmoded economic system. But all proposals made and measures taken for changing that system must themselves be democratic. We cannot expect undemocratic means to produce democratic results. It is in accordance with these principles that practices are to be judged American or un-American, It is in accordance with the same principles that the Dies Committee must itself be judged, for by these same principles it should have governed itself. This it has not done. If the work is to be continued it should be under other management. If there is more work to be done, MR. DIES is not the one to do it.

W. H. K.

THE PROBLEM OF MINORITIES

Margaret Mead

The achievement of social equality is a theme that runs throughout the writings of the social reconstructionists. In this article, the anthropologist Margaret Mead challenges the artificial racial distinctions made between different European, and in turn, immigrant groups to the United States. Following a similar line of thought, she argues that racial distinctions in terms of intelligence and ability are largely meaningless in regard to African-Americans and Native Americans. Overall, she concludes that racially based abilities are an artificial social construction, rather than something that is genetically passed on within a group.

*　　*　　*

For the last quarter of a century the fight against race prejudice particularly as it applies to minority groups in Europe and America, has been characterized by devotion and zeal and a singular lack of success. Anthropologists have painstakingly documented the essential meaninglessness of the concept of race, as applied to European sub-groups; they have shown how tremendous is the over-lapping of traits between the alleged European sub-races, the "Nordic" and "Alpine" and "Mediterranean" types, so that it is possible to find Italians with blond hair and blue eyes and Swedes with black hair and black eyes. The history of western Europe has been invoked to show how heterogeneous is the composition of every European sub-group, and how much of their ancestry the different family lines in different countries have in common. When these un-real distinctions between European groups were claimed to be upheld in the performance of different groups on the Army Alpha and Beta tests during the war (where the "Nordics" made scores conspicuously higher than the "Mediterraneans," etc.), these results have been painstakingly examined; it has been shown how the determining factors in this poorer score are degree of linguistic and cultural assimilation and economic status. The relationship of I.Q. to factors such as these and also to the tradition of the group has been shown, so that it is a fair hypothesis that a minority group of one tradition, e.g. the immigrant Russian Jews' tradition of upward mobility through the use of verbal skills, will react to a minority status by putting forth greater efforts, while another group, e.g. Sicilian peasants with an expectation of upward mobility through a shift from agriculture to factory labor, will have no such premium upon verbal skills and not make a comparable attempt to master the language of the new country. At every turn it has been possible to muster careful documented studies to support the position that no fixed abilities can be assigned to any of these groups in terms of their biologically inherited constitutions, that in fact it is incorrect to think of inheritance in group terms at all.

Each sub-group must be regarded as a collection of different family lines, in each of which definite potentialities are inherited. The similarities between the members of different family lines can be laid partly to inter-marriage in recent generations, partly to a large percentage of common ancestry, and to some selection for physical type so that in one group the blond and in another the brunette is the preferred type with the best marital chances. But most of all to similarities in culture, to a common character structure which results in a similar response to similar conditions, such as immigration to a new country or economic discrimination couched in terms of a theory of racial inferiority.

When it is a question, none of these sub-groups which can lay no claim to being considered as separate races possessing non-overlapping traits, but of members of the different major divisions of mankind, Negroes and American Indians as compared with Caucasians, again scientific research has documented the absence of any proof of reliable differences in intelligence and emotional make-up; differences, that is, which are impervious to the forces of cultural change. It has been shown that the intelligence scores of Northern Negro children are superior to the scores of Southern underprivileged white children, that Indians approach white norms in definite ratio to their experience of white culture forms. Years of patient research and careful development of investigatory techniques have gone into the demonstration, by students of the problem, that we have no evidence for attributing any biologically hereditary differences to members of these different races beyond those of physical characteristics, differences in pigmentation and hairiness, etc., which were the basis of the original classification. From the research materials vivid bits with propaganda value have been selected such as the fact that the Negro has the most human, i.e. unapelike lips, or that members of the Mongolian Race lead the march away from the ape, in being the least hairy of peoples.

Students of those primitive peoples, who add to their differences in physical form and their membership in other than Caucasian races conspicuous differences in level of civilization, have maintained over and over again, on the basis of their intimate study of these peoples, that primitive peoples do not differ in innate capacity from their more socially advanced conquerors. They have claimed that a Samoan or an Eskimo or a Baganda baby, reared without prejudice and with full opportunities offered by modern civilization, would show no differences which could be attributed to his biological inheritance as a member of his group. He would merely be intelligent or stupid, quick or slow, within the normal limits of human variability, depending upon his own immediate inheritance from well endowed or poorly endowed ancestors.

Persistent experimental investigation of the problem has yielded no reliable evidence of the possibility of inheriting acquired characters so we have no reason to believe that because one hundred generations of Eskimos have lived at a low cultural level, any biological trace of this low level will appear in the members of the next generation. On the other hand, every hour that an Eskimo baby spends with his parents will make him more of an Eskimo, more of a specialized sort of human being, well adapted to his parents' form of culture and less able to adapt to any other cultural form.

Yet, in the face of all this documentation, all this research and exposition, the belief in race differences remains a part of the ordinary attitudinal equipment of the main in the street.

The white man continues to insist upon the inferiority of the Negro and the special character of the Mongolian; the typical Nordic continues to preen himself at the expense of the darker complexioned members of the group; the Negro continues to accord more respect to the quadroon than to the mulatto and to the mulatto than to the full blood; the South Sea Islander washes his baby with the white man's soap so that it will be fairer than its parents; the Melbourne business man, worsted by the superior application of refugee competitors, insists that the Jews must be dishonest because no one could honestly learn to speak a strange language in three months, he couldn't. All of this diversified behavior goes back to the same roots: the belief that intellectual, emotional and moral differences are ineradicably associated with distinguishing physical traits, whenever those traits characterize the members of an identifiable social group.

Here it is fruitful to compare the attribution of special abilities to members of groups who differ physically from ourselves with the tendency to attribute special traits to individuals who differ markedly from the norm: who are dwarfed or albinoid or giantesque. Here we find a remarkable scatter of attitudes. Some peoples will regard a dwarf as specially gifted or blessed, another as defective or accursed, but there is no "race" of dwarfs about which a consistent social judgment can be built up which they themselves can share with their detractors. The difference in position between the group which differs from another group, and the individuals in the disapproved minority group who vary in physique in the direction of the approved group from the individual physical deviant, was sharply pointed up by the discovery of the White Indians of Mount Darian; these proved to be Albino Indians who had been segregated from their tribe and reproduced themselves until they formed a group with a definite culture of their own, about which definite social attitudes could form.

The psychologists who try to explain race hatred on the basis of the fear of the stranger or the strange, ignore this essential ingredient of genuine racial intolerance: the need for there to be a group of people towards whom disapproval or approval, contempt or slavish emulation, is felt. In fact, genuine racial or sub-racial intolerance only comes into existence when there are enough members of the minority group to become familiar objects about whom standard social attitudes can form. Members of a minority group may of course become familiar objects through their continual appearance in literature or upon the stage; it is not necessary to have a resident minority group in a community for the members of that community to display well organized attitudes of prejudice and intolerance. This circumstance again demonstrates that it is not spontaneous fear of a stranger but organized attitudes toward a group of people with common and identifiable physical characteristics which are responsible for race prejudice. Children may cry spontaneously when confronted with a giant, but for every child in a given group to have a standard attitude on the subject of skin color, there must be a group of predominantly lighter and a group of predominantly darker people who can pass on their attitudes to their children, as a part of their social inheritance. The solitary albino may be disapproved and left aside, he or she may never marry and die an unhappy outcast, but when the next albino appears, two, generations hence, attitudes towards him will have to be developed all over again.

There are two other scientific findings which are worth considering in this discussion. One is the record Professor Linton brought back from Madagascar of two neighboring tribes. The members of one tribe were much darker in skin color than the members of the neighboring tribe; the darker tribe valued its deeper pigmentation as much as the lighter tribe valued its lighter skin color. In each tribe infants whose skin color varied too far away from the norm were killed; too dark infants were put to death in the lighter tribe and too light ones in the dark tribe. But both peoples gave the same rationalization for their behavior, that a child whose physical appearance varied too markedly would grow up to be a social misfit, a sorcerer, a thief, a leper or one who committed incest. This instance is illuminating because it so rarely happens that two groups which differ physically can come in contact with one another without a differential premium being set, by both groups, upon one variation as compared with the other. In speaking of race prejudice there is always a tendency to distort the issue by assuming that the invidious comparisons are made only by the disapproving group, that they are a sort of attitudinal ammunition directed at the disapproved group. The Madagascar instance illustrates clearly that if actually only one of the two groups felt the premium upon the observed difference, preference for their own type which could be handled constructively and socially would be the result, instead of the hostility and overbearingness on the one hand and inferiority feelings and resentment on the other which characterize most contacts between groups which differ physically and socially from each other. Dr. E. J. Lindgren has reported an instance of Cossacks and Tungus who live side by side, each respecting the other's difference, without putting any premium upon that difference. But these instances where difference from others is regarded as a simple positive value, neither enhancing nor diminishing the desirability of the own group's physical traits are so rare that they merely point up the almost universal occurrence of the other point of view.

A second relevant finding was that of Dr. Moreno in his experiments in the behavior of mixed groups of Negro and white girls in a reform school environment. If he placed one Negro girl in a group of white girls, she was treated well, made a pet of, and her difference in color was rather an asset than a liability, although both the white girls and the Negro girl shared of course the American attitude that a white skin is superior to a black skin. But when a second Negro girl was introduced into such a group the situation changed; the two Negroes clung together and became a minority, and the existence of an invidious distinction based on skin color sharpened the distinction between the minority of two and the majority of ten or fifteen; a situation comparable to the usual minority one grew up. Moreno also found that girls who had been accustomed to having active and engrossing love affairs with boys and who missed these contacts when they were shut up, tended to develop crushes on Negro girls, to write them notes and court their devotion. Difference in race was substituted for difference in sex, and could be substituted for it easily because both difference in race and difference in sex, in our society, are differences which are expected to carry with them marked contrasts in behavior and attitude. Both of these findings point up the fact that we, in common with most but not all human cultures, tend to attach special significance to consistent differences in physical type.

So we have, on the one hand, the dispassionate findings of a large number of investigators to show that there is no evidence for differences in biologically inherited capacity being associated with differences in the types of physical traits upon which our racial classifications are based; on the other hand, we have habits of mind which persistently do associate such differences in physique with inevitable differences in behavior, and continue to attribute to any group of people who are different in physique other traits which are usually regarded as either more desirable or less desirable than the traits of the group with whom they are compared. Through the years the findings of the scientist have had remarkably small effect upon the attitudes of the members of either the majority or the minority group. So little effect have they had that some an-thropologists have been inclined to give the matter up as a bad job, and to say that social attitudes will never be affected by scientific findings, that social atti-tudes are essentially irrational, that it is useless to try to influence them by any presentation of determined facts. This pessimism is amply justified by the his-tory of the campaign against race prejudice, but it ignores one persistent dis-tortion which has been introduced into the propagandic use of scientific materials. The anthropologist says: There is no proof that different races or different sub-racial groups differ in potential capacity. The man in the street says: The members of this or that group are inferior or superior in achieve-ment to me. Both are quite sure of their ground, both have evidence to sup-port their positions. But the opponent of race prejudice takes the findings of the scientist and directs them against the man in the street only after adding a falsification. He says not, "There is no physical inherited basis for the observed differences in achievement level between groups," but "There ARE no differ-ences." The propagandist treats what is as if it were what might be, and the man in the street goes away firmly convinced that the scientist has tried to prove that the average adult American Negro in 1940 has an equal capacity to succeed in performing the skills which win approval in American society. The man in the street knows that this is not true, just as the opponent of women's suffrage and equal rights for women knew that women weren't equal to men, if one considered adult women brought up as men's inferiors.

If the propagandist would shift his ground and deal more realistically with the problem of changing social attitudes, he might have much more effect. If his propaganda consisted in the effect of membership in a minority group on the development of feelings of inferiority, if he documented the slow rot of hopelessness which creeps over the minds of Indian and Negro children as they approach adolescence and come to realize how long the odds are against them, perhaps this would be material to which the man in the street would listen. For the man in the street has been carefully trained to think in matter-of-fact terms. He is amenable to any statement of social costs provided it is stated clearly enough in terms of money costs. He can be roused to the prob-lem of the mental defective or the schizophrenic or even to the problem of the gifted child in the public schools if he is told that the present method of ignor-ing defects and special abilities is not only socially expensive but expensive in the only terms he knows: dollars and cents.

Just as race prejudice rages most fiercely in those areas of society where economic competition is strongest and in those periods of depression when economic anxiety is deepest, the prejudiced propaganda hits at an audience of practical men who have been told that their economic security is being endangered by minority groups. Such an audience has neither time nor tolerance for detached intellectual statements in favor of tolerance for groups who would be as skilled or as ambitious, as aggressive or as unaggressive as themselves if only they were given a fair chance. But they might be reached by a statement of human waste and its cost to the citizen taxpayer if the propagandist faced frankly that a minority group, the members of which share the majority belief that they are inferior or conspicuously and undesirably different from the majority, will undoubtedly display just those traits which are attributed to them. Let the propagandist stress that the criminality records will be highest from the minorities which we brand as natural law breakers; the breakdown records will be highest from the groups which we regard as emotionally unstable; the costs for hospitalizing paresis will be high from the groups which we regard as immoral and therefore do not attempt to educate in the prevention of syphilis; the costs of schooling will be raised among the groups where birth control propaganda is regarded as useless, society and its respectable members will be swindled by those we regard as natural swindlers.

To the man in the street who is a citizen and a tax payer, the scientist student of race can say, "To the extent that you label any human being in terms of the color of his skin or the shape of his head or the language he speaks or the name he bears, as socially undesirable, you make him so." Of course minority groups display endless undesirable traits varying from an unwillingness to make the necessary effort to learn which resembles mental defect, to a willingness to use any method to attain success which looks like hereditary dishonesty. Any group labeled as inferior in such a way that no member of that group can escape the stigma, will be inferior, generation after generation, until the man in the street stops assisting in the expensive habit of manufacturing social misfits.

TEACHERS AND POLITICS—1940 *

by Jesse H. Newlon

J esse H. Newlon was a prominent public school administrator and then a member of the
faculty at Teachers College during the 1930s. Like other social reconstructionists, he felt
strongly that the schools had an obligation to teach students about the problems faced
by society and how to address those problems. He begins the article by arguing strongly
against the idea that teachers in a democratic culture should remain neutral. He argues that
freedom of inquiry and speech is essential to schools and the promotion of democracy,
and that people can achieve "a democratic reconstruction of economic and social life only
as they understand conditions, trends, necessities and possibilities: in a word, the causes
of our ills and the merits of proposed remedies." Participation in civic life is essential if democratic ideals are to be achieved.

Newlon outlines four major threats to democracy that teachers need to address, including the need to combat the rise of dictatorships such as that of Hitler, the need to reconstruct the failed economy, the need to defend civil liberties and free speech, and finally,
the need to extend the control and financing of education beyond the state and local level
to that of the federal government.

*   *   *

A myth of American education that almost hardened into a compelling tradition has been the notion that teachers should be political neutrals. Traditionally teachers have voted for the candidates and measures of their preference
but have generally refrained from giving voice, except in private circles, to political faith or party allegiance. In like manner they have attempted an impossible neutrality in the classroom. In recent years this has been called "teaching
to think, but not what to think."

These attitudes are dissolving. These always have been many exceptions.
Horace Mann cried out against social conditions in early factory towns and
reentered political life to continue his fight against slavery. In this century, the
organized profession has become increasingly active in public affairs and now
wields much influence with the public in shaping educational policies. There
are strong educational lobbies in every state capitol and at Washington. The
profession has expressed itself vigorously against such social abuses as child labor and has made a number of important discoveries. It has found for example, that adequate financial support of schools involves tax policies that strike
deep into the economic life of the country. It is encouraging to see a state

---

* **Source:** *Frontiers of Democracy*, Volume 7, Number 55, 1940, p. 22–24.

teachers association waging a successful battle in close cooperation with farmer, labor and other liberal groups for an amendment to a state constitution, authorizing a graduated income tax.

The educational profession has grown in political experience and wisdom. There is some evidence that it is approaching political maturity. The consequences of the fact that a million teachers constitute one of the most important functional groups in our society are inescapable. They will play their part in political affairs, if only through inaction. They have the same rights and obligations that other citizens have in the solution of the critical economic and social problems that beset us. This does not mean that teachers should use their classrooms for political propaganda nor that as a body they should at this time affiliate with a particular political party, but it does call for a much more vigorous participation in civic life.

Adequate financial support for education will be utterly impossible so long as the national income is in the seventy billion brackets. Adequate educational opportunity is today denied millions of youth, either because the schools of their communities are inadequately supported financially, or because of the low economic status of their families, or for both reasons. Equal opportunity can come only with an economic reconstruction that will release the productive capacities of our country, push the national income to the one hundred fifty billions now within reach, and make available decent incomes for all families by making available to every citizen not only a job at decent wages but security in this job. Talk about equal educational opportunity will become but idle prattle if we are unwilling to face up to these facts and act accordingly.

The welfare of education is, then, dependent on the economic well being of the people. But the people can achieve a democratic reconstruction of economic and social life only as they understand conditions, trends, necessities and possibilities: in a word, the causes of our ills and the merits of proposed remedies. To make their essential contribution to this understanding, schools must be intellectually free: free to make objective and searching analyses of our economic life in the light, always, of the meaning of democracy in all its bearings. In this century encouraging progress has been made in this direction. The profession was never so sensitive to the social implications and responsibilities of education. It is undeniable, however, that such objective study of our culture frequently encounters strong and even bitter resistance. This comes partly from inertia, partly from ignorance on the part of those who shrink from studies that may bring into question inherited attitudes, beliefs and modes of behavior. Such opposition is not so difficult to overcome.

What is needed is more education about democracy and education. But this opposition comes also from entrenched interests that are determined to protect their favored positions and that do not propose to tolerate study in the schools that may bring the status quo into question. We are all too familiar with the operation of these pressures. Teachers have been driven out of the schools because they have attempted with their classes honest analyses of social conditions, or for their political views and activities. The current attack on the Rugg social science books is a case in point, and is one of the most sinister developments in the history of American education. It is doubtful if a drop of honesty can be found at the source of this attack, even though some well-intentioned persons may be taken in by it.

The inevitable conclusion is that control and financial support of schools and the maintenance of freedom of teaching are political problems of the first magnitude. Upon teachers rests, of necessity in our complex industrial society, the chief responsibility for leadership in securing an adequate economic base for the schools, in bringing about genuine equality of opportunity, and in the achievement and maintenance of intellectual freedom in all our educational institutions. This takes the teachers squarely into politics. As a matter of fact, teachers are already deep in politics through the activities of their local, state, and national organizations. It is time that they recognize this fact and face up squarely to all its implications. It is high time that they began to work more forthrightly with those groups that are striving to affect a democratic solution of our economic and social problems.

If teachers are to win and keep the confidence and respect of the people, they must operate squarely in the American democratic tradition. They must spurn all methods that are not democratic. They must deny membership in their professional organizations to those individuals and groups, fortunately small in number, who, carried away by ideologies that serve as underpinning for contemporary dictatorships, persist in attempts to control these organizations through deceit intrigue. There is no place in American democracy for conspiratorial and undemocratic methods. The party line imposed with military authority by the party bureaucracy makes of the party member r an intellectual slave and destroys all democrat y. Teachers, of all people, should denounce such methods and all doctrines that point in the direction of dictatorship—whether the "dictatorship of the proletariat" or the dictatorship of the "elite." All these doctrines are poison to our way of life.

Few members of the profession question that complete military preparation on the part of the United States is today an imperative necessity. Teachers should remember, however, that French democracy was destroyed not only by the Nazi army but by its internal weaknesses. The French nation lacked unity.

It had failed to come to grips with critical economic and political problems. It is just as true that our democracy can be defended in the future only as we solve our economic problems democratically. The public schools are the people's schools. The very nature of the work of teachers demands that their sympathies should lie with the great masses of the people, with the common people. No group should be more deeply stirred by the lot of the economically depressed which today comprises one-third or more of our population.

What does all this mean when translated into action? Limitation of space compels the briefest of answers. Teachers still are bound too much by the myth of neutrality. The political education of all members of the profession is, therefore, a first essential. And it must be remembered that civic behavior will be the only valid test of this education. Here is a challenge to the Progressive Education Association, for only a profession that has the courage to assume its social and political responsibilities can in the future be called truly progressive. It means that each individual must actively support the forces working pragmatically for the realization of economic democracy. In 1940, the presidential candidates and their supporters must be judged by this test. Does the main support of the candidate come from forces that, however honest they may be, are chiefly concerned with maintaining their own favorable position in society? Does the candidate comprehend the nature of the crisis that grips the world today? Does he speak for the common people or for privilege? Does he seek a solution that is democratic in spirit and method? Is he an impracticable doctrinaire? Or does he represent a party that in its purposes or methods actually rejects democracy. Upon each teacher rests the responsibility for making such an analysis and acting accordingly, with courage. Furthermore, the organized profession must have the courage to take its stand on critical issues affecting democracy, as do industrialists, farmers, labor and other organized groups. Finally, the organized profession must draw closer to those groups that are most vital to the preservation of democracy: to labor, to the farmers, to socially-minded middle class groups, professional and political, and to the underprivileged, unorganized and inarticulate masses. Working alliances will often be essential to the protection of the values teachers hold dear. Let them be effected. Only in union and in numbers can come the strength essential to the protection of our democratic values. The American Federation of Teachers is already organically a part of the labor movement. The overwhelming defeat of the Communist element in this organization at its recent annual meeting in Buffalo is a good omen. The Federation has a positive and avowed liberal social orientation. The National Education Association, the Progressive Education Association and most of the state educational associations have been moving in the right direction in recent years.

More specifically, what are some major problems with which teachers should be especially concerned? I shall mention four. The first is the threat to democracy, to the United States, and to civilization itself inherent in the onward sweep of European and Asiatic dictatorship and in Hitler's military might. The second is the defense of democracy at home through a pragmatic reconstruction of our economy. This reconstruction must be gradually effected, but rapidly enough to prevent the piling up of a discontent that will give ear to demagoguery and end in the destruction of democracy. Upon the teaching profession lies an especial responsibility to help the people to an understanding of the fact that this reconstruction cannot be accomplished either through a return to historic laissez faire or by sudden wholesale socialization; that whatever of private enterprise serves well should be kept, but that those sectors of the economy in which "private enterprise" is failing or is thwarting the public interest must be brought under effective public control; that through extensive development of social services and through social investment government must play a more creative role in our economy. Third, the processes of democracy and our civil liberties must be jealously and courageously guarded. This is the realm in which propaganda most dangerously operates to make it appear that the worst is the best cause that necessary changes lead to totalitarianism. Finally, a new economic configuration makes generous federal support of education an absolute necessity. This support must be obtained without erecting a federal system of education paralleling the existing public school system, or without extending federal control over the existing system, and without making public funds available for schools not directly and completely controlled by the public. With all these problems teachers should concern themselves, as teachers and as citizens. In all this I am not concerned with blue prints, and let no one accuse me of holding that the profession should arrogate to itself the direction of social change. I do say that we cannot abdicate our social responsibilities, for what the million of us do, or fail to do, will have its effects for good or ill.

What are the chief obstacles to overcome? The first, of course, is lethargy and that fear that leads to attempted neutrality. The second is that tendency toward appeasement too often characteristic of educational leadership. The third comes from those unfortunate sentimental liberals who cannot make up their minds that political groups operating on the principle of the "party line," but masquerading in liberal disguise, must be condemned for what they are, wolves in sheep's clothing. Some of the worst fence sitters in American life today are to be found in this neighborhood. These are the individuals who are dividing the liberal forces, and in so doing they assume a terrible responsibility. Many of them profess to see little difference between Britain and Nazi

Germany or Soviet Russia, and they are unable to see that the destruction of British political democracy would be a calamity for us and for civilization. An even greater danger is that teachers will not recognize the fascist tendencies in certain sections of big business, in certain chauvinistic "patriotic" organizations, and in other homegrown reactionary groups. Some of these groups already have the temerity to propose measures thoroughly undemocratic and to question democracy as the American way of life. Some openly preach religious and racial hatreds.

Finally, there is the danger that always comes from liberals who are so doctrinaire that they cannot put first things first, that they cannot cooperate with honest conservatives in the defense of civil liberties and other democratic values and institutions, that they are unable, in a crisis, to abjure their perfectionist illusions and join with all men of good will in the defense of the very processes of political democracy. A genuine liberal does not regard himself as omniscient. He knows that many men of more conservative economic outlook than he are just as devoted to democracy. He knows that in the present critical moment in our history the hope of American democracy lies in that fact.

The crisis has suddenly made many of us aware of democratic values that we have long taken too much for granted. Defense of democracy is very popular today. But the voices of many leaders, whose cries now sound out above all others, were but a little while ago scarcely heard in protest against the economic conditions that endangered these values. Some indeed were known as reactionaries. In many instances the awakening is real, and many genuine conversions are occurring. But the shouting of platitudes will not save us. The defense of democracy calls for a fundamental reordering of our economic life at many points. This is the first lesson in political and social wisdom for teachers today. It is the test by which all our professions and actions will inevitably be judged at the bar of history. And the fate of American democracy for generations to come is likely to be decided in the next ten years.

It is a lamentable fact that many leaders of American education have failed to see that the improvement of our economic and social life, the realization of democracy in the age of technology, is fundamentally a problem for political democracy, and that, though they are different processes, education and politics are inseparably connected. This blindness is in considerable measure due to their professional education, but that is another story. It is now imperative that the profession concern itself not merely with the social objectives of education but with the underlying conditions essential to the realization of these objectives. It will be interesting to note which of our comprehensive national teachers organizations will have the courage to attack this political problem.

THIS HAS HAPPENED BEFORE *

Harold Rugg

This article is based on chapters VII and VIII of Harold Rugg's book *That Men May Understand: An American in the Long Armistice* (New York: Doubleday, Doran & Company, Inc.,1941). It argues that the current conservative attacks on education are nothing new and that they have taken place at least five times since the end of the First World War. Beginning with the Red Scare of 1919–1921, Rugg outlines the various attacks on American education and how they were part of a larger conservative political movement led by "professional publicity men and patrioteers."

*   *   *

The current attack on modern education is not the first of its kind. It is true that this present one is nation-wide, more virulent, and promises to last longer and to set back the work of the schools more than any previous one. But it has happened before—five times since the World War! In 1918 there was an isolated, short-lived attack on a single small group . . . in 1921-1926, a prolonged and fairly widespread one . . . in 1927 a local one upon my own group . . . and in 1934-1935 a much bigger and more powerful one. Five times in two decades, including the vast one beginning in 1939, a wave of censorship has rolled up on the schools. If these were plotted on a time-line they would coincide fairly closely with the ups and downs of the curves of social hysteria and conflict.

Since the summer of 1940 I have written the story of witch-hunting in the schools from a four-foot shelf of conflict about "Un-Americanism." It is a twenty-year documentary record—newspaper clippings . . . articles and cartoons from national magazines . . . scrapbooks and folders . . . pamphlets, bulletins and official reports . . . chapters clipped from books . . . transcriptions of records of hearings . . . stenographic records of Hearst newspaper interviews, what-not. Altogether there are thousands of items covering the five recurring waves of social hysteria since 1918. It is, of course, but a meagre sample of the national literature of conflict; but it is a representative sample and contains the key items. This history not only throws the present attacks on schools in perspective but provides an hypothesis for understanding them in their true light.

An hypothesis for a documentary study of these cycles might run something like this:

---

* **Source:** *The Frontiers of Democracy*, Volume 7, Number 58, 1941, pp. 105–108.

Following, or in connection with, each major war or domestic crisis there ensues a dangerous period of restlessness, agitation, discontent and revolt. Labor troubles, strikes, riots, lynchings, near-financial panics, and witch-hunts of aliens, liberals and racial and religious out-groups are all manifestations of this unrest. If the rise and fall of these were shown on a graph, such a graph would, I feel sure, rise quickly to its peak within two or three years, then slowly taper off through some years to a longer period of comparative quiet.

THE RED SCARE OF 1919–1921

This is what happened following the close of the World War of 1914–1918. Within a year a near panic had spread across the country. A wave of labor strikes broke out in the stockyards, shipyards, and subways, on the docks of the harbors, in the shoe factories, and in the building construction industry. At one moment in 1919 two million workers were out on strike.

Labor leaders were not only asking better wages and working conditions, they were asking for drastic social changes as well. In the coal industry, for example, they were demanding government ownership of mines. Defenders of "free enterprise" marshalled their forces against labor, against "radicals," against "East Side Jews." The newspapers were blazoned with scare headlines.

In the winter of 1919–1920 frightening rumors of impending attack on American institutions began to spread. These were accentuated by a series of bombings, in one of which the home of United States Attorney General A. Mitchell Palmer in Washington was damaged. Using the war-time Sedition Act as authority, Palmer had been making raids on aliens, more than 6,000 of whom were arrested and kept in jail. The "Red Scare" lasted about two years. By the end of the summer of 1920, social conditions were getting better. Production was rising, the unemployed were going back to work. Some witch-hunting of aliens and liberals continued through 1921, but by 1922—except for the schools—it had died out, not to appear again for over a decade.

Attacks upon the schools started as the hysteria in other areas declined. There is documentation for the hypothesis that trends for education tend to lag behind those affecting the people more directly. This is what happened in the early 1920's. The school witch-hunters became active in 1921 and their hunt lasted until about 1926. It was manufactured in much the same way as the present one. It was kept going by persons with much the same kind of background, interest and philosophy. And the methods used in spreading and prolonging the attack were almost identical.

THE PATRIOTEERS ATTACK THE "NEW HISTORIANS," 1921–1926[1]

After the close of the War the social soil was perfectly prepared for the launching of a concerted attack upon the writers of school histories. The Red Scare of 1919–1921 had set the mood of many people. The defeat of Germany and the confirmation of British domination over the world stimulated the pro-Ally groups into increased activity. German-Americans and Irish-Americans in general were still alert to seize upon any chance to attack Britain; among these were politicians in power, like Mayor Thompson in Chicago and New York City's Tammany Mayor Hylan, whose primary interest was votes.

Three additional factors helped to pave the way for the attack. First, the controversy had sharpened over the "new" interpretation of American history, evidence for which had been accumulating for several decades. Second, professional publicity persons were at hand ready to dramatize attack and sell it to newspapers and magazines. Third, chiefs of "Americanization" units of national patriotic organizations were becoming increasingly active in propagandizing against any actual or imagined "subversive" influence.

The attacks upon the school immediately after the War cannot be understood unless one remembers that it was in this period that the content of the history program was being made over. "History" had long been little more than a build-up of unthinking patriotism, a eulogy of patriots who had fought the Revolutionary War and founded the country. In the 1890's historians, economists, sociologists, anthropologists and others at such Universities as Chicago, Columbia, and Wisconsin began the publication of the findings of more impartial research—at Wisconsin, F. J. Turner and his *The Significance of the Frontier in American History*; at Chicago, William I. Thomas, J. H. Breasted, and Thorstein Veblen, building the foundations for a new sociology, investigating the origins of civilization, and carrying on economic and social-psychological studies; in the Field Museum Franz Boas, working in anthropology; at Columbia, James Harvey Robinson, developing his studies of western European history, and the younger Charles A. Beard, preparing his now classic monograph on *An Economic Determination of the Constitution of the United States*. Taken all together, these and other students produced, between the 1880's and the World War, materials for a whole new history of Man.

This "new history" began to get into school textbooks by the 1910's. The Colonial period, the Revolutionary War, and the Founding Fathers were given a more objective treatment. Military exploits and political details were minimized. New viewpoints, and particularly new economic and social emphases, were brought out. New content was introduced. The frontier was played up, as were the westward movement, land and industrial history, even "the arts."

It was this new history which became the target of attack. In the uncertainty brought about by the Red Scare of 1921 Charles Grant Miller, a Hearst syndicate writer, started to attack the textbooks of David S. Muzzey,[2] and seven other school historians. Then, as now, the books were called "treason texts" . . . "unfit for public school use, because subversive of American spirit" . . . "un-American" . . . "grossly defamatory," and the like.

Miller formed in 1932 "The Patriot League for the Preservation of American History," a propaganda organization composed of the executive officials of such patriotic organizations as the National Society of the Sons of the American Revolution, the Veterans of Foreign Wars, the American Legion, the United Spanish War Veterans, and the Early Settlers of America.

Meanwhile, in New York City a committee of teachers was appointed to look into the "new history." It held open hearings, at which Miller and other publicists and several officials of patriotic organizations appeared and made charges. In January, 1922, the committee made a report, finding that: "there is no evidence to support the charge that any of the textbook writers whose books were examined is unpatriotic" and no evidence "of organized propaganda."

This report was accepted by the Board of Education, but "Tammany" politicians were not satisfied; they wanted a report more clearly adverse to the new interpretation which seemed to them to be pro-British. One Joseph Devlin[3] was hired by the Tammany Commissioner of Accounts, David Hirshfield, to conduct an investigation of the books, but he too cleared them of un-American taints. Hirshfield, however, shelved Devlin's report and engaged no less than Mr. Miller, an "expert" on such matters, to make a new study. This time a satisfactorily denunciatory report[4] was forthcoming, and Hirshfield published it under his own name.

In 1924, the officials of the American Legion, under the guidance of Garland W. Powell, the chief of the National Americanism Commission of the Legion, decided to write an "American History." They secured the cooperation of some fifty patriotic organizations and hired Charles F. Home, editorial director of the Legion and Professor of English at the College of the City of New York, to prepare the manuscript. It was published in 1926, but in spite of wide publicity never obtained much use in the schools.

Following the unsuccessful attack upon Muzzey, et al., there was a decade-long lull in witch-hunting. As for my own work, I recall no more than four or five instances in the seven years from 1922 to 1929 in which the Social Science Pamphlets (the experimental materials I developed in the Lincoln School of Teachers College) were seriously questioned.

In the spring of 1927 came the only serious attack—one made by the director of research of the "industrial relations" department of one of our largest corporations. The charges in their long briefs ran according to the usual formula: The Pamphlets were called "subversive" and "un-American"; some 200 items had been taken out of context and labelled in such ways as "unbalanced emphasis" . . . "sensationalism" . . . "exaggeration" . . . "misrepresentation" . . . "generalization" . . . "misstatements of fact." My analysis of the 200 items showed that in only three excerpts had we made misstatements of fact (one was actually a misprint) or, from the standpoint of the "new history" which we accepted, had given misinterpretations! In ninety-eight per cent of the items in the briefs the attacker himself was guilty of misinterpretation of the author's meaning, or gross lifting-out-of-context, or sheer ignorance of the purposes and methods employed in the preparation and use of the Pamphlets in the school. This attack never got beyond the offices of Lincoln School, Teachers College, and the General Education Board, for we were able to confer directly with the officers of the corporation and convince them of the validity of what we were doing in bringing the study of American life into the schools.[5]

The 1927 episode caused no regional or nationwide repercussions. Authors of other textbooks have reported to me approximately the same findings with respect to their own enterprises. Attacks upon teachers and professors, and upon academic freedom in general, were few and far between.

The chief explanation for the lull in the late Twenties, I feel confident, is the nature of the period. It was an era of optimism, of speculation, of ebullience. There was little tension among the people. The mood was feverish, but this was more from over-indulgence than from fear of insecurity. For the moment, then, witch-hunting was out; bigotry was at a new low.

Then in 1929–1933 came the first shocking events of the Great Depression, and yet until 1934 there were almost no attacks on the schools. Why? I think that those who manufacture them and keep them alive were otherwise engaged—saving the wrecks of their own enterprises, their fortunes, their minds, their souls. And this leads me to pose another hypothesis for the psychologists of the public mind to document, and refute or confirm; namely—witch-hunting in the schools flourishes neither in times of great prosperity nor in times of great depression. In the one period excitement brought about by the promise of personal gain is so intense that people cannot be bothered with "trivialities in the schools." In periods of great unrest, panic, economic anxiety, the interest of the people in such campaigns just cannot be captured; they are too worried over other matters. The very economic-social scene itself is so "subverted" that the interests of the hunters are diverted in other directions.

1934–1935: ANOTHER WAVE OF ATTACKS

The renewal of slashing attacks in 1934–1935 throws even more light on the combination of factors favorable to the rise of witch-hunting. Between 1930 and 1934 a liberal New Statecraft in government and social reform became generally very active. The social engineering mind got into government as never before in American history. Liberals became vigorous and vocal Progressive educational leaders organized widespread movements for adult education, new societies for the study of our changing civilization, and new magazines for the discussion of it.

As I appraise the work of the New Statecraft and the dramatic action of the liberals in education during the early 1930's I can see more clearly than ever before how inevitable it was that witch-hunting would begin again.

By the autumn of 1934 the public mood was properly prepared. Suspicion was in the air. Growing numbers were beginning to cry out against the "experiments" being tried in Washington. Groups like M. K. Hart's were out to cut taxes even if that meant hampering the schools. Business men were talking about being "hamstrung." In education sincere defenders of the disciplinary tradition sought to put "progressivism" out of the schools. These and other factors paved the way for the fire of the opponents of change in educational practice.

The targets had become conspicuous enough to hit—and hit they did—the Hearst newspapers, Elizabeth Dilling, the Americanism units of the American Legion, the Sons of American Revolution, the Daughters of American Revolution, the Veterans of Foreign Wars, and other patriotic organizations.

In 1934 Elizabeth Dilling, a middle-west concert harpist and housewife, published a little handbook called *The Red Network*. It was a kind of "Who's Who of Radicalism" for "patriots." It listed 460 suspected organizations and 1300 persons, including, in the words of one reviewer, practically everyone in America who "has ever worked for social progress, freedom, and humanitarianism." I am listed in it, because of my reference to the Russian Youth movement in my 1933 *Herald Tribune* speech which was quoted in *The Daily Worker*. I must confess that I should now be quite chagrined had I been left out of it; after all—1300 liberals!

In the winter of 1934–1935 the Hearst Newspapers renewed their liberal-baiting in the schools. Stenographic accounts in my possession prove that Hearst reporters admitted, in interviewing Professors Kilpatrick and Counts of Teachers College, that they were "red-baiters" and that "Hearst is engaged at present in conducting a 'Red Scare.'"

All winter the fight between Hearst and our group of progressive educators went on. I hardly need remind the readers of this journal of our famous

1935 Atlantic City meeting for the discussion of how to stop Hearst liberal-baiting in the schools nor the magnificent denunciation of Hearst by Dr. Beard.

During the same winter and spring of 1935 a similar attack was made by patriotic organizations in various regions of the country, in Washington, D. C, and Cedar Rapids, Iowa. Both of these conspicuous attacks were unsuccessful; my books were investigated by Boards of Education and as a result were retained in the schools. Because of his recent notoriety, it is interesting to note that for five years Verne Marshall, editor of The Cedar Rapids (Iowa) *Gazette*, tried to eliminate my books from the local schools. Like M. K. Hart in New York State, Marshall in Iowa was regarded by university and school men as their principal enemy. For five years Marshall failed to oust my books; in 1940 he succeeded, due, I am confident, to the nation-wide social hysteria that has now rolled across the country. Behind the nation-wide attacks, however, there is reason to believe that the "Americanism" chiefs of national patriotic organizations are the directing hands.

SUMMING UP THEN

Those who have read the article by Alonzo Myers in the October issue of this magazine can now see that "this has happened before." The raids on the schools since 1939 are almost exact replicas of the earlier ones:

- they were initiated by professional publicity men and patrioteers.

- the charges were "un-Americanism," "subversiveness."

- Hearst newspapers, national popular magazines, and the "Americanization" chiefs of national patriotic organizations broadcast the attack.

- they were kept alive artificially.

- special propaganda organizations were formed which inspired and sponsored bills censoring the schools in the legislatures of various states.

- certain publishers of competing texts sent their agents into schools armed with detailed materials to keep the strife stirred up.

- local political factions used the fight to aid them in ousting local school officials.

- associations of teachers and other liberal groups appointed committees and passed resolutions counter-attacking the accusers and supporting the historians.

References

1. In the writing of the chapters of *That Men May Understand* dealing with the history of such attacks on the schools I was greatly aided by being given access to Dr. J. Montgomery Gambrill's file covering the years, 1921–26.
2. Then, as in my case today, Ginn and Company were the progressive publishers involved. In this episode of witch-hunting in the schools they and Dr. Muzzey won a signal victory.
3. The *New York Tribune*, November 5–12, 1923.
4. It is interesting to note that Major General Amos A. Fries is still using this episode and report to buttress his attack on the schools. See his Bulletin, Friends of the Public Schools, March, 1940.
5. In sharp contrast to this tolerant attitude is the blunt refusal in 1939–1940 of A. G. Rudd and B. C. Forbes—leaders in the current attacks on my work—to confer face-to-face. I am convinced that they and their associates do not desire to find agreements with the educational liberals; they wish only to stir up and perpetuate conflict rather than to work out solutions.

THIS WAR AND AMERICAN EDUCATION *

The Editorial Board

I n this editorial the journal's editorial board outlines the basic guiding principles concerning the war and the role of education in solving the social problems that led to the war and that will have to be addressed once peace returns. It emphasizes the fear that the military situation has the potential to lead to "the introduction of the fascist pattern" into American "ways of thought and action." It stresses that democracy will suffer, not only immediately, but in the future, if cultural, educational and political processes are inhibited and restricted as part of the crisis brought on by the war. Finally, the idea that education, in a time of crisis, is not a luxury, but a basic necessity is emphasized.

* * *

Basic Guiding Principles

1. Democratic civilization is in a struggle for survival throughout the world. We regard the winning of both the war and the peace essential to the preservation and the extension of this democratic civilization. Since this democratic way of life also provides both the foundation and the goal of our educational effort, we urge full participation of all educational forces in the present struggle against totalitarianism.

2. We believe that the manner in which our country organizes on the home and war fronts to carry this struggle through to victory will profoundly condition the kind of peace we can create after the Axis Powers are defeated. The cause of democracy cannot prosper during this period if we suspend its cultural, educational, and political processes. Hence it is imperative that we see that all policy-making bodies—local, state and national—are manned by leaders who will be alert to test every aspect of our domestic and foreign program by the democratic criterion. Primary and demanding as are the military aspects of the problem, they cannot be successfully divorced from the social, educational and political factors. We must not let the crucial necessities of the military situation become the occasion for the introduction of the fascist pattern into our own ways of thought and action. The liberal elements in our present able political leadership should be supported and strengthened.

3. We need to cultivate in the people of our country a sense of democratic initiative and advance, not one of defense and retrenchment. This attitude of confidence and bold initiative is particularly needed in the field of education.

---

* **Source:** *The Frontiers of Democracy*, Volume 8, Number 66, 1942, p. 102.

We should in no sense regard education as a luxury at this time. It is both an essential expression of that democracy for which we fight, and a fundamental instrumentality for the defense and extension of democracy during the war and post-war period. Educators therefore should unite with all other forces concerned with the public welfare to see:

A. That the full productive energies of our nation are released so that the essential war and civilian needs may he adequately met. Neither owners nor workers shall be permitted to limit our productive possibilities in this life and death struggle.

B. That the long-run interests of democracy are not impaired by our failure to provide for the physical, intellectual, emotional and social development of the children and youth of our country.

C. That national, state and local health, welfare and educational agencies and activities are coordinated in the most efficient manner to meet the total needs of the young.

D. That a vital and comprehensive program of adult education is developed. Without an alert and enlightened public we cannot achieve the kind of democratic outcomes we need to justify the huge sacrifices of this war. If we are to win both the peace and the war, the democratic processes of inquiry, discussion, criticism, clarification and formulation of aims and programs must be extended, not abridged or adjourned.

EDUCATION AND TOTAL WAR [*]

The Editorial Board

The editorial board for the journal takes the position in this editorial piece that the world is in a profound process of social transformation as a result of the Second World War. They declare that: "We who are concerned with social reconstruction must recognize that reconstruction has already begun. What American communities are now doing, the organization and upheavals which they are now experiencing—these in very fact form part and parcel of the social endeavor to build a juster world." As a result of the war, and the peace that will hopefully follow, American society and its institutions will be radically redefined.

The editors call "for an education which is realistic, vital, comprehensive, an education which is an integral part of the life of the community and the nation, an education geared to the fast-changing social and economic life of the nation, an education which meets in fact the needs of the individual and of society."

Referencing the "Nine Freedoms" that the National Resources Planing Board emphasized in their report of 1942, the editors of the journal add a tenth freedom, "the right to equality of treatment." In doing so, they anticipate the Civil Rights Movement of the 1950s and 1960s, and the extent to which the schools and the educational system at large could no longer remain seemingly neutral in terms of issues of social justice and equality.

* * *

This total war, the first worldwide total war in history. It is a war in which all the resources—both human and material—of each nation are needed for the Every man, woman, youth and child is in—It is a war in which battle lines are everywhere; the home front and the war front are inextricably interwoven. It is a war in which we are all bound together in the conflict and equally bound together in the peace. This "total war" involves all of us for all our futures.

Already the war effort has brought many dislocations in American life— Men have been drawn from home and community to serve in the armed forces. Taxes have risen many fold. The manufacture of consumer goods has been restricted and even prohibited. Each and every one of us and each and every community has in some way already been seriously affected.

But these present dislocations are merely a scratch on the surface in comparison with what is to come. The number of men drafted for armed service will be multiplied many times; men, women and youth workers will be drafted for "work" service and sent to critical spots on our war production map. Professional people will be called for their war effort. Doctors and nurses will be

[*] **Source:** *The Frontiers of Democracy* Volume 8, Number 70, 1942, p. 228–229

needed in great numbers with the result that health services will be seriously affected and careful plans must be made to protect communities from epidemics. It is estimated that one out of every ten teachers now in our schools will be missing as schools open in the fall. Taxes will be doubled and tripled. Consumer goods of all types will be rationed. Wages, profits, rents, and the cost of essentials will be frozen by law. All this effort to plan American production and consumption is necessary, for America has become the final source of supply for all our allies. Today we are only at the threshold of the period when every expenditure of physical resources and human energy must be carefully scrutinized to justify its relation to our total war effort.

In this total war effort, the social and economic patterns of America are undergoing drastic change; in many respects these changes will be permanent. We cannot draft men for the war and after the war is over be unconcerned that they are unemployed or poorly clothed or ill fed and ill housed. War is always a rapid transition period in the history of social evolution. Our social changes in fact began long before December 7th and the resulting social patterns and the planning which now are part of our war effort will not cease when peace is declared. What we can do to wage war, we can do to make a decent peace. We who are concerned with social reconstruction must recognize that reconstruction has already begun. What American communities are now doing, the organization and upheavals which they are now experiencing—these in very fact form part and parcel of the social endeavor to build a juster world.

In this drastic reorganization of American society, educational institutions and organizations are bound to be seriously affected. Some will sigh for the old carefree days but schools cannot remain isolated from the currents and tides of community reconstruction. The only question is as to how well they do their part. We who are concerned that education should play a proper role in world reconstruction will accept the opportunity to rebuild educational institutions and practices so that they may really play an important role in winning the "total war." And we will not stop with winning the war. We must go on also to win the peace. For the war is only the first stage of the larger effort to regain and upbuild a decent civilization.

The schools of America stand now at a vital crossroad and a choice must be made quickly. There are two directions in which they may go. One is to retrench and retreat into isolation. They can let budgets be cut, salaries be reduced and the curriculum become the dry skeleton of out-moded academic learning. If this course be followed during the war emergency, it will continue during the post-war period of reconstruction. This means either that our boys and girls will grow up ignorant of the problems of the nation and so fail the community when the need arises, or that other agencies created by society will inadequately attempt the necessary task which the schools have failed to perform.

The other possible direction is one of aggressive action. In this period of war emergency it is possible for educational institutions to effect a more rapid transformation than in normal times. The basic changes which the war is right now bringing into our society allow and even require basic changes in the educational patterns for children and youth. The problems and responsibilities of the present and the future call for an education which is realistic, vital, comprehensive, an education which is an integral part of the life of the community and the nation, an education geared to the fast-changing social and economic life of the nation, an education which meets in fact the needs of the individual and of society.

If education is thus to share in the campaign for victory and for a just and lasting peace to follow, it must be a new kind of education. The schools can no longer work in isolation but must become an integral part of the community and the nation. Such planning must be locally done and on a total community basis.

Already many leaders have foreseen that changes must be made in our schools. The Educational Policies Commission of the NEA, the American Youth Commission, the AF of T, the PEA and other organizations have issued statesman-like documents on the general direction education should take and have charted its course in many areas for the present emergency and the period of reconstruction. This good advice has not been followed, however. The evidence is overwhelming that these statements have not affected general school practices in as rapid and in as effective a way as is necessary. In part this failure is because these policies and programs have not been created by the teachers and citizens of the communities who must execute them. War or no war, ideas be effective must be the ideas of those who are to put them into practice. A better education has long recognized that in dealing with either young or old, participation in planning programs is an essential. It is this idea we must now nationally accept.

Some steps can be suggested. In each local community a School-Community Council can be set up: (1) to study what the community should be doing for war and peace, and (a) to get community and school to work carrying out the plans. Such a Council should consist of school people, social workers, parent-teacher representatives and the like, with plans to get groups of citizens and pupils working at actual social problems and efforts. In a small community there might be one or two such Councils; in a small city several; and in large cities many. District, state, and national organizations should be effected. Back and forth between local councils and the successive headquarters ideas can flow and efforts be coordinated in one great democratic enterprise.

It is in such ways as this that ideas can really get into effective operation. This is democratic education at its best. We hope that this magazine and Progressive Education may later have more specific steps to suggest.

The Nine Freedoms

The national resources planning board formulated the nine freedoms to which this issue of our magazine is devoted. Taken together these constitute a new and advanced charter for our national life. In a true sense they represent the reconstruction of our institutional outlook referred to in the earlier part of this discussion. Up to ten years ago no American government could have promulgated half of what is implied in the statement of these freedoms. We are even now in the midst of peaceful revolutionary change. The war hastens but by psychological, not violent means. The School-Community Councils suggested above could do well to base much of their work on the foundation of these freedoms. There is no community but has far to go to live up to them. Youth can greatly profit by the study of them to put them into fuller operation in the local neighborhood. We must bring up a generation to understand them so thoroughly as to be willing to accept them to live by.

A Tenth Freedom

Naturally, no limited list can include everything. Back of the nine rights lies one even more fundamental which was assumed as unnecessary to state, namely the right to equality of treatment in respect to all these nine freedoms. These rights are to hold equally for all our citizens irrespective of race, color or creed. That they do not so equally hold in our land we know only too well, be it said to our shame. This magazine has often called attention to the failure of our American civilization in respect to the treatment of minorities.

It is, however, an international complication to which we here call attention. On the statute books of our country we profess to treat all our citizens alike; in our international relationships we do not even profess it. We refuse to recognize the yellow and brown peoples as deserving of equal legal treatment with white and black. We refuse to let immigrants from the Orient become citizens. For us so to act can only affront. At the Versailles Conference the Japanese sought urgently to get official recognition of racial equality of treatment. It was refused. We cannot refuse it at the close of this war when China and India sit at the peace table with us. The sooner we remove these citizenship restrictions the better for all concerned. This war is a war for the ethically equal treatment of all people. India hesitates now. Our step would help. We must remove these humiliating restrictions or seriously endanger our cause.

ESSENTIALS OF EDUCATION FOR A PEOPLE'S PEACE *

B. Othanel Smith

A leading figure in educational research and a teacher during the 1950s, B. Othanel Smith spent most of his career at the University of Illinois, Urbana, where he taught in the School of Education. In this article, he calls for "making the struggle for universal peace a central theme of mass education." In a statement that resonates clearly with contemporary educational and social conditions, he argues that: "The opposition, especially our native fascists, may yet win and in so doing plunge the world into a prolonged period of slavery or into a century of terrorism and despair." He further believes that education as a field must take sides in the struggle for a more peaceful world and outlines the basic steps that must be undertaken to accomplish this goal.

*   *   *

A tranquil world cannot be established once and for all at a conference table. Although what is done at the peace parley is extremely important, peace can be maintained only, by the creative use of the years that come after the victory.

Since peace is no more dependent upon immediate political action than upon the shape we give to future domestic and foreign policies, the schools can make a significant contribution to the continued peace of the world by making the struggle for universal peace a central theme of mass education. This can be done effectively only if the character of the times is clearly sensed and used in shaping the educational program.

We are witnessing a period of profound social change, as significant as that which saw the fall of the Roman Empire, the birth of modern capitalist society, or the rise of the middle class to power in 1789. It is a period of world revolt against economic injustices, against the predatory anarchic nation-state, against the domination of the white man. It is an era of great endeavor, the greatest the human race has made, to democratize economic power and to establish a world community of racial, social and political equalities. Aside from the dynamic power of democracy, its driving force is the impact upon the masses of the inability of the prevailing economy to release the tremendous productive capacity at our command.

The deepest issues of our time center about this great endeavor. Both the war and the bitter domestic conflict among social groups and classes go back to the fact that individuals and organized groups and nations have taken sides for or against the fulfillment of the purposes that give this historic period its

* **Source:** *Frontiers of Democracy*, Volume 10, Number 79, 1943, p. 27–28.

particular significance. The outcome of this intense and far-reaching struggle is unpredictable. The opposition, especially our native fascists, may yet win and in so doing plunge the world into a prolonged period of slavery or into a century of terrorism and despair.

In this struggle education must take sides. Education for peace, for a better world, must of necessity seek the alteration of men on a mass scale in the interest of the fight against fascists and the battle to democratize economic and political power. The content and the method of education must be profoundly altered and the spirit and structure of the whole school must be made to conform to the new ideals and to the new content.

Let us therefore build an educational program that will—

1. Be Dedicated to the Development of Social Vision and Unity of Purpose

Despite the fact that we are living in a period in which the fundamental alternatives are a further democratization of life or a further constriction of human welfare, social purposes are confused and vision of the future is too often clouded by the glories of the past. This is due partly to the nature of the time and partly to lack of discipline in thinking about common goals. In an era of intense social unrest, such as we are now experiencing, the very ends of existence are the primary points of controversy. At such a time men everywhere are confused and in conflict, not so much about the ways in which they should fulfill their purposes as about what purposes they should attempt to fulfill. In the rebuilt curriculum we must recognize and repudiate the half-truth that as a people we are agreed upon ends but not upon means. Anyone who has given the slightest attention in the last few years to efforts to improve housing conditions, to extend medical care to all persons, to turn the wheels of industry at full capacity, to wipe out fascist influence at home and in the world must surely have realized that failure has resulted from no lack of technical knowledge, no deficiency of materials or of manpower, no lack of political information and prestige. The failure lies rather in the fact that as a people we are agreed upon these things only in the abstract, only so long as they are desired in isolation from other things. This is clear the moment the slightest effort is made to attain them. For then it becomes painfully evident that some individuals and social groups want these ends only if they can be attained without the loss of the special privileges and powers they now enjoy. The curriculum must realistically recognize that we can have such social gains only by overcoming the resistance of those whose loyalties and interests are selfishly embedded in the system of things as they are. It must drive home the idea that the price of peace, as well as of victory, is that we cannot preserve the world as it was between the Great Wars.

It must necessarily follow from what has been said that the rebuilding of universal human purposes amid sharp social conflicts must be one of the central problems of a curriculum devoted to a peace made in the interest of the common people. For fully a half a century the schools have failed to do this. Instead they have dwelt upon what man has done to the exclusion of what he is trying to do or should be trying to do. They have stressed facts and abstract generalizations while ignoring the tragic truth that, in the absence of a clearly defined and accepted set of social purposes and ideals, such knowledge may serve Mammon and God, the sinner and the saint, the fascist and the democrat equally well. In the curriculum for our times we must build a common vision of things to strive for. We must focus the eyes and ambitions of youth upon the stars of our forefathers rather than upon the embers of their dying campfires. We must everlastingly keep before youth the all-important question: What kind of a world should we, not as isolated individuals but as a people, strive to build?

Let us be specific. Let us build a curriculum from which youth can learn that we can and should achieve full employment and an excellent standard of life—food, clothing, housing, education, recreation and health—for everyone regardless of race, social position, or nationality; that all of this is possible for the whole world as science and technology are applied to the development of the industrially backward peoples; that all of this can be attained not by surrendering the hard-won freedoms of ordinary people but by extending those freedoms and equalities in many new directions and to all peoples. The vision that they must see is a world in which democracy has remade economic, political, and social relations among individuals, social groups and nations. Let us build an educational program that will—

2. Make the Democratic Values the Universal Basis of Social Decision and Action

If the curriculum is to be an instrument for the development of social purposes and vision, it should be no less an instrument for the development of social judgment to choose wisely among the various proposals and plans for realizing the vistas thus built. Few things are now more puzzling to youth and adult alike than the question of how to know which side is right in a social conflict, which course of action is best among those proposed by sincere men for the resolution of issues, which plan is best for the realization of social purposes. The particular social situation makes this an unusually perplexing question today, one which is closely related to the problem of attaining common purposes. When the social orientation of a people is more or less stable social decisions are easy to make. For the fundamental principles upon which the tightness of choice rests are understood and commonly accepted. In a period of deep social cleavages, however, the meaning of these principles is relative to the social position and interests of individuals and groups. Social judgment and decision then become complex and difficult tasks. The automatic process of choice prevalent in a stably developing society must then be brought under conscious control.

Under such circumstances the curriculum must provide situations in which loyalties are not only studied and reconstructed but also used critically as the moral basis of social choice and action. From such situations youth will learn that the ultimate criterion of social choice is: Which of the proposed courses of action expands human equalities and freedoms and extends them to a larger and larger number of people? There can be no social intelligence, no political maturity in a democratic people undisciplined in the application of this principle to their daily choices and actions.

Much is being said about social planning today, which indicates that it is used as a neutral concept, equally applicable to the restriction of human welfare and to its expansion. Social planning as such means an increase of well being for the masses only if it is made to conform to democratic principles. The best safeguard against the abuse of social planning in the interest of special groups and classes is a people whose will to action is disciplined by democratic ideals.

Let us build a curriculum which will make the great social issues of today a central concern, and let us deal with these issues, not in an air of objective detachment, but as burning social conflicts involving the vital prejudices of youth and adults as well as the perspectives and designs of conflicting social groups and classes. Let us reach conclusions and evaluate them in terms of the democratic values rather than by their effects upon dominant vested interests, or upon personal ambitions. Thus discipline will be developed in the making of social decisions, a discipline without which domestic and international peace and progress are impossible in an age of social conflict.

Let us build an educational program that will—

3. Provide a Socially Positive Subject Matter

The nature of our times requires not only a dedication of the curriculum to new purposes and to the development of the powers of social judgment, but also a new content compatible with these dedications. The present curriculum, even in the most advanced reconstructions of it, largely ignores two kinds of subject matter, which are absolutely essential to the realization of the progressive potentialities of industrial society. The first of these is the moral content of our culture. What is needed is the inclusion of the principles of social morality as objects of intensive study. They must become as explicitly a part of the curriculum as the principles of science or of mathematics.

The second kind of content, which the curriculum must include if people are to understand and deal successfully with the problems that arise in the fulfillment of common social goals, consists of the facts about the productive capacity of modern industry and the forces, conditions, and special interests that prevent the full utilization of that capacity. Likewise the facts about international policies must be realistically presented. It is becoming clear that our foreign policies have been directed more by the wishes and interests of special groups than by the broad principles of international justice. The very men who are allied against the democratization of economic life at home are allied against the realization of mutual relations in the world at large. Facts about these groups and their strategies must have a conspicuous place in the education of the masses.

Effective reconstruction of the educational program along the lines here suggested assumes a complete reorientation of the curriculum—from the victories of the past to the battles yet unwon; from verbal worship of democracy to the actual use of its principles and its dynamic powers in shaping the course of events; from a bloodless, neutral content to a content vibrant with moral imperatives; from facts about abstract social processes to knowledge about social and political strategies of organized groups and classes. This is part of the price, which the educator must pay for a people's peace.

THE DIRECTORS OF THE PROGRESSIVE EDUCATION ASSOCIATION VOTE 12 TO 3 TO DISCONTINUE PUBLICATION *

Directors of the Progressive Education Association

In the notice included below, the Directors of the Progressive Education Association call by a vote of 12 to 3, to discontinue publishing *Frontiers of Democracy*. Financial limitations are given as the reason for discontinuing the journal. The notice suggests that while the Association will "continue to report progress in education and to give help to teachers," it will also "increasingly reflect the new direction in which the Association will move in the future." This, and other statements, suggest that the Association was deliberately setting itself apart from the social reconstructionist perspective of Rugg, Counts and their followers.

THE DIRECTORS OF THE PROGRESSIVE EDUCATION ASSOCIATION VOTE 12 TO 3 TO DISCONTINUE PUBLICATION

The Progressive Education Association announces with regret that FRONTIERS OF DEMOCRACY has been discontinued as a publication of the Association.

For years FRONTIERS OF DEMOCRACY has been published only by the employment of deficit planning which in view of our present financial situation can no longer be practiced. Had we continued the publication of FRONTIERS OF DEMOCRACY we would have faced a deficit at the end of this year of at least $2,200 for this publication alone. Under present conditions, elimination of FRONTIERS OF DEMOCRACY as one step in a necessary program of economy was inevitable.

The Board of Directors in taking this action desires to reaffirm its belief in the statement of Position and Program of FRONTIERS OF DEMOCRACY, which appeared on pages 3 to 5 of the October issue. The Board further desires to officially express its deep appreciation, to Dr. Harold Rugg for his unceasing efforts on behalf of the journal and the Association and for his notable contribution to the cause of American liberalism.

PROGRESSIVE EDUCATION will be substituted for FRONTIERS OF DEMOCRACY for all who subscribed exclusively to the latter journal. For those members who subscribed to FRONTIERS OF DEMOCRACY in combination with PROGRESSIVE EDUCATION we shall extend membership and subscription to PROGRESSIVE EDUCATION to cover the contractual

* **Source:** *Frontiers of Democracy*, Volume 10, Number 81, 1943, p. 70.

period for which no issues of FRONTIERS OF DEMOCRACY will be forthcoming.

The remaining journal—PROGRESSIVE EDUCATION—will not only continue to report progress in education and to give help to teachers, but will increasingly reflect the new direction in which the Association will move in the future. Moreover, it will use its influence to promote all constructive endeavors that make for better education and for a democratic society.

Virgil Rogers
President

VINAL H. TIBBETTS
Director

WE ACCEPT IN PRINCIPLE BUT REJECT IN PRACTICE. IS THIS LEADERSHIP?[*]

Harold Rugg

H arold Rugg in this editorial responds to the Progressive Education Association's discontinuing the publication of *Frontiers of Democracy*. Rejecting the idea that ending publication of the journal was simply a financial issue, Rugg maintains that the Association is abolishing the journal because of a lack of commitment on their part and "the fear of the Officers that *Frontiers* would endanger the new program that they were making for the Association, and in addition would endanger their own personal security." Rugg maintains that it is the duty of progressive educators to defend the principles of democracy from "menacing fascists and false patrioteers." Rather than exploring the frontiers of democracy and "controversial issues of community life," Rugg maintains that the Association is simply interested in maintaining the status quo—i.e., popularizing "accepted truths" rather than developing "new ones."

*　　*　　*

This is the last issue of *Frontiers*. The directors of the Progressive Education Association have voted, 12 to 3, to discontinue publication.

My colleagues and I are compelled to acquiesce in the Board's decision. Following the action of the Executive Committee several New York Editors and members of the group that created the SOCIAL FRONTIER in 1934 and developed and financed it for five years (Messrs. Kilpatrick, Childs, Counts, Elliott, Johnson and Rugg) seriously considered the possibility of taking over the journal again. With heavy hearts we have been forced to the conclusion that the financial burden would be too great for us to carry. We cannot send this third and last issue to press, however, without asking our readers to consider what this action means for liberal educational leadership in the United States.

Why did the Directors abolish *Frontiers*? One of their reasons, that given on the adjoining page, is lack of money. It is true that the Directors are finding it difficult to finance the work of the Association. The Officers now assert that *Frontiers*, which was being published by deficit financing, cannot be continued because this year's added deficit would be $2200.00. But other activities of the Association have been carried on for years by deficit financing; its other magazine, PROGRESSIVE EDUCATION, confronts the Association with an estimated loss this year of $2700.00, yet no proposal has been made to

---

[*] **Source:** *Frontiers of Democracy* Volume 10, Number 81, 1943, p. 71-72.

discontinue publication. It is clear, therefore, that other factors have played a major part in the Directors' decision to discontinue *Frontiers*.

These other factors are far more subtle and powerful than inability to raise a few thousand dollars for the journal. They are psychological, not economic. They are human desires and human fears—the mainsprings of men's actions. What men do and avoid doing is primarily the product of what they want most and what they fear most. The Directors have abolished *Frontiers* because they don't want it enough to work for it, or to fight for it. They fear that to continue its publication would prevent them from doing what they want most to do.

What do they want most? Naturally, as loyal directors they want first, to keep the Association alive in this difficult period. They want to raise a large enough annual budget to finance a paid Director, to conduct conferences, to maintain an office, to sell their publications and to do the other things that the P.E.A. has done in the past. While serving the Association they also want to avoid doing anything that will hurt their own professional security.

But these drives are very general, and would not, taken alone, have brought about the striking decision of the Officers and Directors to rid themselves of *Frontiers*. The one factor that led directly to the decision was special. It was the fear of the Officers that *Frontiers* would endanger the new program that they were making for the Association, and in addition would endanger their own personal security. The Editors had said to the Officers, Directors and members through October *Frontiers*: One of the greatest functions that the Progressive Education Association can exercise in the critical years ahead is to lead educators in the building of an enlightened America. To do that directly and effectively we must use our magazine and our conferences for the frank study of social issues. Our treasured American way of life is in great danger, not only from menacing fascists and false patrioteers, but primarily because our people, standing baffled and bewildered on the threshold of abundance are unable to bring about such a life. They are helpless because they don't understand the problem. It is the duty as well as the thrilling opportunity of progressive educators to lead in building consent among the people by a nationwide program of youth and adult education. The one sure foundation of government by the consent of the governed is a program of action based on understanding.

Moreover, said *Frontiers*: Understanding can be built among the people only if they study the vital issues of their social system. The people of America, in company with those of all the United Nations, are engaged in a deep struggle for power. It is the duty of progressive educators everywhere to grasp the essential nature of that struggle and to lead the people of their communities in the study of it and in building programs of action to deal with it. *Frontiers* was direct and explicit about this: the struggle has two realistic facets—mobilizing peace-time production for full-employment (as Henry Wallace put it, building a "capitalism of abundance, full-employment, and democracy for the many instead of the few") . . . and mobilizing the American people to participate vigorously in world cooperation. In the October *Frontiers* we documented the task clearly. We said we would do what we could to help clear away the fog of uncertainty. With drastic issues confronting us, no man, no group, no social instrument whose energies are to count in this struggle can be neutral. *Frontiers* will not be neutral. On no human issue will it compromise. Every month it will point a direction. It will not delude itself that it has achieved solutions. But it will probe to the conceptual roots of our changing, productive system and of our transforming institutions.

Thus the Editors proposed to the Progressive Education Association, that it should work vigorously on the social frontier—that it should deal frankly with matters of social controversy. At their Chicago meeting the Officers and Directors studied the documentation of the October issue carefully, and accepted it, at least by implication, for they unanimously voted *Frontiers* a thousand dollars toward its clerical expenses. Two months later they accepted it formally, for they approved by a 10 to 4 mail vote (the Editor and three others not voting) the Statement of Position and Program on pages 3 to 5 of October *Frontiers*. But on the same ballot they voted 12 to 3 to discontinue the magazine! That is, the Directors accept the social function in principle but reject it in practice. They say, in effect: "We grant that the times are critical and that progressive educators should lead their communities in the study of controversial issues. But we are not willing to do it ourselves, and we will not commit the Progressive Education Association to doing it."

As it has been for fifteen years, social study is still today the bugaboo of Progressive Education.

The Directors have contradicted themselves; they have rejected a social program made by several of their number, and they now propose to steer the Association onto a totally different tack. Their program has not yet been presented in written form but it has been discussed among the members of the Board sufficiently so that its outlines can be seen. It is essentially a proposal to enlarge the membership many-fold ... to concentrate on the task of clarifying progressive education for the citizens of their local communities ... to build a new conception of community-life-as-education among laymen and teachers and administrators who have been slow to adopt new ideas.

The Directors are really proposing that the Association abandon its historic pioneering function. Their program commits us to spreading out over old ground rather than pushing forward into new territory, especially onto the one frontier on which new educational trails must now be blazed. They propose that progressive education shall popularize accepted truths rather than develop new ones. But most important of all their program avoids the controversial issues of community life; it is safe. It is merely the echo of a time-honored battle cry of education. This is the stock-in-trade of the massive entrenched organizations, not of adventuring groups like the P.E.A.

This rejection of today's challenge to education; this quick retreat in the face of a tough job to be done puts the problem of leadership and program squarely up to the membership of the Association. Progressive educators must now, by the democratic process of free and full discussion, appraise the needs of our time, make up their minds what they want the Association to do and choose officers and directors who will do it. They must confront one central question: Is the Progressive Education Association to be a pioneering organization working directly and wisely at the most insistent problems of the people? Is it to extend the magnificent record of the Association of the past quarter century into the post-war years? Since 1919 it has cultivated one area of new ground after another. In the 1920s, the first decade of its corporate life, its members won brilliant victories applying in the elementary school, the new psychological knowledge of the human individual. In the 1930s, its second decade, it pushed forward into the secondary and college fields, and with vast endowments from the Carnegie and Rockefeller Foundations achieved splendid successes through the work of four of its commissions.[2] The frontier, on which the Schools and the Association chose to work in this decade as well as in the 1920s, was that of the individual human being; it was primarily the psychological and pedagogical frontier. During the earlier years there was not perhaps the insistent demand inherent in the social situation today that progressive educators employ education in social reconstruction. Certainly there was enough pioneering to be done in the freeing of the schools from the regimentation of mass-education, from the slavish worship of the dead "classic" past and from commitment to a false mechanical and atomistic psychology. Looking back on it we hail the P.E.A. for a good job, well done.

But the great world depression of the 1930s and the war and post-war crisis of the 1940s have presented to the leaders of progressive education a very different problem. If they are to lead, they must work on the social frontier. No longer can they stand aloof from the insistent social problems of their country. This present crisis penetrates so deeply into the uttermost reaches of American life that every man and woman of liberal tendencies should throw himself into meeting it. Certainly no progressive educational worker should hold back for they alone are equipped to do the things that must be done.

Will the Progressive Education Association accept this challenge? Is there latent leadership within it that will shake it out of its lethargy and build a post-war program that liberals can embrace and work for without stint? Or is it, as some have been saying recently, too old? . . . Too tired? . . . Too timid? . . . Is its work done? Should it balance its books, glad of its surplus on the credit side of the ledger, and pass gracefully into educational history?

We shall soon have the answer to these questions. The problem of electing officers for the coming year will confront the Association this month. The progressives must make up their minds whether they will drift with the tide of complacent inertia or act vigorously, voting in a new, young leadership–a leadership prepared to make a strong social-educational program for post-war America.

One prediction I will venture: If the P.E.A. does not recognize that it has come to the end of the main-traveled roads . . . if it does not provide now the sounding board from which the clear vigorous voice of a socially-minded America can be heard, young Americans who have been preparing for this moment will step forward and build a new and a very different one. I know these young people. I've seen the contempt on their faces for those who are satisfied to do nothing in such critical times. I've seen their impatience with the business of accepting social programs in principle and rejecting them in practice. Mark my words: these young people are going to do something definite about these things . . . soon.

Their voices, uttering the words of a new world statement, take us back 25 years to 1918-19 . . . to the founding of the Progressive Education Association by another little group of young people. They take us back even four years earlier, to a place behind the battle lines at the beginning of the Thirty Years War, where three young world citizens–the British Beatrice Ensor . . . the French Adolph Ferriere . . . the German Elizabeth Rotten–founded the New Education Fellowship. These young people accepted both in principle and in practice.

Today we stand close to the end of that Thirty Years War . . . on the threshold of a new world. Is educational history about to repeat itself, but on a higher level of the culture spiral? I think so. Shortly, a strong new American Educational Fellowship will be created.

Rollo Brown tells you in his beautiful little book that
"There must be a new song."
I say to you the new song is being sung . . .
The greatest poems are being written . . .
The singers are coming to life . . .
The Answerers are speaking.

The American is the maker of poems,
The Answerer.
What can be answered . . . he answers.
America is Answerers.

Notes

1. Three members, including the Editor, did not vote. This action was initiated by the President, Mr. Rogers, at a called meeting of the Executive Committee in New York ten days after the full membership of the Board had approved the expenditure of $1,000.00 for the editing of *Frontiers* at its Chicago meeting, October 15–17, 1943. The editing of *Frontiers* on this nominal sum—the real cost being several thousands of dollars more—was being made possible by the fact that the Editor's Research Staff, listed on the mast-head was contributing its services without pay.

2. The Commission of the Relation Between School and College . . . the Commission on Adolescence . . . The Commission on the Reorganization of Secondary Education . . . and the Commission on Human Relation.

In Retrospect [*]

The Editorial Board

In this final editorial for the journal, its editorial board reviews the original purpose of the journal, which was not about methods of teaching, but instead "an assembly of diverse ideas and opinion, and—even more important—an instrument for positive fashioning of programs and philosophies." Emphasized was the idea of helping to make teachers and other readers of the journal critical thinkers whose actions would have meaning in the real world. In this context, the journal and its purpose anticipated the Social Foundations Movement in Education and its emphasis on teachers as intellectual and critical thinkers. An appeal for further funding to keep the journal afloat concludes the editorial, one which ultimately did not succeed, as priorities involving the Second World War and an increasing growth of conservatism contributed to the failure to keep the journal operational.

*   *   *

Looking back over *Frontiers*' ten-year history it seems as though this journal's existence is being cut short at the very moment it was coming of age. Born of the aftermath of the Great Depression, *Frontiers* has been deeply concerned with the crises in social, economic and political affairs throughout the thirties, and the strategic war-election year of 1944 offered the greatest challenge of all. (In another part of this final number Dr. Rugg describes the program that had been planned for 1944.)

The first issue of *The Social Frontier* appeared in October 1934, boldly proclaiming itself an independent "journal of educational criticism and reconstruction" and thus the founding "frontier thinkers" definitely lined themselves up with the liberal and progressive forces. It "took sides" from the very beginning: cautioning teachers to be alert for fascist forces in the United States, denouncing the Ives Law, praising the progressive measures of the New Deal. But by no means did the Editors presume to "indoctrinate" their readers. As John Dewey stated in an early issue: *The Social Frontier* was designed to help teachers and other educators "to make a conscious choice on the basis of intelligent study." In line with this policy, there appeared articles expressing such diverse views as those of Reinhold Niebuhr, Lawrence Dennis, Bruce Bliven, Earl Browder, Harry Gideonse and Arthur Garfield Hays. Here indeed was an unusual educational magazine: none of the trite "new ideas" in methods of teaching, but an assembly of diverse ideas and opinion, and—even more

---

[*] **Source:** *The Frontiers of Democracy*, Volume 10, Number 81, 1943, p. 100.

important—an instrument for positive fashioning of programs and philosophies.

Frontiers' financial situation—now in its final crisis—has always been a precarious one. Its main assets have always been the faith and enthusiasm of its patrons, and the unremunerated services of its editors and contributors.

At the beginning two small Foundations granted a total of $900, and the editors made up the difference by personal contributions. These personal responsibilities were considerably lightened in 1939 through the affiliation of *Frontiers* and the Progressive Education Association. Long aware of their mutual interests, these two organizations had decided the time was ripe for "fusion." W. Ryan Carson, Jr., President of PEA at that time, wrote in *Frontiers*: "When *The Social Frontier* was independently launched the Progressive Education Association was on the verge of publishing a journal that would do for the educational world what *The Social Frontier* has so ably done in the last half decade. . . . It is with great pleasure on the part of the Boards of both organizations that we announce the joining of forces." During these four years *Frontiers* found a friendly sponsor in the like-minded PEA—always willing to offer its resources in the solving of technical problems, but never attempting to influence editorial policy, and most generous in carrying the burden of *Frontiers'* deficit.

A TESTAMENT OF FAITH

It has not been the function of the Editor's Research Staff to issue pronouncements—we felt honored to be the wheel horses of what was to us the most forward-looking journal in the field of education.

When we reflect, however, on the tremendous promise *Frontiers* held for the future, and on the gallant efforts of Harold Rugg who gave of his soul, time and substance for the past half year, we feel we would have been unworthy of our posts were we not to make this statement and proposal.

Sidney Hook has well said: "Among the most poignant tragedies of history are those in which men cried 'impossible' too soon." While we would not infer that the present tragedy is of cosmic proportions, the place that *Frontiers* held, and what is more important—promised to hold—for the progressive and liberal elements in American education allows small dispute. You who have been reading *Frontiers*—what is it worth to you, that this journal which has so consistently upheld the liberal tradition in your profession may continue to be what Professor Kilpatrick called "a medium for the development of a constructive social consciousness among educational workers"? That this promise may not be stillborn, we propose the following:

1. That $5000 be raised forthwith to constitute a working fund to insure publication of *Frontiers of Democracy* for another year.

2. That this sum be raised by all who consider themselves friends of liberal, realistic, American education. This can be done in any one of a number of ways: If 500 persons contribute $10 each we can go on; if 200 contribute $25 each we can go on; if 2000 contribute $2.50 each we can go on.

3. That when this sum of $5000 is raised, the donors shall, in keeping with the democratic ideals of this journal, elect an editor.

To carry out the above proposal we suggest you make a pledge to contribute what you can. Please mail your pledge to Miss Ursula Reinhardt, 66 West 12th Street, New York 11, N. Y., by March 31, 1944. If the pledges total the needed $5000 they will be called in May.

G. M. Coke
George Freimarck
Walter R. Mahler
Ursula Reinhardt
T. Earl Tilley
Mary Wollner
Louise Yuill

Bibliography

The following bibliography is intended for readers interested in the writings of the Social Reconstructivist movement and its commentators.

American Historical Association, Commission on the Social Studies, *A Charter for the Social Studies*. New York: Charles Scribner's Sons, 1932.

Beard, Charles A. "The Society in an Age of Conflicts," *School and Society* 43, (February 1936.)

Bowers, C. A. *The Progressive Educator and the Depression: The Radical Years*. New York: Random House. 1969.

———, "The Social Frontier Journal: A Historical Sketch," *History of Education Quarterly*, Volume 4, Number 3, 1964, pp. 167–180.

———, "Social Reconstructionism: Views from the Left and the Right, 1932–1942." *History of Education Quarterly*, X, 1970, 22-52.

Cremin, Lawrence A., *The Transformation of the School*. New York: Vintage Books, 1964.

Cremin, Lawrence A. et al., *A History of Teachers College, Columbia University*. New York: Columbia University Press, 1954.

Counts, George S., *A Call to the Teachers of the Nation*. New York: John Day Company, 1933,

———. *Dare the School Build a New Social Order?* New York: John Day Co. 1936.

Dennis, Lawrence J. and William E. Eaton. George S. Counts, *Educator for a New Age*. Carbondale, Illinois : Southern Illinois University Press, 1980.

Educational Policies Commission, *The Unique Function of Education in American Democracy*. Washington, DC, 1937.

Educational Policies Commission, *Research Memorandum on Education in the Depression*, Social Science Research Council Bulletin 28, 1937 (New York, 1937).

Educational Policies Commission, *The Purposes of Education in American Democracy* Washington, DC, 1938.

Educational Policies Commission, *Federal Activities in Education*, Washington, DC, 1939.

Evans, Ronald W., *The Social Studies Wars: What We Should Teach Our Children*. New York: Teachers College Press, 2004.

———, *This Happened in America: Harold Rugg and the Censure of Social Studies*. Charlotte, N.C.: Information Age Publishing, 2007.

Goodenow, Ronald K. and Wayne J. Urban, "George S. Counts: A Critical Appreciation," *The Educational Forum*, Volume 41, Number 2, 1977, pp. 167–174.

Graham, Patricia Albjerg, *Progressive Education: From Arcady to Academe, A History of the Progressive Education Association, 1919–1955*. New York: Teachers College Press, 1967.

Gutek, Gerald Lee, *The Educational Theory of George S. Counts*. Columbus, Ohio State University Press, 1971.

Harrison, George J., "An Historical Analysis of the Social Frontier: A Journal of Educational Criticism and Reconstruction," Dissertation. Dissertation, Rutgers, The State University of New Jersey, 1968.

James, Michael E., editor, *Social Reconstruction Through Education: The Philosophy, History, and Curricula of a Radical Idea*. Norwood, N.J.: Ablex Publishing Company, 1995. Included in the James work is James R. Giarelli's essay, "The Social Frontier 1934–1943: Retrospect and Prospect."

Kilpatrick, William H. *Education and the Social Crisis: A Proposed Program*. New York: Liveright, 1932.

Kilpatrick, William H., et al. *The Educational Frontier*. New York: Arno Press and the New York Times. 1969.

Lagemann. Ellen C. "Prophecy or Profession? George S. Counts and the Social Study of Education," *American Journal of Education*, Volume 100, Number 2, 1992, pp. 137–165.

Null, J. Wesley and Diane Ravitch, *Forgotten Heroes of American Education: The Great Tradition of Teaching Teachers*. Greenwich, CT: Information Age Publishing, 2005.

O'Neill, Maureen, *The Social Frontier and Frontiers of Democracy, 1934–1943: Visions for Curricular Reconstruction*. Doctoral dissertation, Rutgers, the State University of New Jersey, 1985.

Perlstein, Daniel, "There is No Escape... from the Ogre of Indoctrination": George Counts and the Civil Dilemmas of Democratic Educators." In *Reconstructing the Common Good in Education: Coping with Intractable American Dilemmas*, edited by Larry Cuban and Dorothy Shipps. Stanford, CA: Stanford University Press, 2000.

Rowan, J. E., *The Social Frontier (1934–43): Journal of Educational Criticism and Reconstruction*. Dissertation, Case Western Reserve University, 1969.

Tyack, D., Lowe R., and E. Hansot, *Public Schools in Hard Times: The Great Depression and Recent Years*. Cambridge, MA: Harvard University Press, 1984.

THIS SERIES EXPLORES THE HISTORY OF SCHOOLS AND SCHOOLING in the United States and other countries. Books in this series examine the historical development of schools and educational processes, with special emphasis on issues of educational policy, curriculum and pedagogy, as well as issues relating to race, class, gender, and ethnicity. Special emphasis will be placed on the lessons to be learned from the past for contemporary educational reform and policy. Although the series will publish books related to education in the broadest societal and cultural context, it especially seeks books on the history of specific schools and on the lives of educational leaders and school founders.

For additional information about this series or for the submission of manuscripts, please contact the general editors:

Alan R. Sadovnik   Susan F. Semel
Rutgers University-Newark   The City College of New York, CUNY
Education Dept.   138th Street and Convent Avenue
155 Conklin Hall   NAC 5/208
175 University Avenue   New York, NY 10031
Newark, NJ 07102

To order other books in this series, please contact our Customer Service Department:

800-770-LANG (within the U.S.)
212-647-7706 (outside the U.S.)
212-647-7707 FAX

Or browse online by series at:

www.peterlang.com